Todd Swanson

LEANINGS 2

LEANINGS 2

GREAT STORIES BY AMERICA'S FAVORITE MOTORCYCLE WRITER

PETER EGAN

MOTORBOOKS

First published in 2005 by Motorbooks, an imprint of MBI Publishing Company, Galtier Plaza, Suite 200, 380 Jackson Street, St. Paul, MN 55101-3885 USA

ISBN-13: 978-0-7603-2164-5
ISBN-10: 0-7603-2164-7

Editors: Lee Klancher and Leah Noel
Designer: Tom Heffron

Printed in the United States

On the cover: *Cycle World* columnist Peter Egan consulting the map over his next motorcycle destination. *Keith May*

On the back cover: More of Eganibilia, evidence of a lifelong love of all things motorcycle. *Nick Cedar*

Inside photography: Eganibilia on display, photographed by Nick Cedar and Lee Klancher.

Section break photography, pages 11 and 51: *Keith May*

DEDICATION

To Barb

CONTENTS

Foreword
A PERFECT MATCH

by David Edwards,
editor-in-chief *Cycle World* magazine

True story . . . it's happened more than once. Peter Egan and I had ridden a couple of *Cycle World* testbikes 30 miles up the coast to San Pedro for the annual Father's Day open house at Century Cycles, one of the fixtures on the Southern California classic-bike scene. I immediately vectored for the food line while Peter wandered off to ogle a particularly tasty Triumph or Norton. Before I made it to the potato salad, though, I was intercepted by an earnest-looking fellow with questions.

"You're David Edwards, right?" he said.

I pled guilty and shook the man's hand.

"Er, I wonder if I can ask you something?" he wanted to know.

This happens all the time. Someone seeking my learned counsel on all matters motorcycle. Perhaps he was having a tough time deciding between two new bikes. Maybe he wanted advice on riding gear. How much to pay for an old Ducati? The Rockies or the Pyrenees? What's the best viewing spot at Laguna Seca? The secret to kick-starting a BSA Victor 441? Perhaps he wanted an autograph.

"Sure," I said, happy to pass on any hard-earned knowledge. "What's up?"

He checked over both shoulders, took a step closer, and lowered his voice. This was serious.

"Well, can you please introduce me to Peter Egan . . ."

Which, in print, is what I've been asked to do here for *Leanings 2,* his second compilation of motorcycle stories.

I've read Peter's words for 28 years, worked with him for 20, ridden with him everywhere from Route 66 to the Alps, and here's the thing about Egan: *If he didn't exist, we'd have to invent him.*

For a magazine like *Cycle World*, one of the last remaining to cover (as its title purports) the entire world of motorcycling, Peter is the perfect writer. He's best known for his folksy feature stories and slice-of-life columns, of course, but Peter actually began his career at *CW* in the technical editor's seat, putting the skills he acquired as a line mechanic at a foreign-car repair shop to good use. As far as bike interests go, Peter's range wide. He's done a nut-and-bolt restoration on a 1967 high-pipe Triumph Trophy 650 and track days on a 996 Ducati. He's as happy bouncing down the Baja peninsula on a Suzuki DR400 as he is rolling across the Great Plains on a Harley Road King. He's also the guy who rescued a cute little 50cc Honda Spree scooter from the city dump and parked it alongside his hulking Kawasaki ZX-11, then the reigning steamroller of speed. Peter's love of motorcycling is deep and non-denominational.

But then, many of us love motorcycles. It's what Peter does with a keyboard that sets him apart from anyone in the bike-mag biz, and the reason, presumably, you've purchased this book. My job as editor-in-chief at *Cycle World* brings with it many privileges, one of those being that I'm the very first person (other than wife Barb) to read Peter's monthly column, fresh from his computer. It's a treat I hope to have for many years to come.

So without any further ramblings from me then, ladies and gentlemen, I present to you Peter Egan. I would wish you good reading, but that's a given.

Section I
THE FEATURES

2003 edition of Cycle World*'s* Adventures *magazine*

THE SEARCH FOR ROBERT JOHNSON

All of us who travel away from home, I think, have a few favorite places we return to any time we have the chance—landscapes that hold some special meaning for us, either historically, scenically, or spiritually, or all three. One of those places, for me, is the Blues Country of the Mississippi Delta. It's an odd place to tour on a motorcycle, really, because its flat agricultural landscape doesn't have many of the traits that normally draw motorcyclists—no curving mountain roads or scenic seacoasts. What it has is a history of producing some of the world's greatest and most haunting music, against all odds.

If you love that music, the place has a resonance that transcends the normal rules of tourism. It's a place where, as Antoine de Saint-Exupery said, "that which is essential is invisible to the eye."

I didn't have a hellhound on my trail, but my bike was leaving a pretty good rooster tail of rainwater. Mounted atop a brand-new Triumph Bonneville, I was cruising down Highway 100 through the hills of western Tennessee in a cold, steady rain. Pockets of ghostly fog drifted through the hills, causing moments of sudden blindness.

A shame, really, because Highway 100 is a nice, curvy road, full of forested dips and rises and old bridges over rivers with romantic Chickasaw Indian names. It was a wonderful road for an agile bike like the Bonneville.

But as I neared Memphis, the country began to flatten out and the deep forest melted away. West of the Loosahtachie River Canal on Highway 64, I began to see cotton fields. The sky cleared, a warm sun dried the roads, and I stopped to take off my rain suit at a gas station. A crop duster swept over a nearby field.

Out of the Appalachians and into the Mississippi Delta. Goodbye, curves.

But then, I hadn't come here for the curves. I was looking for the roots of that uniquely American musical phenomenon, the blues.

For reasons that have never been adequately explained, this 200-mile stretch of rich southern bottomland between the Yazoo and Mississippi rivers has been home to about eighty-five percent of all the great blues musicians who ever lived—Charlie Patton, Son House, Howlin' Wolf, Muddy Waters, B. B. King, Sonny Boy Williamson, John Lee Hooker, Mississippi John Hurt, and a hundred others. Many of them moved north to Chicago or Detroit, but the sound they took with them came right out of Mississippi.

And, I must confess, this sound is my favorite kind of music. Has been since I was first exposed to its haunting tones and lyrics by the Rolling Stones as a young northern white boy back in the early 1960s.

So, when editor Beau Pacheco called and said he'd like someone to pick up a new Triumph Bonneville in Nashville and take it down to the Delta on "a search for Robert Johnson," I signed on approximately at the speed of light.

"A search for whom?" you say.

Robert Johnson, for those not baptized in these deep, mystical waters, is to the blues roughly what Hank Williams is to country music. He was a thin, handsome black musician who died at the age of twenty-seven, back in 1938, when a jealous husband at a juke joint supposedly poisoned his whiskey. He did only two recording sessions, but managed to lay down such classic tracks as "Cross Road Blues," "Love in Vain," "Come on in My Kitchen," "Hellhound on My Trail," and twenty-five other songs that have been recorded by everybody on Earth.

Legend says that Johnson went to the crossroads at Highways 61 and 49 one midnight and sold his soul to the devil in exchange for his extraordinary musical talent. (I've tried this trick several times myself, but no one ever shows up.)

There is much controversy surrounding Robert Johnson's final resting place—several books and film documentaries have been made about the search for Johnson—so I thought it best to add to the confusion by heading south to see if I could straighten things out. And maybe hear a little live music at the same time.

On a cold Wisconsin October morning, I climbed on my Harley Electra Glide, rode to Nashville in fourteen numbing hours, and swapped for the Triumph at a place called Castle Motorsports.

I hadn't ridden a modern Bonneville for a couple of years and had forgotten what a delightful, all-purpose standard motorcycle it is. It has a perfectly flat seat, so you can move anywhere on the saddle; there's plenty of legroom, and the bars and pegs put you in a slight forward lean, ideal for a road bike with no fairing. The gas tank is really the gas tank, the replaceable handlebar is tubular, and the styling has not been contrived to prove that the designer is an avant-garde genius. It's a compact, yet roomy bike, flickable and fun to ride.

Late in the afternoon, I hit the four-lane blacktop into Memphis, making my way to the famous old Peabody Hotel. I had deemed this a good starting point because the Mississippi Delta, it is said, "begins in the lobby of the Peabody Hotel in Memphis and ends on Catfish Row in Vicksburg."

The Peabody is also just one block off Beale Street, the traditional blues club row of Memphis. It's a grand old hotel, even if they charge $175 per night and have neither coffeemakers in the room nor free coffee in the lobby.

This shortcoming was quickly pointed out to me by Keith May, our caffeine-addicted photographer and art director, who flew in from California. Keith and his camera-packed rental car would be meeting me along the route to snap pictures of whatever scenic locales I would happen to blunder upon.

That evening, we walked down Beale Street looking for food and drink. We ambled in to the Blues City Café for some of the best seafood gumbo I've ever had, and later heard a good guitar player named Earl the Pearl and his band.

As we stepped out into the warm night, I looked down Beale Street at the bright neon lights, tourist-crowded bars, shops, and cafes and said to Keith, "You should have seen this place when I rode through here twenty-five years ago on my Honda CB400F. It was bombed out. Vacant lots, broken glass, closed-down bail-bond stores with bars on the windows. But they've brought it back from the dead."

We passed under the crown-shaped neon sign for B. B. King's club, and I thought maybe the street finally looked more like it did when B. B. himself came here to seek his fortune. Half a century later, the exact same music was bringing people back again.

The next morning, we rambled a few blocks east to the little brick building that houses the famous Sun recording studio.

Sam Phillips, founder of Sun Studio, once remarked that if you could find a white singer who had a "black feel," you could make a million dollars. Lo and behold, young Elvis walked in. As well as Jerry Lee Lewis, Carl Perkins, Johnny Cash, and Roy Orbison. A magical place, from the very dawn of rock 'n' roll, and the original recording studio is still there, apparently unchanged, with its perforated white acoustical tile. Musicians still come to pay homage and record. U2 did a session there a few years ago.

When you stand in the studio, you can see why. There's still a vibe to the place, a distant thrumming in those walls, a time-machine sense of suddenly finding yourself in a simpler era. And Sun still draws true believers.

On our tour of the studio were two young German-speaking guys with well-greased Gene Vincent ducktails, big sideburns, skinny belts, and rolled-up cuffs on their blue jeans. One of them looked just like the guy who took my sister to the prom in 1958.

Here was a whole new 1950s' twist on William Faulkner's famous comment that in the South, "the past is never dead. It's not even past."

I climbed on the Triumph and cruised down Second Street, to Huling, and found myself suddenly confronted with the chilling edifice of the Lorraine Motel, where Martin Luther King Jr. was gunned down. There's a wreath on the second-floor balcony to mark the spot.

The motel is closed now, the original structure having been absorbed into the larger National Civil Rights Museum. Before leaving, I pondered that balcony for a while and marveled at King's courage. It's a risky business being hated by J. Edgar Hoover and every homicidal maniac in America just because you would like to vote. Or stay at a better motel.

On a slightly lighter note, I cruised down the famous Elvis Presley Boulevard and parked at Graceland. Keith met me there, and we took a guided tour, visiting the graves of Elvis and his parents.

One thing that immediately strikes you about Graceland is that the mansion is not very big, compared with the ridiculous palaces perfectly ordinary Americans are building for themselves these days. You get the feeling that Elvis just wanted a comfortable place to hang out with his friends and family, rather than to show off his wealth. A nearly lost concept.

I cut across to Highway 61 and motored south past bail-bond offices, used-car lots, and liquor stores. At the Mississippi state line, the new four-lane highway suddenly exploded with huge, garish signs for huge, garish gambling casinos. Ballys! Harrahs! Seafood Buffet at Sam's Town!

Gambling came to the northern edge of the Delta about ten years ago, and it has transformed the landscape. The new gambling resorts dwarf the old cotton plantations, shacks, and warehouses, making them look like quaint, sepia-toned leftovers from another century. Gigantic casinos sit uncomfortably in the middle of cotton fields "like space ships filled with money," as author Peter Applebome once remarked.

Just south of Highway 304, however, the gambling stops and the Delta returns to its old self. I pulled into the tiny village of Robinsonville for lunch and found a charming old restaurant called the Hollywood Café, famously mentioned in several John Grisham novels. I wanted to see Robinsonville because Robert Johnson had grown up nearby on the Abbay and Leatherman Plantation. While Keith and I were eating the catfish lunch special, we started talking with the people at the next table and found out one of them was none other than Bobby Leatherman, heir to and owner of the plantation.

"Yes, Robert Johnson's house was just down the levee from our place," he told me. "The house is gone now, but it was just kitty-corner from the Exxon station down the road. My father knew him very well. He worked for our family."

I rode down to the station and found that the place where Johnson's house once stood is now nearly buried under the entrance road to Sam's Town Casino. As I rode away, a sign along the highway said Kenny Loggins was coming to one of the casinos. Delta showbiz, old and new.

Swinging back onto Highway 61, I cruised down to Clarksdale, population 19,717, Ground Zero for the blues. Every black musician in the Delta seemingly was born in Clarksdale—or on the nearby Dockery Farms or Stovall Plantation. The Delta Blues Museum is located in the old train station in Clarksdale. There are record shops there, too, as well as a recording studio and several clubs—one of them called Ground Zero, no less.

There's a blues-theme "motel" just east of town on Highway 49, called the Shack Up Inn, where Keith and I found rooms for the night. It's essentially a row of artfully restored old sharecropper shacks lined up behind the cotton gin and seed houses of the old Hopson Plantation. They look like the real thing, but have carefully hidden amenities for the modern traveler, such as hot running water, air conditioning, and VCRs. It's just the kind of place at which Robert Johnson would have stayed, if he'd had a cell phone to make reservations. It's a friendly, laid-back place that bills itself as the Delta's "oldest B&B—Beer and Breakfast." So we ordered a beer and joined a group of other guests sitting around in a circle of lawn chairs outside, watching the sun go down over the cotton fields.

The next day, I visited the Delta Blues Museum—notable for having Muddy Waters' boyhood log cabin assembled within its walls—and then rode south to Highway 7 and the metropolis of Quito. This is just a wide spot in the road with a derelict garage, a few houses, and a neat little church called the Payne Chapel next to a cemetery. One small block of granite has a guitar engraved in the stone, and it reads, "Robert Johnson, May 8, 1911–Aug. 16, 1938, Resting in the Blues."

Except, of course, no one knows if he's resting there, blue or otherwise. He was murdered at the Three Forks Store, a juke joint just a few miles up a side road, and quickly buried somewhere nearby—most people think here, or at the Zion Church a few miles south. A fan put this headstone over an unmarked grave sometime in the 1970s.

There was a Hohner Blues Harp harmonica lying on the grave, with the initials "J.H." drawn on it in Magic Marker.

I paid my tentative respects to this probable monument, then rode down the highway to a junction where the old Three Forks juke joint used to be.

Alas, since I was here last, the very building in which Johnson was poisoned had been bulldozed into a nearby swamp to make a turnaround spot for trucks. Too bad. If I'd known the building was worth so little, I'd have bought it myself. Maybe started a blues bar.

From there, I rode three miles south to Zion Church, which is just east of the road. This cemetery has a much larger headstone, an obelisk with an engraved portrait of Johnson, and a list of his great songs. It reads, "King of the Delta Blues Singers, his music struck a chord that continues to resonate. His blues addressed generations he would never know and made poetry of visions and fears."

Nicely put. And there was another Blues Harp on the grave, with "J.H." on it. Also a bottle of Beam's Eight Star Kentucky Whiskey.

If Johnson—or any other real bluesman—were still around, I thought to myself, that bottle would be history. Yet out of respect—or fear of poison—I did not drink it.

Instead, I headed back to Clarksdale for a drink and some live blues. Keith and I stopped for a rib dinner at the junction of Highways 61 and 49, reputed to be the place where Johnson sold his soul. These days, he'd be run over by truck traffic and muscle cars with rap music pulsing from their doors at nosebleed volume. I guess it was quieter in the 1930s.

We went over to Ground Zero, had a few beers, and listened to a phenomenal Texas guitarist named Catherine Denise, then walked back to our lodgings for the night, the famous old Riverside Hotel. This slightly weather-beaten place is a former black hospital, the place where Bessie Smith died after her car accident in 1937.

As the only black hotel in town, it was the natural stopping place for all the traveling bluesmen—Sonny Boy Williamson, Robert Nighthawk, Ike Turner, and others. The owner, Frank "Rat" Ratliff, gave us a tour and showed us Bessie Smith's old hospital room. Our rooms, just down the hall, were clean, plain, and neat. I read somewhere that there's still a morgue in the basement, but I didn't ask to see it. Such places give me the blues, which are possibly related to the creeps.

In the morning, I rode southeast to the little town of Tutwiler on Highway 3. Tutwiler is famous for two things: The famous bandleader, W. C. Handy, waited here for a train one hot night in 1903 and heard a black man playing slide guitar blues with a jackknife and was quite taken by "the weirdest music I had ever heard." It was the first time this music had ever attracted the attention of a professional, big-time musician.

Tutwiler is also famous as the final resting place of Sonny Boy Williamson II (a.k.a. Aleck "Rice" Miller), who I think was the best blues harmonica player who ever lived. He recorded with Eric Clapton and others during the blues boom of the 1960s and died in 1965—about the time I discovered his music. There's a map painted on the Tutwiler train station showing how to reach his grave, which is next to an abandoned church a few miles from town.

The church is gone now. Recently burned down. But the grave is still there, neatly kept, with a list of Williamson's great songs chiseled in stone. My favorite is "One Way Out," which my own garage band has in its vast repertoire of bad imitations. On Williamson's grave was another harmonica left by the ubiquitous "J.H."

I checked out of the Riverside Hotel the next morning, said goodbye to Rat, and swung south under a dark, rainy sky for one last day in the Delta and two more holy shrines to visit. Following Highway 1 down the river, I rode to the little town of Rosedale, which I wanted to see only because it's mentioned in one version of "Cross Road Blues."

Rosedale is a little town with neat, shaded suburbs and a crumbling Third-World downtown slumbering beneath a vine-covered water tower. I walked up onto the nearby levee in a pouring rain for a view of the river, but it was entirely invisible through the trees, as it often is. I suspect that many Delta dwellers live for years at a time without ever seeing the Mississippi unless it floods. Then they see it in their kitchens.

So, I had finally seen Rosedale. Big deal, you say, but now I could die happy.

Almost. I still had to find the grave of another musical hero, Mississippi John Hurt. When I was in college, every guitar player I knew was trying to fingerpick like John Hurt. He was said to be buried in the St. James churchyard, in Avalon.

But when I got to this little roadside settlement on Highway 7, no one seemed to know anything about him, or the church. The local mail carrier and several local farmers shook their heads and looked blank. A tractor driver finally told me that there was a small church on a dirt road along the creek.

When I turned onto the dirt road, I found no church, but rather a black family disembarking from an SUV to go fishing. I asked the man of the family about St. James Church.

"Why do you want to go there?" he asked.

"I'm looking for the grave of Mississippi John Hurt."

The man looked surprised. "I'm his great-grandson!" he said. "My name's T. Kimball," he added, shaking my hand.

Kimball's wife shouted from the car, "Who's he looking for?"

"Grandpa John!" Kimball shouted back.

She made a face. "He'll never find that grave," she said. "It's way back in the woods." They gave me complex directions to the cemetery nonetheless.

And find it I did, after many missed turns and much backtracking. The cemetery was nowhere near the church, but in a small, mosquito-infested clearing in the woods, high on the bluffs overlooking the Delta. The cemetery looked like a stage set from a John Fogarty concert, and the road to it was a single-lane dirt trail, overgrown with vines and forest. Any bike larger or less nimble than the Triumph wouldn't have made it. Shades of my Triumph Trophy 500—a bike that can go anywhere.

A simple headstone between two trees said, "John S. Hurt, born Mar. 8, 1892, died Nov. 2, 1966." There were some faded flowers on the grave—and a harmonica from J.H. again. A true and hard-core blues fan, J.H. I was beginning to like the guy, and I'd never even met him. Or her. We had the same heroes.

It was a little sad, I suddenly realized, how much our homage to the blues had become mostly a series of visits to gravesites. A bit macabre, perhaps, but then I suppose culture is mostly a matter of honoring the dead. In every generation, there are only a few people who do really great work, and if you don't keep their memories alive, you have no history and no standards to lean on or learn from. These men buried in the Delta had changed my life, and they were all long gone. Only the songs and legends remained.

And they'll outlive us all. Especially those of us who died of West Nile virus from all the mosquito bites we got while standing around old cemeteries in Mississippi. Time to go.

As I climbed out of the Delta and into the hill country, it turned cold and began raining harder. I found myself humming "Hellhound on My Trail" inside my steamed-up helmet, though there was nothing in my mirrors but that big rooster tail of rainwater again, and those same eerie patches of fog moving over the highway. "Got to keep on movin'," I sang quietly to myself, heading inexorably north toward winter, "Blues fallin' down like hail."

August 2003

WHERE THE SIDEWALK ENDS

The reader will note there are two Baja off-road stories in this volume. That's because the Baja peninsula is an addictive place, and the more you go there, the more you want to go there. Also, it's generally warm, dry, and sunny in the winter, which my home in Wisconsin is not.

My friend Pat Donnelly and I were not in the greatest shape when we made this trip. He'd just had a recent false-alarm cancer scare and was still getting over the flu, and I was feeling mysteriously dragged out and tired myself, being diagnosed a short time later with hepatitis C. Nevertheless, we had a great time and rebounded two years later to take another trip the full length of Baja. Proof that riding, sunlight, and big clouds of dust are good for you.

"How's that GPS working?" I asked my buddy Pat Donnelly as I sawed at the wheel of my blue Ford Econoline van. Pat stared at the tiny screen of the hand-held Garmin and shook his head slowly. "It says we're still where we used to be . . ."

That was bad news, because we were at that moment in the middle of a blizzard in central Illinois, blasting through clouds of wind-driven snow, and if there was one place we did not want to be, it was where we used to be. Which, just hours ago, was back home in Wisconsin, loading our bikes in the gloom and chill of a February dawn.

Where we wanted to be was basking under the warm desert sun in the Mexican state of Baja California, some 2,000 miles to the southwest.

Pat and I had been planning our getaway trip to Baja for a full year, and, typically, we'd finally managed to leave on the worst day of winter. Hunkered in the back of my van were a pair of Suzuki DR-Z400S dual-sport bikes. Pat's was yellow and mine was blue, both 2001 models.

We'd spent several months prepping the bikes, making nearly identical modifications—oversized four-gallon IMS plastic gas tanks, full aluminum skid plates, Pirelli MT21 knobbies, and brush-cutter handguards. Our toolbags were crammed with extra tire tools, patch kits, and CO_2 cartridges. In the duffel bags with our riding gear were backpacks with Camelback water bladders, spare heavy-duty tubes, J-B Weld, sunscreen, hats, and a wide assortment of high-octane energy bars laced with caffeine.

Pat had even ordered an off-road route guide called the *Baja GPS Guidebook*, put out by an intrepid woman explorer named Kacey Smith, complete with maps, GPS waypoints, and much good advice. Using GPS would be a first for both of us. Pat and I had done a 1,000-mile off-road Jeep trip to the tip of Baja (and 1,000 back) in 1985 and had discovered that our AAA map was a little light on details when you got into the real outback. Baja is a land of many unexpected forks in the trail, and one of them is always wrong.

You are never really *lost* in Baja—the peninsula's too narrow for that—but it's possible to be confused until you run out of gas. Or daylight. Hence the GPS.

Essentially, we'd planned, researched, and shopped ourselves to death, and we were ready.

The plan was to drive the van into Baja and leave it at a couple of strategically located motels while we did two-day loops to distant overnight lodgings in the mountains. That way the van could serve as Mother Ship, a place to store extra tools, water, oil, dirty socks, etc., while we traveled with relatively light backpacks.

Three days after leaving home, we crossed into California just past Yuma, Arizona, stopped at a Shell station in Jacumba to fill up all tanks and buy Mexican insurance for the van and bikes. You must have Mexican insurance in Baja, by law, and it costs about six dollars a day, per vehicle, for liability insurance only, more if you want theft protection. We opted for the whole package, which cost $234, van and bikes, for seven days.

Taking scenic Highway 94 down to the border crossing at Tecate, we changed our money (about ten pesos to the dollar) and bought tourist cards for eighteen dollars each (good for six months). Tecate is my favorite border crossing because it's a small town with light traffic and almost no waiting. Tijuana, on the other hand, can be a nightmare, and Mexicali is not much better.

Late in the afternoon, we drove east thirty miles to El Hongo, then took a washboard dirt road south about twenty miles to a resort motel called Hacienda Santa Veronica.

Washboard roads, incidentally, are a specialty of Baja. They have a Department of Washboard Research (DWR) with a full staff of civil engineers who have figured out exactly how far apart the ridges have to be to shake every nut and bolt loose on your vehicle. Driving my van down to Santa Veronica was like piloting an air chisel.

The DWR is always in competition with the Office of Pothole Development, a friendly rivalry not unlike that between our own FBI and CIA. The dirt roads in Baja would be tragic if they weren't so funny. You see middle-aged couples hammering along in their dented Omnis and Fiestas with their hats jittering on their heads and wonder if they ever ask why their roads are so bad. It's all a matter of low population and tax revenue, of course. Baja is a big place with few people and long distances, which is why we go there. If the roads were better, we'd stay home.

Hacienda Santa Veronica had a cold, empty feel when we got there. It was the hired help's day off, and there were no other guests, as an off-road tour group was not slated to arrive until the next day. Nevertheless, a woman named Lourdes cheerfully opened the bar and restaurant, made a warm fire in the fireplace, whipped up some margaritas, and cooked (after making the sign of the cross) us a great machaca beef dinner with fresh tortillas.

Pat and I unloaded the bikes, and in the morning headed out on a 150-mile ride to Laguna Hanson, a lake up in the mountains. It was all narrow dirt road of varying quality, with just enough sand, rocks, rain ruts, and water crossings to keep our attention. This was Pat's second dirt ride ever, and I hadn't been off-road in Baja on a motorcycle for twenty-two years, so we both needed a good break-in day of only moderate brutality.

We tried a stretch of single-track up a canyon, but heavy rains from the previous week had washed the trail into a jumble of boulders and tree roots, so we turned around and headed for the little village of Ojos Negros, where there was said to be gas.

We spotted a homemade cardboard *gasolina* sign in the courtyard of a house and tractor-repair shop, but a woman came out and said they had no gas. She pointed at another house diagonally across town and said they had gas. They didn't, but pointed at another house. They didn't either. Finally, I saw a guy standing on his rooftop, waving his arms and pointing into his yard. Just like a neon sign for the Golden Nugget in Las Vegas, only live.

The man had a drum of gasoline in the back of an old pickup, and he sucked on a hose and siphoned fuel into a plastic milk jug. Each of our bikes took one jug, at a cost of about $2.50 a gallon.

Fueled up, we made the last climb to Laguna Hanson, but it turned out to be a *laguna seca*—a dry lake. Last time I was here, it was a sky-blue diamond in a setting of tall pines, but last year's drought had left the basin dry. We headed back in late afternoon, with a chill in the air and the sun low, hustling to the lodge just before dark. The tour group had arrived, New Yorkers on ATVs, led by a German ex-motocrosser from San Diego named Sven. Sven rode the only two-wheeler in the group, a Honda XR400, and kidded his clients that he was still too young to ride an ATV.

"Those DR-Zs are nice bikes," Sven said, looking at our Suzukis, "but in Baja, in the middle of nowhere, I like air-cooling. Less to go wrong. XRs are tough."

I agreed with him, but had to admit I was addicted to my DR-Z's electric starting. We retired to the restaurant, had another great dinner, and sat around the fireplace all evening comparing brands of tequila and telling incredible but partly true stories.

The next day, Pat and I loaded our bikes into the van, juddered back to the highway and headed east on Mex. 2, taking the four-lane toll road over the spectacular Rumerosa Grade, whose flanks are a graveyard of smashed and burned cars. Crosses and memorials to the dead line the road; it's the Flanders Fields of highways. Descending onto the coastal plain, we motored into Mexicali.

Mexicali's suburbs are a zone of bad construction, stray dogs, junked cars, Tecate Beer signs, and blowing plastic bag—the air redolent with the aroma of sulfur and trash. But when you get to the center, it's a bustling industrial town with a Wal-Mart and McDonald's and lots of American-named factories, part of the NAFTA miracle that has cost us so many jobs in Wisconsin.

We turned down Mex. 5 toward San Felipe and just south of Mexicali motored through a vast city dump in the desert flats—burning tires, trash half-buried. For miles and miles there are old tires everywhere, far as the eye can see, like spilled black Cheerios. Mexico's border with the United States is never a pretty place.

But it quickly gets better. As you head along the salt marshes of the Gulf of California, traffic tapers off and after about 100 miles you come into the little fishing and tourist town of San Felipe, which sits charmingly on a white sand bay. The place is full of *mariscos* (seafood) restaurants and bars, with lots of retired gringos living in cottages and motor homes on the nearby beaches.

We checked into the Hotel El Capitan, a clean, modern place with an enclosed courtyard to protect bikes and trucks from prying eyes. After unloading the bikes, we headed off for dinner on a warm, balmy evening with the surf lapping the beach and a breeze rustling the palm trees. I suddenly realized that for the first time in months I was fully relaxed and not hunching my neck down into my collar to keep warm.

"There is a vast distance, geographically and psychically," I said to Pat, "between this place and, say, Springfield, Missouri, during a blizzard."

"Almost another planet," he said.

In front of the International Restaurant (which advertised Mexican food!), we met Jeff Allen, a *Cycle World* photographer who'd ridden down from the home office in Newport Beach to join our little expedition for a day of riding and shooting photos that would capture our almost indescribable riding skills against the mystical Baja landscape. Jeff is a superb dirt rider who could easily zip ahead of us on the trail, with plenty of time (hours) to set up his camera gear and catch us roosting down the dusty trail.

Jeff was also mounted on a DR-Z400S, a brand-new test bike with the small stock 2.6-gallon tank, so he had a couple of plastic gas bottles bungeed to the sides of his seat. He'd made it all the way from the office in one day, riding on dirt roads over the mountains rather than cruising down on the paved highway. Yet he looked completely relaxed and rested. Pat and I were dumbfounded.

In the morning, we gassed up, slung on our backpacks, and headed off into the mountains on a two-day loop that would take us to the legendary Mike's Sky Ranch and back. We rode out of town past the city dump without taking advantage of the many opportunities for tire puncture on old nails, metal scraps, cans, barbed wire, etc., and soon found ourselves following Jeff through miles of deep sand whoops across the valley floor.

To a person of fifty-five from Wisconsin who has gained twelve pounds over the winter and has had no exercise except to walk the dogs on those rare days when it's above zero, several miles of repetitious sand whoops are the equivalent to your first day in basic training—all pushups and deep knee bends. But we did not melt down and eventually got into the rhythm of riding in the sand, which is simply a form of fatalism. You abandon yourself to the constant sensation of imminent crashing, sit back on the saddle loose as a goose, and keep the power on.

Pat caught onto this very quickly, and was soon riding faster than I was. I have an Early Tankslapper Warning System (ETWS) embedded in my brain that, tragically, prevents me from really dialing it on in deep sand. It has its roots in a high-speed face-plant I managed in the Barstow-to-Vegas dual-purpose ride one year. Yes, in the sand I am damaged goods.

In mid-morning, the trail opened on to a huge dry lake bed called Laguna Diablo (*si*, the dreaded Lagoon of the Devil; many enter but few return) and we pegged the throttles wide open. My bike would pull about seventy miles per hour in fourth, but bog in fifth. Pat, with a Yoshimura pipe, richer jetting, and K&N filter, could go about five miles per hour faster and use top gear. But my stocker started and idled better, by way of feeble compensation.

We stopped halfway across the lake bed at a cluster of rustic buildings where the inhabitant, a small Mexican man, sells cold drinks and snacks. He had a pot of something mysterious brewing on an oil-drum stove. His house had a slightly evil smell, and the garage was festooned with a couple of severed goats' heads, hanging from strings and dangling in the wind. Something about the place reminded me of either the last half-hour of *Apocalypse Now* or an old Rolling Stones album I have. Perhaps this man was, in fact, the devil himself, and the pot contained genuine goat head soup. Or perhaps he was just an avid Stones fan.

In any case, the Cokes were ice-cold, and we got to pet several yellow dogs as we shooed away the flies. Soon another tour group arrived, fathers and sons all on motorcycles, led by a guide named Bruce Anderson, who was a fellow car and motorcycle roadracer when I lived in California in the early 1980s. Good to see him again.

Like Rick's place in *Casablanca*, sooner or later everyone comes to Baja. Or at least all the usual suspects do.

After more sand trails, we hit a short stretch of paved road on Mex. 3, then turned off on a dirt road with a sign for Mike's Sky Ranch. It was a beautiful road in the late afternoon sun, gradually turning just hilly, rocky, and twisty enough to be fun as you approach Mike's. We took a single-track detour for several miles through the pucker-bushes, just to build character, and I went wide in a corner and neatly sheared off an ocotillo tree with the brush-cutter on my left handguard.

Handguards are good, I noted. Otherwise, I would have smashed every finger in my left hand, and taken the clutch lever off.

We finally came over a rise and saw Mike's, a lovely rancho/motel built around a pool in the palm of a high mountain valley. When we got off the bikes, it was Miller Time in a big way. Actually, Pacifica Clara time. We were tired and blissfully happy to be there. As we sat by the pool with a beer, it felt like the Promised Land.

Mike's was originally conceived as a fly-in trout-fishing resort, and there's a small airstrip, now closed (supposedly at the suggestion of the DEA) on the nearby mountaintop. But it was off-roaders more than fishermen who converged, making the place a Baja institution. The bar is plastered with business cards and bumper stickers from every off-road race team, bike maker, buggy builder, and dirt rider in the world, with several generations of *Cycle World* decals in the mix.

Mike Sr., who looked like Caesar Romero, died a few years back with his wife in a car accident, but his son, Mike Jr., has kept the spirit of the place and fixed it up better than ever. The rooms are clean, and furnished in elegantly simple Spanish style.

We had the traditional Mike's dinner of steaks cooked over a mesquite fire, then returned to the bar for a beer and to watch Baja 1000 videos on TV with a big crowd of other riders who'd shown up in small groups.

Among them was none other than Jerry Platt. Jerry is an old Baja hand and *Cycle World* contributor, with whom I first rode to Mike's twenty-three years ago on our annual *CW* Baja Trek. Jerry ran the first Baja 1000 in 1967 on a magazine-sponsored Norton 750 P11 scrambler, and his old race partner Vern Hancock was also in the bar. Traveling with them were Vic Wilson, who won the first Baja 1000 outright in a Meyers Manx, and his wife Betty Jean, former wife of the late Joe Parkhurst and co-founder of *Cycle World*. Baja royalty. They had all arrived in buggies and trucks.

The old Rick's place syndrome again. Bruce Anderson was there, too. It felt like the bar at a class reunion.

The next morning, Jeff split for home, and Pat and I filled our Camelbacks and mounted up. Incidentally, I'd never used one of these "hydration systems" with a hose and mouthpiece before, and it made a huge difference in how much water I drank because I didn't have to take my helmet and goggles off to get a drink each time. Pat and I had brought lots of bottled water along in the van, but I ended up filling my Camelback bladder with tap water at all our hotels, without problem. Water is supposed to be good everywhere in Baja.

In fact, the only time I ever got sick here was from eating unwashed salad greens in Ensenada in 1982, just before a ride to Mike's. Nature called so often it sounded like an echo chamber.

Pat and I cruised back to San Felipe on many of the same trails, and a few new ones, had a shrimp taco dinner that night at a little outdoor seafront cafe, then braced ourselves for the Big Ride the next day.

Rising early (for us), we rode down the gulf coast about 100 miles on a mixture of increasingly neglected roads and dirt trails, refueled at Bahia San Luis Gonzaga, then turned southwest on single-track trails. Our plan was to climb over the mountain divide, hit the main highway, and head back north to the village of Catavina that night. On this leg, we decided to challenge ourselves a bit and take a trail marked on our map as "difficult" over the mountains.

And it was.

Picture fifteen miles of steep stairs made of loose rock and boulders in a V-shaped canyon.

Which is another way of saying we beat ourselves to death for about three hours climbing out. I crashed into the side of the canyon wall while trying to loft my front wheel over a boulder about the size of a prize-winning hog. The sudden stop split my plastic gas tank at the rear mount and smacked my ribs into the left grip (the bruise is still there, in festive shades of iodine and Vicks-bottle blue). Gas trickled down onto my swingarm like a babbling brook, but at least I was left with half a tank after the fuel level sank below the split seam.

Pat crashed about three times and hit his chest on the bars, hard. I heard his engine stop once and went back to find him splayed on the rocks with his arms and legs out and his bike lying on its side. "I'm just resting," he said.

We got out of the canyon in a series of thirty-yard banzai attacks on the rocks, punctuated by five-minute rests in relatively flat areas. About an hour before dark, we finally crested the grade and found ourselves on beautiful high-desert trails, with a mist of rain moving in.

At an abandoned mine called "Mine Camp" (which I immediately dubbed *Mein Kampf,* after our struggle up the mountain), we took a wrong fork in the growing darkness, but Pat's GPS unit came to the rescue, pointing us back to the camp and off on a different trail.

Without Kacey Smith's GPS coordinates, we'd probably still be out there, eating grubs and seeds, these pages would be tragically blank, and our wives would be out shopping with the insurance money.

We passed an amazing little Baja institution called Coco's Corner, a rancho and snack stop festooned with aluminum cans hanging from all the fences, glittering in the wind. Coco himself came to the gate and advised us not to press onward toward Catavina because *(a)* it was about fifty miles away, *(b)* it would be much colder on the Pacific side of the mountains, and *(c)* it was almost dark and about to rain. He advised us to ride back down to Gonzaga Bay, whence we had come, a mere thirty miles away on the graded dirt road.

But just as Hillary and Tensing did not turn back from Everest, Pat and I pressed on into the gloom. Mainly because we wanted to have a margarita and stay at the upscale (for Baja) Hotel La Pinta, which I remembered as the best and only lodging in Catavina. In fact, it was almost the only building, miles from anywhere, in a spectacular setting of cactus and boulder fields—one of the most beautiful spots in Baja.

We got there, damp, cold, and exhausted about 8 p.m. and found the place was full, as two large tour groups of BMW streetbikes were staying there, having come down the smoothly paved Mex. 1, the cowards. I naturally hadn't gotten reservations because I'd never seen the place full.

Pat and I were very sad. Speechless, in fact.

But the clerk told us in Spanish (which I both speak and listen to brokenly) that there was, in fact, another little motel about 400 meters up the road called Cabanas Linda, so we went there and found a room. Cheap (twenty dollars for a double), clean, and simple—two beds, a chair, and a sort of shower nozzle/pipe-in-the-wall that actually emitted steaming hot water. There was no room heat, but the beds had lots of blankets, which is the normal Baja answer to the national furnace shortage.

As I fell asleep that night, after popping a Vicodin for my injured ribs, I said, "This is the best motel I've ever known."

We had breakfast at La Pinta the next morning and I filled my leaking tank at the nearby Pemex station, reasoning that our J-B Weld and duct tape probably wouldn't stick to the soft, greasy plastic. We then hotfooted it 160 miles back over the mountains, taking the "easy" road this time, with my bike stinking of gas fumes. We refueled in Gonzaga Bay and stutter-bumped back up the coast to San Felipe.

Late in the afternoon, we finally got back to our trusty Hotel El Capitan, where the owner had kindly let us leave our van. My bike had just gone on reserve.

We climbed off the bikes stiffly, took off our dusty goggles, looked at each other like a couple of weary raccoons, and shook hands. End of the Baja ride. Still walking upright, more or less, bikes still working.

Over fish tacos and beers on the waterfront that evening, Pat and I agreed we'd been lucky not to get stranded the day before. At one point in the rocky canyon we were about thirty difficult miles in any direction from another human being, a telephone, or even a standing wall. A broken wrist or a broken bike would have been a Very Bad Thing.

Most amazing, though, over all those hard miles, was the toughness of our Suzukis. Pat said, "I cannot believe the beating these bikes take without failing."

Our skid plates helped, of course. Both of us smacked into boulders several times, hard enough to break the cases or clip off a water pump housing. And my left radiator had been bent like a banana, but had fortunately not sprung a leak. Sven, with his preference for air-cooled bikes, probably had a point. Still, we both made it with no trouble other than a pair of lost chain guard bolts, which we replaced with nylon tie-wraps.

Beyond the bikes' capacity to absorb punishment was their ability to soldier through so many types of terrain without stalling, overheating, or being deflected from the trail. The DR-Z400S has an amazingly plush ride and seems to soak up shock loads from rocks and rain ruts, while maintaining its direction, in a way that at times seems to defy physics. It wants to go where you point it, and the engine is like a bulldog crossed with a greyhound; it just never quits grinding out forward motion at the bottom end, yet feels lively at the top.

We were both worried about having only batteries and starter buttons—no kick starters—before we left for Baja, but the little red buttons never let us down. And there is something wonderful about restarting a bike on a steep hillside with the push of a button, rather than backing it down to a level spot. One of the unwritten laws of kick-starting a dirt bike is that you usually have to do it when you're so tired you can't.

Overall, I would have to say that the DR-Z is a great trail bike, and an easy bike to handle for riders at our level. Or, apparently, at any level. Jeff liked his, and *CW*'s dirt ace Jimmy Lewis owns one. In any case, my hat is off to the Suzuki engineers who cooked up this particular brew. Pat and I did 700 miles off-road in Baja, and our bikes got us out of a lot of tight spots.

With our week of Mexican insurance about to run out, we loaded up the bikes in San Felipe and headed north. At a clogged border crossing in Mexicali, we encountered an American customs agent who was so rude I told Pat I thought he was just testing to see if we would fight back. "Maybe if you don't flash a little anger, they know you're hiding drugs."

"No," Pat said wearily, "he's just an unhappy guy."

While the agent carefully inspected the contents of our van, people were passing money and documents back and forth through the iron bars of the border fence, fifty feet away. No wonder the guy was unhappy; he'd been given a hopeless job.

Not a very pleasant welcome home, but maybe we'd just been spoiled by the quiet, dignified politeness of the people farther south in Baja, away from the border.

And the food. And the beer. And the weather, too.

We hit yet another blizzard at the Missouri border on our three-day drive home, and arrived at my house on an evening when it was eighteen degrees.

It's a long drive in your van from Wisconsin to San Felipe and back—our round trip was 4,600 miles—but worth it. I'd do it again, and probably will.

There's no place like Baja. It's a big, dry, mountainous land, a wilderness large enough to perpetually frustrate easy commerce and settlement. The peninsula itself is like one of the desert plants that grow there—durable, spiny, and full of defensive thorns. You can admire it, but it's not easy to handle. It's a place that resists domestication and change. I first rode there twenty-three years ago, and it's just as good now as it was then.

Bad roads, of course, deserve most of the credit for this ageless charm.

May they never improve.

2005 edition of Cycle World's Adventures *magazine*

A THOUSAND MILES FROM NOWHERE

I've watched my old VHS copy of On Any Sunday *so many times the tape is about worn out, and my favorite part is always the footage of Malcolm Smith blazing across the empty spaces of Baja. But even those skillfully shot, sprawling scenes don't really give you an accurate idea of what a big and beautiful place the Baja peninsula really is, and what it means to ride 1,000 miles on dirt roads and two-track trails through desert and mountains.*

This is a bike trip I've wanted to make for many years, along with my friends Pat Donnelly and Jim Wargula, and last fall we finally quit making excuses and pulled it off. All of us realized we aren't getting any younger, and, while Baja never seems to change, we do. It was time to go and quit talking about it.

It was almost Halloween, and the baggage handlers unloading our plane in San Diego were wearing clown masks. A little unsettling in this age of terrorism and bad chain saw movies, but our luggage arrived unmolested.

We quickly hoisted our three huge duffel bags of riding gear from the carousel and lugged them out into the warm California sunshine.

Palm trees rattled in the light ocean breeze. Deeply tanned women who'd stepped right out of a fitness video were flagging down cabs, or climbing into Mercedes convertibles with guys who looked like Kid Rock or Prince Bandar.

Simultaneously, we all put on our sunglasses.

About five minutes later, a spotless white Chevy pickup towing a double-axle trailer loaded with bright red motorcycles came skidding to a stop in front of the baggage claim. The truck said "GoBajaRidin" on the door.

"I think that's our ride," Pat Donnelly said. Jim Wargula and I picked up our bags and headed toward the curb.

This was more like it.

Only two years ago, my buddy Donnelly and I had done a 700-mile, off-road loop through northern Baja on our own Suzuki DRZ-400s. It was a great trip, but more than half of our vacation time was spent hauling our bikes across the United States in my Ford van. By the time we got home, our off-roading adventure had almost become a dim memory, like trying to remember your exact bank balance right after a bad plane crash.

"Next time," Pat said, as we pulled into his driveway, "I think we should fly out to California and rent some bikes. That tour group we met at Mike's Sky Ranch seemed like the way to go."

So last summer, Pat, who is a lot more computer savvy that I am (which is also true of our senile dachshund, Tuffy), got on the Internet and tracked down the folks whose path we'd crossed at Mike's, an outfit called GoBajaRidin Tours (www.gobajaridin.com). The owner of the company, Bruce Anderson, said he would be happy to organize whatever kind of trek we had in mind.

"Here's the deal," Pat told me, after gathering all the facts. "You pay your money, fly into San Diego, and they drive you down to a hotel in Ensenada. You start riding the next morning. They provide Honda XR400s, hotels, fuel, and meals. Everything's included except your drinks and airline tickets. They have a support truck for tools and spares, and to carry your luggage to the next hotel. Most of their guided tours are three- or four-day loops in northern Baja, but Bruce said they could take us on a five-day run down the whole peninsula to La Paz because they want to pre-run this year's Baja 1000 route."

"Perfect," I said. "Now all we have to do is get Jim to go along."

The Jim in question was Jim Wargula, a trail riding buddy who, like Pat and me, had just gotten back into dirt riding a couple of years ago. We went way back, Jim, Pat, and I. We'd all played in the same clueless loud garage band back in the 1960s, and we were still playing together now, in an only slightly quieter version of the same group. Three guitar players, three motorcyclists, three old gringos: The *Tres Amigos*.

"I'll have to put the pressure on Jim," I told Pat. "He won't want to spend the money because he just bought a Honda XR650 and some new motocross boots. Also, he's cheaper than ten Scotsmen."

So I called Jim and used what I call the Mortality Argument.

"I really shouldn't go," Jim said. "I can't afford it right now."

"Well, look at the bright side," I said. "We'll all be dead soon and then we won't have to decide whether to go on THE RIDE OF A LIFETIME WITH OUR BEST FRIENDS or not."

A few days later, Jim called and said he'd go. Terror of the void works every time on people over fifty-five.

So we maxed out our credit cards (GoBajaRidin prices range from $1,750 per person for the four-day loop of northern Baja to $3,700 for a six-day run to Cabo San Lucas), packed our riding gear, cashed in our frequent flier miles, and flew into San Diego. Minutes after arrival, that white Chevy pickup drove into view, towing its trailer load of Hondas.

Bruce "Bruno" Anderson, a big, hearty guy who looks vaguely like Kris Kristofferson (but can probably hold a note more accurately), bounded out and shook hands with us. "Let's throw your luggage on the roof rack and head for Mexico," he said.

We cleared customs at the border and drove across into Mexico. Small clusters of young men were sitting on earthen embankments next to the highway, tying rubber tubing around their biceps and shooting up in broad daylight.

"Look at all these guys shooting heroin," Bruce said.

"Why here?" I asked.

"Because it's cheap and the cops don't care."

We cruised out of the sunbaked bordertown tackiness of Tijuana and down sixty miles of scenic highway to Ensenada, where the Pacific was glistening under sunny skies. We passed the seaside Fox movie studio where nautical scenes from *Titanic* were filmed. The icebergs, apparently, had melted.

At Ensenada, we unloaded our bikes and met two of Bruno's assistants, Manuel Santana and Ricardo Lopez, who would alternatively be riding sweep and looking after our bikes. We checked into rooms at the San Nicolas Hotel and walked to dinner. The town was jumping, and a big Tecate sign over the street said, "Welcome SCORE 1000, Nov. 17-18."

Over a plate of great fish tacos, Bruce said, "Larry will be joining us in the morning, just before we leave."

This was none other than Larry Roeseler—ten-time overall winner of the Baja 1000, six-time ISDT gold medalist, and twelfth-place finisher in his first Paris-Dakar race last year. One of the greatest off-road motorcyclists on Earth. In recent years, he'd started racing off-road trucks for the Terrible Herbst team, and was doing just as well in those.

Larry would be riding with us partly for fun and partly to scout this year's Baja 1000 route, which he, Bruce, and Santana would all be running in a few weeks. Bruce had run the race four times on bikes and won his class twice with four-wheelers, while Santana had done it twenty-five times, finishing third in class on an XR600.

This was a fast bunch we were riding with. Especially considering the almost tragically limited dirt experience of the *Tres Amigos*.

On our walk back to the hotel from dinner, Bruce pointed out the traditional starting point of the Baja 1000, a city street that immediately hooked down into a river valley and headed up a wide, shallow river bed. He explained that we would be skipping this immediate baptism in the crystal waters of the Arroyo de Ensenada and hitting the trail just east of town in the morning.

"Get some sleep," he said at the hotel, "We've got a big day tomorrow." It was not the last time we'd hear that phrase.

We congregated at our bikes in the morning, suited up, and got ready to go. Bruce requires full body armor for all participants—motocross boots, knee protectors, chest protector, elbow pads, full helmet, goggles, etc. A good idea, as it turned out.

Larry Roeseler showed up and unloaded his personal mount, a KTM 625 EXC. I'd never met Larry before, and he turned out to be a great guy—articulate, funny, and very sharp, but also modest and self-effacing. Funny how the best people in motorsports almost always turn out to be this way.

We learned the starting drill on our XR400s (choke when cold, ease just past TDC with the compression release, then kick like you mean it, all the way through), pulled our goggles down over our eyes (or tri-focals, in my case), and hit the road in the direction of San Felipe on the eastern, Sea of Cortez side of the peninsula.

A few miles later, we turned off the highway onto a rocky, rutted two-track road through the mountains. Time to get it on, as they say in old *Shaft* movies.

And Bruce, who was leading our group, did just that. The pace was fast.

It took me about five minutes to warm up and wish I hadn't worn my enduro jacket. "This ain't no disco," I wheezed into my helmet while standing on the pegs and leaping around a rock-infested puddle. "This ain't no foolin' around."

Larry went by me with his rear tire occasionally touching the earth in a sort of wheelie-dance, and he disappeared into the distance. I gripped the bars, sucked in, and cranked on some more throttle. "Only about 992 miles to go," I noted cheerfully.

That day followed a pattern repeated often during the trip. I'd feel old, slow, and useless in the morning, then get into the rhythm of riding and feel more energetic in the afternoon. Some days were better than others. (I have Hepatitis C, and my energy level takes wild swings, like the laugh-meter in a cheap sitcom.) But by the end of the trip I felt great, and was ready to ride to Tierra del Fuego. If you don't break your leg, dirt riding is always therapeutic.

Meanwhile, Jim would ride like a bat out of hell in the morning, then he'd tire in the afternoon, and I'd pass him. Pat rode fast all the time. Being a good, natural powder-skier, he was very comfortable in loose, deep sand—of which we would have many, many miles.

Regardless of position, we rode most of the fast, straight sections about an eighth of a mile apart to stay out the previous guy's dust cloud—good for both lungs and air filters. We were a long dust train, burning up the open space.

We looped upward into the pine country of the Sierra de Juarez, through El Coyote and Santa Catarina, then hit a short stretch of paved Highway 3 before dropping into sand whoops (where Jim crashed in a deep sand wash, saving me the trouble) leading onto the mirage-ridden expanse of Diablo dry lake. More miles of sand and dirt road, through the existential city dump, and into San Felipe on the Sea of Cortez. We pulled into a nice motel called George's with a protected courtyard for parking and climbed off the bikes. I was wringing wet with sweat from the last ten miles of sand whoops.

"I'm glad I didn't put this trip off until I was seventy-two," I told Pat.

We cleaned up, came out at dusk, and found ourselves surrounded by little ghosts, mummies, witches, pumpkins, and zombies. No baggage handlers. It was Halloween night in San Felipe, and the town's parents had gone all-out on their kids' costumes. We had a beer on the boardwalk near the beach and watched these apparitions trick-or-treating in all the stores and shops. To see families interact in Baja is to go back to the 1940s and 1950s in the United States—the kids are respectful, unspoiled, and a little shy around adults, not encouraged to see themselves as royalty.

We had our own Halloween treat—dinner at the famous old El Nido steakhouse. There we met Jim Dickinson, a three-time GoBajaRidin client who had flown in from Maryland and was just joining our intrepid troupe. He turned out to be a lively, high-energy guy and an excellent rider, adding a whole new element of fun to the trip. Arriving with Jim was another guide, a tall, easy-going surfer/skier/rider (what season is it?) named Clark Hudson. Now we were nine.

"Gotta leave early in the morning," Bruce said. "We've got a really big day tomorrow."

During the night our bikes had magically been fueled, cleaned, and lubed by the crew, and we headed south out of San Felipe just as the first sun rays were breaking over the Sea of Cortez. At the edge of town, Bruce suddenly cut left over a huge sand dune and we all followed him, sliding back down onto the highway.

The coast highway south of San Felipe starts out paved, then gets steadily worse all day long, until you are riding on a mixture of loose gravel and rocks held together with potholes, seismic faults, igneous extrusions, and Permian hogbacks—not too many lava flows. The Honda XR400s, I must say, handled all this in stride.

Bruce and Clark prepped the bikes with bigger plastic IMS 4.3-gallon gas tanks, taller gearing, heavy-duty tubes, O-ring chains, much richer jetting (160 main), K&N air filters, and tall Moose seats with heavy racing foam from Guts. Forks and shocks were reworked by Precision Concepts and revalved with "way stiffer" springs from Eibach.

And their bikes did take a beating, mile after mile of it, without complaint. They were a little less flickable than my KTM 525, and somewhat wound-out on paved highway, but they handled the dirt with good stability, poshness of ride, and had nice power delivery on the trail. Kick-starting and air-cooling keeps them simple, basic, and tough. Great Baja bikes, they built more respect with each passing mile.

Morning sun helped to warm us despite an eerie thirty-five-mile-per-hour gale that blew our dust clouds away in small horizontal twisters. We stopped to take a break at the only ugly spot on the coast, a little godforsaken concrete-and-rebar village called Puertecitos. There were no humans to be seen and the broken sign in the closed Pemex station creaked in the wind. Somewhere a cat ran away. The place gave me the creeps, like a post-nuclear town from *On the Beach*.

We climbed on our bikes and hammered south, fueling up at Gonzaga Bay, a fly-in fishing village. We stopped for lunch at a famous (only) restaurant called Alfonsina's. The owner told us they had just stopped serving lunch.

But, as we were their only customers, he started again. Good business plan. Good fish tacos, too.

We struck inland toward the mountains, climbing to a place called Coco's Corners at a remote junction of roads. Coco is a notorious character, a wild man who runs a little snack stand and campsite decorated with tin cans, hubcaps, Baja 1000 stickers, women's underwear, goat's heads, and dead scorpions. Picture a Mexican John Belushi in a high desert version of *Animal House*.

We had a Coke and I asked Coco if there was anyplace to take a leak. He waved his arm at the great outdoors. "Everywhere the ground needs water." I looked around and saw that he was right.

Another forty miles of scenic bliss, up canyons and riverbeds, brought us to the highway and a short distance from our destination, the famous little fishing town of Bahia de los Angeles. We hit our friendly little motel right at sunset and met up with our late-arriving, hard-riding photographer Jeff Allen, who'd brought his own Suzuki DRZ400S. We all kicked back for a few beers in the courtyard, then walked to a beachside restaurant called Guillermo's—great fish.

In fact, nearly everywhere in Baja has great fish. The Sea of Cortez is one of the richest fisheries in the world, a fact that didn't elude the great author and sometime marine biologist John Steinbeck, who came to Bahia de los Angeles in 1940. Even then, he noted, there were a lot of Americans in town, fishing. He didn't mention dirt bikes.

"Better get a good night's sleep," Bruce said on our walk back to the motel. "We've got a really long day of riding tomorrow."

In the morning we looped inland along a mountain ridge, then descended a steep valley to Punta San Francisquito for lunch in a little seaside outdoor cafe under a palm-covered roof. The afternoon was spent climbing back through the mountains, up beautiful valleys washed by creeks and surrounded by stunning Sonoran desert plant life—big cardon cactus, ocotillo, and the famously weird boojum trees of Baja, which look like twisted, twenty-foot-tall candles. In one of these valleys, we stopped for a breather and were passed by none other than Robby Gordon in his pre-runner truck, scouting for the upcoming 1000.

At El Mujica we hit Highway 1 and "burned pavement," as Bruce would say, for the last thirty miles to the La Pinta Hotel in San Ignacio. This little town is one of my favorite places in Baja. A green oasis in a deep valley, it has a lovely old mission church and a quiet little square with shops around it, like something in an old Peckinpah Western. When I retire, I just might move to San Ignacio.

As we headed back to our rooms after dinner, Bruce said, "Get a good night's sleep. We've got a really big day tomorrow, and we have to leave before sunrise." I turned on the TV in my room, where votes were being counted in the Kerry-Bush race for president. No results yet. Good. I needed sleep. And ibuprofen.

We met by our bikes in chilly pitch-darkness, fired up, and headed out of town. Before the trip, Bruce had recommended clear-lens goggles. I neglected to buy any before the trip and brought tinted goggles. Big mistake. For the first hour out of San Ignacio, I had to ride through the darkness with my goggles off, squinting through the dust clouds to see where I was going. By the time the sun came up, my eyeballs felt like they'd been on loan to Erwin Rommel.

Southwest we rode, toward the Pacific coast, on endlessly long sandy roads flanked by cacti, turning south at the coast through a series of small, remote fishing camps. Lunch found us at San Juanico, eating under a *palapa* (thatched hut) at the famous surfer's camp called Scorpion Bay, a stunning spot surrounded by blue water and drenched in sun, like something from a Jimmy Buffett album cover.

An American in surf baggies sat at a nearby table, clacking away on a satellite-linked portable computer. "Well, it's final," he said. "Bush has won the election."

The news caused quiet elation in some of our group and speechless despair in others. I won't tell which camp I was in, except to say that I had voted for a candidate who I believed was *not* dumber than a pail of mink food. You'll have to draw your own conclusions.

From there we rode south along the hard-packed sand beach—an exercise in pure elation and freedom—then cut toward the other coast on rugged sand and dirt roads toward Loreto. With shadows long, we descended to the coast through one of the most beautiful canyons I've ever seen—mystically deep and misty green. It had an ancient colonial road hacked into cliffs (by Indian slaves) on the opposite wall, so the Spanish padre and soldiers could cross the mountains. To build more roads. To find more Indian laborers whose souls needed saving, and so on. Most of the Indian population of Baja was wiped out by smallpox, so the missions here were left with few parishioners, but large graveyards.

The canyon opened up to the coast, and we found our hotel—a big seaside golf course resort, just south of Loreto. This was the most swanky hotel of the trip, but my least favorite. Too removed from the gritty reality of Baja for my humble soul. I like the mom-and-pop places, where your bike is just outside your room.

In the dark, early morning, we backtracked up that same spectacular canyon and forked south to the beautiful San Javier mission, nestled in the mountains like a jewel lighted by the rising sun. On the gate of the mission was a business card from Larry Roeseler, who'd left earlier to do some scouting. On the card he'd written, "What took you guys so long?"

From San Javier we zigged to the Pacific coast, then headed across the peninsula's narrow waist to our final destination, burning some highway toward the Bahia de la Paz.

This was the best day of the trip for me. I felt good, and finally started feeling relaxed with the throttle wide open on deeply sanded roads with the bike squirming queasily but harmlessly across the endless miles of desert and beach sand. This is what it takes to go faster in Baja: confidence under conditions of disconnected looseness, but without losing your concentration or readiness to deal with sudden surprises. Of which we had several that day—washouts, buried boulders, sudden turns over blind rises, etc.

When we got into La Paz, just at dark, we'd covered 274 miles that day. This, folks, is a long way to go on a dirt bike. We'd averaged well over 200 miles a day, and covered just over 1,150 total miles, what with all our backtracking to hotels at night.

How far is that? Well, it's like riding from my home in Wisconsin to Daytona Beach, off road, or twice the length of Florida. I don't know how anybody does it in one continuous ride, or even splitting the Baja 1000 into halves with a co-rider. If you ride at racing speed—especially at night—the opportunities to crash are endless. These guys have my undying admiration and respect.

Even at our more sedate pace, Jim and Pat had each gone over the handlebars once in spectacular fashion—getting only minor bruises—while blitzing through deep sand whoops, and Jim had done a couple of minor get-offs in deep sand wallows. I got through the trip without crashing, but had more than my share of "moments" where I'd abandoned all hope. How Larry Roeseler could *win* this thing year after year without crashing his brains out is beyond me.

As Jim said, "That's why he's Larry Roeseler and we're not."

La Paz, when we finally got there in the gathering darkness, turned out to be a large, rather cosmopolitan city—with lots of good restaurants, upscale shops, and hotels—on a huge blue bay. Our hotel, a beautiful, friendly beachside placed called La Concha, sat on a white sand beach just on the edge of the city.

The crew from GoBajaRidin loaded up and left in the morning, hauling the bikes back up to Los Angeles. The rest of us took a day off for beach lounging, then flew home the next day.

Before he left, Bruce shook my hand and said, "Well, you guys all made it."

I laughed and said, "There were a couple of days when I wasn't so sure we all would."

Bruce nodded. "It's a tough ride, but we do everything we can to make sure no one gives up. People who finish this trip will always remember it and feel like they've really done something, but a guy who quits is ruined forever."

As we flew north along the Sea of Cortez, I looked out at that 1,000-mile coastline and thought to myself that riding here in the dirt is not so much a sport as a parable.

2005 edition of Cycle World's Adventures *magazine*

IN THE MOON OF THE FALLING LEAVES

Author Robert M. Pirsig once pointed out that many of the virtues we've idealized as Americans—self-reliance, direct speech, stoicism in the presence of hardship, and personal freedom—actually originated with the Plains Indians and rubbed off on our white western heroes, the best of whom lived with the Indians and learned their ways.

The area around the Badlands and the Black Hills is, to me, the very center of that highly developed old buffalo hunting culture and the great chiefs who fought to hold on to their land. These people are long gone now, but it seems to me that the further they recede into history, the more we have to learn from them. The opportunity to think about these things has brought me back to this corner of South Dakota many times.

"Sometimes when I ride up to this ridge and look north along the Cheyenne River valley, it's almost as if I can still see the tepees down there on the cottonwood flats, or the blue-coated cavalry camped along the bluffs," rancher Randy Babcock said to me, sweeping his arm along the horizon.

We were sitting on a couple of dirt bikes, Randy on his new Suzuki DRZ400 and me on my KTM 525 EXC. With us were at least a dozen other guys on dirt bikes, lined up along the ridge like some kind of modern-day war party, helmeted and bristling with body armor. We weren't making war on others, however, just administering the usual self-inflicted wounds, testing ourselves against this rugged country just north of the Badlands.

Our engines were off and the wind was whistling soft and steady through out helmets. No one spoke.

Randy was right. You could easily imagine tepees on the river flats below. Maybe that was because we'd been trained by a hundred Western movies to see this landscape as Indian country (*Dances with Wolves* was filmed nearby), or maybe historical places really do resonate with stray energy, even after the warriors are gone.

In any case, I felt lucky to be there, another happy victim of chance in one of those weird connections you find only in the motorcycle world.

My Wisconsin riding buddy Rob Himmelmann met the owner of this fine property, Randy Babcock, several years ago at a swap meet in Sturgis, where they were both admiring the skeletal remains of an old Bultaco Lobito—or some such crusty relic—and got talking about dirt bikes and trail rides. The upshot was that Randy invited Rob and a few of his friends to come riding on his nearby ranch, which has been in his family for three generations.

What Rob found there was an off-road riding paradise. A nice old ranch house, a barn filled with a funky, charismatic assortment of motorcycles, and nearly 7,000 acres of soaring grass pastureland, scenic ridges, shaded valleys full of trees, barely climbable buttes, and steep cattle trails leading down into the river bottoms.

Randy and his family had moved into a newer home nearby, so the old original ranch house had magically mutated into a kind of clubhouse for motorcyclists, decorated with Norton posters, Triumph signs, and other old bike memorabilia. There was a real jukebox in the dining room and a lifetime supply of motorcycle videos and classic John Ford Westerns piled next to the TV in the living room.

Life honed to perfection, in other words.

And into this Nirvana I was invited—through Rob's good graces—a couple of years ago.

It turned out Randy has get-togethers at this ranch three or four times a year, and he invites several dozen of his old riding buddies to converge on the place. They come from all over the West and Midwest, dragging trailer loads of bikes, coolers of beer, grocery bags of food, glistening green bottles of Old Overholt, and other wisdom-producing fluids of only the highest octane. For three or four days, they eat like kings, ride like the wind, then drink like fish at night. Sometimes they take Excedrin in the morning. In any case, it's always a good time.

So when Rob called me at my rural Wisconsin home and asked if I'd like to make a "ranch run" before winter hit, I said, "Yes! And it just so happens I'm up to my ears in Sioux Indian lore right now."

It was true. The history of the Plains Indians has always fascinated me, and I have a small library of books on the subject. Hell, I even have a full-size tepee I put up in our lower pasture every summer. Groups of our friends have campfires there, and we all sleep in the tepee. We smoke a peace pipe I bought at Pipestone, Minnesota. For an Irish guy from the Midwest, I'm fairly well steeped in the spirit of the Great Plains. Half nuts, some would say.

When Rob called, I was actually reading a new biography of Crazy Horse, one of the great Lakota chiefs who gave Custer what Russell Means calls a lesson in "sensitivity training" at Little Bighorn in 1876. (The Sioux called themselves "Lakota" in the western plains, and "Dakota" among the eastern tribes.) I had also recently reread Dee Brown's *Bury My Heart at Wounded Knee*.

I told Rob all this, and he said, "Well, then. We should take our DR650 dual-sport bikes out there—in addition to our dirt bikes, of course—and do some exploring of the country around the ranch. The trail where Chief Big Foot led his people down to Wounded Knee runs right past the ranch, and the old chief's cabin is just north of there. We could even ride down to Wounded Knee. Randy loves this stuff. He was a history major in college."

So early on a dark morning in late autumn I loaded my KTM 525 and Suzuki DR650 into the back of my Ford Econoline, and swung up to Oxford, Wisconsin, to pick up Rob. We hooked up his bike trailer—bearing his trusty ATK 650 and his own DR650. (Rob and I belong to a small, exclusive bike club that believes the simple, cheap, torquey, air-cooled DR650 to be an underappreciated dual-sport classic.)

After pounding the Interstate west for eleven hours, we turned north at Wall, South Dakota (home of famous Wall Drug), hit a long stretch of gravel road, and found ourselves at the ranch just at sunset. There we were met by Randy and his brother-in-law, Butch Knock, a consummate Honda XR600 pilot and part-time cowhand who usually rides in from Montana for these spontaneous motorcycle powwows. Photographer Brian Blades had also just arrived in his rental SUV after flying into Rapid City from California.

I shook hands with Randy, a relaxed, easygoing guy who, some years ago, decided that dirt bikes eat less hay and have fewer vet bills than horses, so he replaced his horses with an XR600 Honda. He rides his fences and herds cattle on the Honda—or on his new Suzuki DRZ-400—and told me he prefers motocross boots and a Belstaff enduro jacket to cowboy boots and traditional western wear. It's this kind of free thinking that can cause one to become a Moto Guzzi owner. Randy had just bought himself a new Le Mans the day before.

We ate a chili dinner, sat outside around the fire ring in the yard, and drank beer with a million stars overhead. Like Montana, South Dakota has a big sky and not much city light to drown out the stars.

In the morning, we saddled up and hit the trail north. Following ranch roads and dirt trails, we rode through the little "town" of Creighton (three houses and a row of mailboxes), turning north along Deep Creek to the former village of Pedro.

Once a thriving little pioneer farm center, there's nothing left now but an empty ranch house, some abandoned cars—including and overturned Volvo 122 with several bullet holes in the roof—and a couple of decaying log cabins.

The worst of the two cabins, now collapsing into the earth, was the home of Chief Big Foot. After the murder of Sitting Bull at Standing Rock, the Lakota decided to flee down from what is now the Cheyenne River Reservation to the Pine Ridge Reservation. They convinced the old and ailing Big Foot to leave his ranch and lead them south in bitterly cold December weather in 1890. Thus began the infamous march down the Big Foot Trail that ultimately led to the near extermination of this rag-tag band by the U.S. Cavalry at Wounded Knee.

"I'm surprised someone doesn't buy this place and restore it," I said. "The cabin could still be reconstructed, even though it's falling over."

Randy nodded. "One of my best friends in high school used to live in the ranch house over there, and we used to play around here when we were kids. But now there's no one out here."

It was the ongoing story of the Great Plains—an ever-diminishing rural population as the descendants of the original homesteaders abandon the dream of owning land and move to cities, where they can operate computers and drink Starbucks coffee instead of checking fences and producing food. Years of low rainfall west of the 100th meridian (where the West is said to begin) have made cattle ranching a tough business at times.

We rode northeast on Wilsey Road along the Cheyenne River to the Four Corners Bridge, a huge structure spanning this wide valley in the middle of nowhere.

"The corner of the Cheyenne River Reservation is right over there," Randy said. "The Indians weren't allowed to do the Ghost Dance on the reservation, so they used to come across the river and camp on this side."

The Ghost Dance was the messianic movement started by a Paiute mystic named Wovoka who preached that the Indians could bring back the buffalo herds and the good old days if they would just gather together and do the Ghost Dance. God would punish the whites for stealing Indian land, burying them under the new grass next spring while rendering Indian shirts bulletproof. All they had to do was *believe*—and dance to exhaustion.

It was a weird mixture of Christian and Indian religious ideas, the last refuge of a desperate and demoralized people. The army saw in it the seeds of further rebellion and decided to clamp down by arresting the leaders of the movement. Fear and suspicion swept over both sides, creating the fevered atmosphere of mistrust that in part led to the showdown at Wounded Knee.

Riding south, we paralleled the Big Foot Trail down Barthold Flat Road, then jogged off onto smaller dirt roads and stopped at Rose Cemetery, where many of the early white settlers are buried. We looked around the old Dowling Baptist Church, then visited a former air force missile silo command center (now owned by Randy's parents) on the edge of the ranch. The underground command bunker has been cemented in, but the upstairs living quarters are still there.

Touring this place makes you realize what the Lakota were up against, technologically speaking. Less than one human lifespan after Wounded Knee, the *wasichus* (whites) placed ICBMs in South Dakota—a couple of miles from Big Foot's cabin—that could vaporize Moscow, halfway around the world. The age of the Winchester was over.

We rode back to the ranch and continued our ride down the Big Foot Trail the next morning, detouring west on Kelly Hill Road, which is part of the old Fort Pierre–Deadwood stage line, and into Wall, Randy on his "Bumblebee" R100GS and Butch on the big-tank Paris-Dakar version of same. Neither seemed to have much trouble handling any road or trail on these big adventure-tourers.

Rob and I, meanwhile, were finding our DR650s just right for this combination of two-track ranch trails, gravel roads, and pavement. We'd both done similar modifications: four-gallon plastic Clarke gas tanks, DOT knobbies, skid plates, handguards, and one less tooth on the countershaft sprocket for better hill climbing. These bikes cruise easily at seventy to eighty miles per hour on the highway and are still light enough to handle rough trails, if you don't overwork the rear suspension with too much speed. As Rob says, "If you can't get there on a DR650, you probably shouldn't be there anyway."

We headed into the "Little Badlands" near Wall, a surreal landscape of eroded gray earth and bullets, where both Randy and Butch learned to ride dirt bikes as kids. From Wall, we descended into the Badlands National Park on Highway 240, swooping down through this beautiful, strange moonscape into the Buffalo Grass National Grasslands and west onto Highway 44 to Scenic.

Just south of town, a few miles off the highway, we climbed a rocky dirt road to the rim of Sheep Mountain Table, where a woman rancher once lived in splendid isolation, bringing all her water up the plateau in barrels. I thought the spectacular view alone was worth the effort, but then I hadn't carried any barrels up there.

Riding back through Scenic, we found the local tavern unaccountably closed, so we lunched on wholesome junk food from a convenience store across the street. Friendly dogs helped us eat Cheetos. When I was here in the early 1970s, a sign on the roof of the bar said, "Indians not welcome." Now the word "not" has been painted out. That's a big change.

Swinging north, we detoured into the Sage Creek Campground and hiked on foot to get a closer look at some grazing buffalo along the creek. I always get some elemental pleasure out of seeing buffalo; they have a prehistoric, dawn-of-time look, like something from the cave paintings at Lascaux, and they're still the perfect symbol of the western plains. My ancestors probably hunted them out of Europe, and it's only by accident we didn't hunt them to extinction in the New World.

One old bull began to snort at us, and that got us quietly discussing our sprinting ability in motocross boots. We gradually retreated toward the bikes, walking backwards.

After this big loop through the Badlands, we got back to the ranch at sunset. It was Wednesday night, and Randy's riding buddies were beginning to arrive in numbers. By Friday night, we would have twenty-eight riders sleeping on every available flat surface in the ranch house, some camping around it in tents and camp trailers.

And for the next two days, we rode the ranch—across sprawling pasturelands like a dream of freedom, down steep cattle trails into the valleys of the Cheyenne River Breaks, and along the river itself. We climbed the imposing Teapot Butte, then stopped at a place we call Borrowed Bike Hill. This is a nearly vertical silt bed/cliff along the river that has been successfully climbed only three times—usually on someone else's bike. Hence the name. Some of the younger guys in our group nearly made it. Others looped and crashed magnificently.

We rode back to the ranch and partied and talked and looked at each other's motorcycles, made big dinners of basic meat products served with hallucinogenic hot sauces, watched *The Horse Soldiers*, and hung around the campfire. I took my turn doing dishes and found the quintessential ranch house fixture—a set of Vise-Grips acting as hot water knob on the kitchen sink.

"Basically," Randy said, "this has become a clubhouse for guys by default, because no decent woman will stay here."

Friday morning arrived fog-bound, cold, and rainy, so most of the guys decided to lie around the ranch house in various states of repose and vegetative squalor, but yours truly, the intrepid reporter, was fixated on the idea of visiting Wounded Knee Cemetery, some 125 miles to the south.

Randy, Butch, Rob, and Brian kindly assented to come along, donning their many layers of Gore-Tex over wool. Jeff Ecker, a guy who will ride anywhere at any time, also decided to come with us on his BMW R100RT, which he'd just ridden in from Colorado.

It seemed like a good day to go to Wounded Knee. The Indians made the trip in bitter December cold, and even the U.S. Cavalry that intercepted them would probably have been happier to stay in the fort on those dark, wintry days just after Christmas in 1890.

So we rode through fog and rain down into the Badlands again, through Big Foot Pass, then down the highway through Potato Creek, Kyle, and Porcupine to the highway junction near Wounded Knee Creek.

There on a hill overlooking the creek was the forlorn little cemetery, with its mass grave of eighty-four men, forty-four women, and eighteen children (another seven Lakota died later of wounds). Twenty-five U.S. soldiers died as well. During the struggle in the camp below, this hill had been an emplacement for an army Hotchkiss gun.

All hell broke loose here when U.S. troops tried to disarm the warriors before escorting them into the Pine Ridge Reservation. One young brave refused to surrender his costly new Winchester and fired a shot. Both sides opened up on each other and the ensuing chaos turned into a general massacre of Indians. Big Foot, already almost dead from pneumonia, was killed. His frozen body was found the next day by a burial detail, along with many others.

Much debate had taken place over the chain of events here, but the simplest fact is probably this: Both sides were sick to death of each other, spring-loaded for violence. Randy commented that the ugly mood on both sides reminded him of Kent State during the Vietnam War. A good analogy, I thought, with chilling features of My Lai thrown in.

Small outbursts of conflict simmered on the plains in the months that followed, but Wounded Knee was really the end of the U.S.-Indian wars, and the end of a way of life for the plains Indians. The old buffalo hunting culture was gone.

We were chilled and hungry at the cemetery, so we asked a couple of high school girls who were selling souvenirs where we could find lunch. They said to go down the road a few miles and turn left up a gravel road to a place called Betty's Kitchen, which we did.

Betty's Kitchen turned out to be a neat double-wide family home in which Betty served home-cooked meals to passersby. We ate fried chicken and buffalo burgers in the dining room while a clothes dryer tumbled nearby. The walls were full of family photos, some of them showing an old chief with full eagle-feather headdress sitting with some young children. "That's my mom as a little girl, with my grandfather, Black Elk," Betty told me.

"You are the granddaughter of Black Elk?" I asked incredulously.

"Yes."

He was a holy man of the Oglala Sioux, made famous by the John G. Neihardt book, *Black Elk Speaks*. It's a classic of Indian history, still in print. I've had my own copy for years.

"He used to live on this hill," Betty said, "and John Neihardt would come up here and interview him."

A worthwhile subject for interview. Black Elk fought in the battle of Little Bighorn when he was thirteen, and he lived to see the end of World War II. His recollected life was a condensed volume of American history, from Crazy Horse to Ike.

We said goodbye, mounted up, and rode north for several hours in the gathering darkness and rain. The ranch house was an orb of light, warmth, and welcome when we got there, well chilled and soaked, after dark. A hot shower was a thing of beauty.

And so was the glass of Bushmills Randy handed me that evening, as our nightly party gathered force. "Washington Square," by the Village Stompers, was playing on the jukebox, and somebody rode a dirt bike through the house, leaving clouds of gray smoke. Gunfire from a ceremonial canon outside frightened the dogs. Grizzled riders with sore muscles popped ibuprofen like candy and washed it down with cheap rye or caffeine-free diet soft drinks. Brian Blades did a surfing demonstration on the kitchen table, while the campfire outside blazed with chunks of wood that looked suspiciously like parts of a barn. Coyotes howled in the hills. Just another quiet night at the ranch.

When we loaded the bikes to go home the next day, I noted the Suzuki DR650's odometer showed it had gone 500 miles, radiating outward and exploring from our base camp at the ranch. I'd done about sixty miles with the KTM on the ranch itself. It was all great riding, but not enough.

This part of South Dakota, surrounded by the Badlands, Black Hills, and the Cheyenne River Breaks, is so full of natural beauty and history you could spend a lifetime exploring the trails and back roads. Like certain parts of New Mexico, it has a strange, mystical quality to the landscape, and you can see why the Sioux and Cheyenne fought so hard to keep it.

The spirits are still here, and Randy's right: You can almost see those tepees from the ridge, even now, as if the clamor of history had passed out of view just moments ago, leaving dust in the air. It's a place to go back whenever you can, or just stay.

Section II

THE COLUMNS

March 1988

GUITARS AND MOTORBIKES

"How many guitars do you have now?" I asked my old friend David Rhodes this summer when I dropped by for a visit. David is a writer who lives on a farm in Wisconsin and collects vintage electric guitars.

"About four dozen," he said.

David and I get along pretty well, probably because I'm one of the few people he knows who doesn't bat an eye at the idea of owning four dozen electric guitars. I not only approve, but applaud. Besides being a kind of fascinating historical archive done in hardwood, varnish, and mother-of-pearl, David's collection has the added value of making my own paltry hoard of six guitars look like the work of a sane man. In other words, my wife thought I was out of my mind until she met David. Now I appear almost normal. Shoplifting pales next to the Great Train Robbery.

It's hard to explain to an outsider why a man would want more than one electric guitar. (In high school, it was hard to explain to my parents why a man would want even *one*.) Unless you are steeped in the history and aesthetics of rock 'n' roll, blues, jazz, or country music, you aren't likely to care that Chuck Berry sounds best on an ES-355 Gibson, or that Fender Stratocasters with maple necks sound and feel different from those with rosewood necks. (Clapton uses a maple-neck version; 'nuff said.) Old guitars are both cultural icons and expressions of mood, so if you feel like playing a Les Paul Gibson and all you've got is a Gretsch Country Gentleman, you're just flat out of luck. Stuck with Greek, when you're hungry for Mexican.

Motorcycles, of course, are the same way. At least for some of us.

It is possible to get by with just one motorcycle, I'm told, and lead a fairly normal life. Single-bike ownership, after all, is the very thing for which dual-purpose motorcycles were created: To go anywhere and do everything reasonably well. Get yourself a good XL or KLR 600 and you can ride to the Arctic Circle, see the dusty side of Baja, commute to work, or carve up a canyon, all on one bike. You're set for life, right?

Wrong. Dual-purpose is about six purposes too few, if life is to have the proper balance and variety. For instance, what if you've got an XL600 in the garage and suddenly take a fancy to the idea of polishing and admiring the kind of inch-deep chrome pipes and mufflers found only on old Nortons and Triumphs? Ever try to find one piece of good chrome on a modern dual-purpose bike? Or what if you do own an old Triumph and want to ride to the Arctic Circle but are not fond of hitchhiking in the cold and living with timber wolves? What if you've got a nice, long-legged BMW for touring, but suddenly get homesick for the insane race bike whoop of a high-revving Japanese four?

Funny you should ask. Those are the very questions I've been asking myself lately.

The reason, as you might have guessed by now, is that I've had the same two bikes for nearly five years—a KZ1000 MkII and an old XL350. Good bikes. Great bikes, even. Trouble-free, competent, honest machines on which I can go almost anywhere, across continents or deep into the desert. The discerning eye will note, however, that there are no British singles or vertical twins in this little collection of two; no American or Italian V-twins; no lightweight canyon screamers with the souls of GP bikes; no tall-geared German Boxers to lope over the open highway with seven-league boots. In other words, I've got some serious gaps here, holes through which you could drive an aesthetic, philosophical, and functional truck.

The cause of the problem is that for the past five years, my wife Barbara and I have been Saving For a House. Yep. The original gold-plated guilt trip. The one you see reflected in the bloodshot eyes of house guests who've slept on the hide-a-bed in the living room once too often (the one with the steel bar across the rib cage, just beneath the Wonder Bread–thin mattress), their mute, accusing stares asking, "How can a guy spend all his money on motorcycles and live in such a tiny excuse for a house? Why doesn't his wife divorce him? And, while we're at it, who's in the bathroom?"

Well, we sold some bikes, saved our money and, just this year, bought the house. Three bedrooms, two bathrooms, family room, nice yard with rose bushes and trees, two-car garage. The world is now safe for house guests and relatives, the dreaded hide-a-bed is gone. I've paid my debt to society, and the guilt trip is over.

Buying the house was Plan A. Now it's time to activate Plan B.

Plan B is a complex, long-imagined strategy in which I make up for lost time and past error by gradually tracking down clean versions of at least three of the bikes I never should have sold, and a few others I've never owned but always admired. First on the list is a late-1960s, high-pipe 650 Triumph TR6C Trophy Special. After that I'll stay flexible, ear to the ground, eyes peeled, for targets of opportunity, like the '74 black-and-gold Norton 850 Commando, and the Honda CB400F, and the . . . well, I won't run on. One thing at a time. I'll find them all, eventually, if there's any money left after house payments.

The only other thing that could possibly slow me down is if I run across a certain Les Paul Gibson, the famous Black Beauty model with three Humbucking pickups. The kind Keith Richards used to play. . . .

May 1988

GARAGE IKEBANA

All I can say is I'm glad there's no such thing as a surprise psychiatric inspection. You know, an unannounced raid on your home, a Freudian version of what the fire inspector does when he suddenly drops in on your place of business and writes you up for having oily rags smoldering in uncovered cans. If psychiatrists did spot checks, I'd have been taken away for sure.

It was a Thursday night and there I was, out in the garage all by myself (wife gone visiting), drinking hot sake, positioning a chair in each corner of the garage like points on a compass, and moving three vehicles around into various experimental poses and juxtapositions—just like a Japanese *ikebana* artist arranging fern stalks and lotus blossoms in the most pleasing and Zenful way.

Funny you should mention Lotus. One of the three machines was a car by that name, a 1964 Lotus Super Seven. The Super Seven is a lightweight English roadster that has been called "a motorcycle on four wheels," which, of course, it isn't. A motorcycle has two wheels and that's that. Never mind that we now have touring bikes that outweigh cars.

But I digress. Let's backtrack a bit. Here's the deal:

About three weeks ago, I traveled to my home state of Wisconsin to pick up the Lotus and trailer it back to California behind a Chevy van. My old friend and employer Chris Beebe agreed to take a short leave from his foreign-car repair shop in Madison and help with the driving. After we'd loaded our luggage and spare Lotus parts, I said to Chris, "Wow, there's a lot of empty space in the back of this van. What else have you got around here that I need?"

"Well, I have two red 1975 400F Hondas," Chris said, grinning, "and I'm using only one." I'd been hinting strongly for about ten years that he might like to sell me his spare 400F, so we wheeled it into the back of the van and hauled the bike to California along with the car.

No sooner had we arrived home and offloaded these treasures than I picked up the local newspaper, perused the motorcycle classifieds as usual, and found my breathing suddenly arrested. Under the heading TRIUMPH, which very seldom appears any more, was an ad that read: "67 TR6C 650cc, stock, classic, immaculate, 13,000 mi., $1,295 obo."

Now, I don't know about you, but I have been looking for a clean, complete, unbent, unraced, unchopped, unchromed, unruined, stock, late-1960s, high-pipe, single-carb Triumph 650 TR6C (or Trophy, as they called it some years) forever. Since 1967, actually. Only a few of these bikes have turned up for sale over the years, and always at the worst possible time, like while I'm standing in line to buy lifeboat tickets on a sinking steamer, or during some similar crisis.

This time wasn't much better. I was almost broke, and there's something wretchedly excessive about stuffing three new/used project vehicles into your garage within any 24-hour period, even for me. But still, a Triumph TR6C . . . The Holy Grail itself.

I called the owner, got directions to his house, found the Triumph to be as clean and original as advertised (the engine was a little clattery, but these things can be fixed), gave him a $100 deposit, and went to the bank. The following evening I paid for the bike and rode it home on the Pacific Coast Highway, the dual side-mufflers booming through the night, waves crashing on the moonlit empty beaches, Lucas headlight flaring and dimming with the rise and fall of revs. It was wonderful.

When I got home and parked the Triumph in the garage, there was no one around to share my elation, but I felt that some sort of celebration was in order. Usually, I open a bottle of Guinness Stout on these occasions, but there was nothing in the refrigerator except a few cans of Coors Light, which seemed too weak a brew for such a heady moment. So I heated up a bottle of sake, which has a certain ceremonial aura about it (never mind that Edward Turner was probably spinning in his grave), and returned to the garage.

It was then, unobserved by anyone except our two cats, that I began the experimental placement of the three machines for most harmonious viewing. Garage *ikebana*, the new art form. After many false chess moves and shuffles, I finally discovered the magic combination. Many personal interpretations are possible, but in the end I concluded that the Lotus looked best from the front left quarter because of its superb nose and fenderline, the Honda 400F from the right front quarter where the sensuous curves of its 4-into-1 headers can be seen, and the Triumph from the left rear, where its pipes and the waspish narrowness of the tank were most visible. With all these angles and elements properly arranged, I sat back for a long time and studied the three machines.

Suddenly I focused in on the Triumph, its pipes, air cleaner, the lovely tank, the perfect chromed bullet headlamp, the just-right curve of the sloping seatback, the artful finning of the cylinder head, and realized that I was seeing perfection within perfection, *dharma* within *dharma*, a garageload of stuff that was fun to look at, where the true pleasure of it began with the smallest things. All three machines were designed in different places by different people, yet each designer knew that beauty starts with a thoughtful sympathy for the pieces that make up the whole. "We're talking *oneness* here," I explained to the cats, "the kind that radiates outward and gravitates inward." They blinked calmly.

I poured another cup of hot sake, held up a toast to the people at Lotus, Honda, and Triumph who cared enough for detail to give us their best, and whispered, prayerlike, "Hot Damn."

June 1988

ALAS, ALBION

I woke up in the night feeling uneasy, half dreaming something in the house was wrong. It was an odor. The human nose has a way of sending wake-up calls to the brain, probably dating back to the caveman's fear and loathing of wolf breath, and mine had phoned a message that something was not quite right.

I sat up in bed and sniffed the air, confused for a moment. Then I relaxed. It was only the Triumph.

Ah, the British.

The aroma that filled our house had its source in the garage, but had somehow found its way to the bedroom through a five-by-seven-inch cat door, across an entire dining room, and down a long hallway to the exact opposite corner of the house. Still, there was no mistaking it for anything other than the distinctive fragrance of leaded gasoline leaking past the float-bowl gasket of an Amal Monobloc carburetor, and from there dripping its way onto the engine cases beneath, like slow Chinese water torture. Even in the dark, I could picture the entire process.

It wasn't merely the smell of raw gasoline. It was a special English smell you get when a perfectly controlled rate of eternal seepage allows gasoline to half-evaporate before it drips, leaving a thick, red deposit of lead and heavy mineral spirits on the underside of a carb body, along with a smell so pungent you suspect that fossil fuel might be reverting to its original state of primordial soup in a warm tropical sea. There are other elements in the aroma, of course, like mildly decayed, cotton-insulated wiring, old foam beneath the vinyl seat cover, and motor oil heated and chilled a hundred times on the outside of the engine; however, the main ingredient, I think, is still gasoline, or whatever remains when the volatile ghost of gasoline has left the scene.

Like a farmer who feels compelled to get up and see why the dogs are barking, I heaved myself out of bed to go check the Triumph, just to make sure I hadn't left a petcock open, flooding the garage floor with fuel. I got dressed and shuffled out to the garage to have a look.

No major leaks or oil spills, just the usual seeps. A warm spring wind was blowing against the garage door, no doubt wafting the smell into our house with more force than usual. I ran my finger along the underside of the Amal, and there was the usual residue, oozing thickly red. Despite my best efforts.

The float-bowl sidecover had been leaking badly when I bought the Triumph, so my first action on the bike's behalf had been an attempted repair. The carburetor had been designed to leak, of course; nobody but a child, inexperienced in the ways of the world, would seriously believe that a flat metal plate, a paper gasket, and three screws would hold back a reservoir full of a sneaky, low-viscosity fluid like gasoline for long, especially if the carburetor were rigidly attached to a hot, vibratory, 650cc vertical-twin motorcycle engine.

"Use two gaskets," my friend Bill Getty at British Parts Old & New had told me. "That usually cures the problem."

So, I'd put on two gaskets, after carefully checking the plate for flatness and filing down the small, raised volcanoes around the screw holes where the metal had pulled through. It still leaked. Next, I would try various glues and gasket cements from my large drawer of same. Sooner or later, I'd find a solution.

What was needed, of course, was a rubber O-ring. Not only a rubber O-ring, but a float bowl designed like a cup rather than a bass drum, allowing the bowl to have its sealing surface above the fuel line. Like the one on my '82 Honda XL500, which sat nearby. (Triumph later switched to a concentric Amal with *real* float bowls that didn't leak as much, except when you deliberately made them overflow by using the starting ticklers.)

What was it, I wondered, that so mystified and eluded British engineers when it came to the design of gaskets, seals, and mated surfaces. They never did get the idea, right up until the end, that fluids belong on the inside of an engine, while fresh air and sunshine belong on the outside, and that there is seldom any real advantage in having these disparate elements swap sides, except in the case of combustion gases.

All of the British bikes and cars I'd owned had leaked one or more fluids from some orifice (I'd never owned a British airplane, but Spitfire pilots tell us in their memoirs that the smell of hot, leaking glycol from that big, water-cooled Merlin is one of their most pungent memories of flight).

Old road tests I'd seen in English publications had actually suggested that oil leakage was a desirable trait in motorcycles and cars because it preserved their lower extremities from rust.

Leakage is so universal in these machines, it has now become part of the lore and romance of owning British; and half the fun of restoring an old Triumph, Norton, or BSA lies in reducing fluid loss to a minimum through careful assembly, subtle filework, double gaskets, aftermarket sealants, and right thinking.

Still, as I sat in the garage and looked at the Triumph, I couldn't help wondering where the British motorcycle industry would be today if they had discovered O-rings, precision surfacing, and horizontally split engine cases. Some people simply won't forgive a motorcycle that wakes them up in the night. Others of us are willing to overlook a little nighttime seepage—provided the bike doesn't put us to sleep during the daytime.

January 1989

THE BUCK-A-DAY 25-YEAR HABIT

"What have you got there?" my wife Barbara asked as I walked in the front door. I was carrying a small rectangular box, holding it slightly away from my body, the way you hold a dead skunk or a small dog who's just been swimming in the pond behind the toxic waste dump.

"A new battery for the Kawasaki," I said. "I just wrote a check for it."

Barb, who adds and subtracts with a little more accuracy than I do (I hope), took the checkbook out of her purse. "How much was it?"

"Thirty-four dollars and nine cents."

A sigh issued forth. Not an annoyed sigh, but one of those life-goes-on types. Barb recorded the amount in the back of the book and said, "I wonder how much we've spent on motorcycles over the years?" She gazed wistfully at the checkbook for a moment and said, "Maybe it's better we don't know."

I went out to the garage to install the battery in the KZ1000, which certainly deserved it. The bike is a 1980 MkII model that I had been kick-starting for two years on a dead battery. I can't think what possessed me to buy a new battery—perhaps the novelty of using the starter button again, or a suspicion that the starter motor might be rusted solid.

As I dropped the new battery heavily into its cradle, I began to think about what Barb had said. How much *had* we (okay, mostly I) spent on motorcycles over the years? It was a fair question, I suppose.

I'd bought and sold quite a few bikes since that first ratty James-Villiers in 1963. Mostly cheap used ones, with only a few expensive new bikes in the mix. Some I'd restored lavishly (Armor-All, fresh chain lube, the whole bit), yet others had required no more than an oil change or a clutch cable during my entire stewardship. I'd hardly ever made money on a motorcycle, but it seemed to me that I hadn't ever lost much on a bike, either.

I'd always avoided adding up the true cost of my obsessions, partly out of guilt, no doubt, but partly because I cling to the ancient philosophy that investments and enthusiasm are two different things. Like fire and water. I prefer a universe where the only significant bottom line is death, and your travel expenses en route don't matter much. Or something.

Nevertheless, I began to think that after a quarter of a century of motorcycling, it might be time for an accounting of sorts. Had my years of motorcycle ownership been merely a fun, affordable hobby? Or was it a passion whose excesses had permanently stunted Barb's and my economic growth, preventing us from owning the oil wells, the steamship companies, and the industrial empire we so richly deserved? If I had invested that $1,800 in blue-chip stocks back in 1975 rather than in a Norton, would we now be skiing in Switzerland with Malcolm Forbes rather than eating at Flo's Airport Cafe with people like Steve Kimball? Perhaps if I hadn't bought the RD350 eight years ago, we could now afford a Chevy van *without* noisy lifters, or even have the cat fixed.

That evening, after installing the battery, I went in the house, got myself a pencil and a yellow legal pad, and began to compute.

I made four columns across the page with the following heads: Bike; Price Paid; Repair/Restoration Cost; and Price Sold For. After adding, subtracting, dividing, and figuring averages to the best of my ability, I came up with some possibly fascinating statistics, depending upon how easily you are fascinated.

First, it turns out I've owned twenty-one motorcycles, with a price range from $50 for the cheapest to $3,700 for the most expensive. When I added them up, the total cost of all these bikes was $19,055, for an average purchase price of $907.38.

Okay, next column. The total repair/restoration costs came to a mere $2,000, which must be wrong because it sounds too cheap, but I haven't been able to invent or recall any other hidden costs. Most of the work I've done on bikes has been labor-intensive—sanding, painting, installing pistons, fork seals, etc.—but the actual parts costs have been remarkably low. Add those costs to the purchase prices, and suddenly my total for all motorcycles is up to $21,055, with an average total cost for each bike being $1,002.62.

A thousand dollars a bike.

Now, then, I added up the selling prices of all the bikes I've sold, plus the current market value of the four I still own (estimated toward the low side—what I could get for them if they had to be sold tomorrow), and got a value of $16,465, or an average selling price of $784.05.

That means my total losses over twenty-five years and twenty-one bikes have been $4,590, or $218.57 per bike.

Dividing that $4,590 by 25, I get an annual cost of $183.60, or $3.53 a week.

That's about fifty cents a day.

The alert reader will notice I have not included the cost of insurance, sales tax, or registration. That's because these fees have varied widely depending on where I was living and the type of insurance carried (liability with or without collision/theft, etc.). But let's assume, for the sake of argument, that these expenses actually double the cost of motorcycling, which they can easily do.

That would drive the cost all the way up to a dollar a day.

After arriving at this astounding conclusion, I was going to suggest that most of us could afford to ride motorcycles simply by giving up some small daily pleasure—a good cigar, a drink in the evening, a movie, or whatever—but I couldn't think of a single worthwhile vice that still costs only a dollar a day.

So, you're on your own. If you can find a cheaper way to throw money around, jump on it.

May 1989

CONVERSION

While reading a recent issue of *Cycle World*, I learned that the original Honda CB750 Four is celebrating its twentieth anniversary this year. I can't say I was surprised—I've now grown used to the numbing succession of anniversaries designed to remind me that I'm not exactly in high school any more—but twenty years is still a long time ago.

I was twenty-one when the bike was introduced, residing in a tropical fun spot called Buu Son, and keeping track of the jerky advance of civilization via the letters and magazines that filtered their way through the Army Post Office (APO).

If you haven't been in the armed forces, the APO works pretty much like its civilian counterpart, except it has a special Package Aging Center, where chocolate melts, cookies mold, and magazines are beaten with chains. This is all done so you don't feel that anything valuable has been damaged when the mail bag is heaved out of a helicopter door.

Anyway, somewhere in my ruined 1969 mail, there arrived a *CW* with the Honda CB750 on what was left of its cover, and I recall being astounded and amazed.

And a little skeptical.

"*Four* carburetors?" I said to LeBlanc, the artillery radio operator, flashing him a photo of the Honda's engine. "How is anybody ever going to keep four carbs in tune?"

LeBlanc shrugged. He didn't know.

No one did.

I puffed on a C-ration Lucky and narrowed my eyes. There were four of everything on the bike—carbs, cylinders, exhaust pipes, mufflers—all of which were fine on a racing bike with a team of trained mechanics, but possibly too many for a street machine. And then there was weight. Five hundred pounds of it. And width; the bike looked as wide as a BMW Boxer Twin—all the way up to the top of the tank. And it looked pretty tall, too. None of it seemed to make much sense, physics-wise, and I figured Honda had built the bike just to prove it *could*, like Cool Hand Luke announcing he could eat fifty eggs.

Magazine editors, however, loved the bike and raved about its smoothness. Smoothness didn't mean much to me at this time because it had never occurred to me that motorcycles vibrated, except in the case of the Norton 750 Atlas, which looked at idle like a heart awaiting transplant. Bikes were supposed to vibrate a little, after all, and it seemed that the big Honda had traded a few vibes for an awful lot of bulk and complexity.

No big, wide, heavy fours for me, thank you. Honda would have a hard sell with this here Enlisted Man. They might as well have been pitching Christianity to Attila the Hun. Nevertheless, these bikes sold like crazy, and by the time I got home they were everywhere.

Once I was firmly settled back into civilian life, my friend Howard the Honda Mechanic insisted that I take a ride on a 750 Four he'd just tuned for a customer friend. I did, and came back with mixed reviews. I owned a Norton 850 Commando at the time, and by comparison the Honda felt big, chunky, and numb. Also, the chrome looked like it had been sprayed out of a can and the gold metalflake paint reminded me of something Wayne Newton might wear.

In the Honda's favor, however, I couldn't help but notice that *(a)* it had 35,000 miles on the odometer; *(b)* it still felt almost like a new bike; *(c)* all four carbs seemed to be perfectly synchronized; *(d)* all those mufflers gave off a nice sound, a race-bike snarl that sounded like something important; and *(e)* it really was smooth.

Gradually, approval came to displace doubt, and by the mid-1970s I actually began to believe that a big-bore, four-cylinder streetbike might not be such a bad thing to own. Furthermore, I began to see the four-pipe 750 as a rather handsome machine, not quite as refined looking as the CB550 or

400F, but blessed with the redeeming quality of horsepower. Also, the old glittery paint had given way to understated, primary colors. There was a growing possibility that I might need one of these bikes.

Necessity reared its ugly head when my friend John Jaeger decided to take an autumn motorcycle trip on his BMW R90S from Madison, Wisconsin, to the U.S. Grand Prix at Watkins Glen, via southern Canada. The old Norton was feeling a little tired, so naturally I was forced to buy a CB750.

The bike was a 1975 model, blue in color, with about 13,000 miles on the odometer. It had been stored for two years, but once I'd sanded the green crud off all the electrical connectors and cleaned the red crud out of the needles and seats (all four), and bled the black crud out of the brake hydraulics, everything worked fine. We took back roads and sped nearly flat out to the Glen and back, hovering above 100 miles per hour for long stretches across the straight, empty farm roads of southern Ontario. By the time we got home, I was composing mental letters to Mr. Honda, apologizing for having doubted his wisdom. For delivering everything it promised, the 750 Four was simply one of the best bikes I ever owned.

These days I still prefer big twins for most kinds of riding, but the old quatrophobia, if you will, is long gone. There is something in the immediacy of a good inline four, in that smooth, instantaneous whoop, that has become for me one of the key notes in the music of motorcycling. I haven't been without some variety of four-cylinder motorcycle for well over a decade.

In defense of my early misgivings, however, I should add that the CB750 marked a peculiar turning point in motorcycle design and a change in marketing philosophy that made me a little uneasy back in 1969, and continues to cast a small shadow even today. It was the first big displacement bike I ever owned that was cheaper and easier to replace than it was to rebuild.

The good part was, I never had to.

July 1989

LEADING THE WITNESS

If my friendly employers should someday see the light and fire me from journalism, there's a chance I could take up an alternate career in law. Specifically, courtroom law. Perry Mason stuff—you've seen it—where relentless, clever questioning causes beads of sweat to pop out on the upper lip of the witness, just before he suddenly stands up and shouts a confession to the entire courtroom.

As it stands right now, I don't know the first thing about law. But I've certainly had plenty of practice drawing the truth, or what passes for it, out of reluctant witnesses.

Where, you ask, would a person like me achieve such experience?

Calling about old Triumphs and Nortons, that's where.

Nearly every day since about 1960, I've gone through the classifieds in the daily paper to see what motorcycles are for sale. And, due to a tragic personality defect, I have never failed to study the ads for Triumphs and Nortons with a certain uncalled-for, riveted attention. And sometimes, when one of them sounds truly irresistible (or cheap), I walk right over to the phone, call the owner, and ask for details. Sometimes I even buy one.

Back when I lived in a small midwestern city, I didn't waste much time on the phone. I'd simply get the address of the seller and run over to his house or garage, look at the thing, and draw my own conclusions. But that was then.

Now, I live in a sprawling landscape of single-story stucco buildings known as The Los Angeles Area, where it's entirely possible to share area codes with a person who lives three hours away because of congested freeways named after Spanish saints. So before you waste an entire Saturday morning running off to look at a completely ruined dud of a motorcycle, you want to do some careful investigation over the phone.

Once, for instance, I saw an ad that said, "1968 Triumph Trophy 500, mint condition, must sell. $1,000."

Now, my understanding of the word "mint" roughly parallels that of coin collectors and Webster, meaning, "unmarred, as if fresh from a mint." In other words, the bike should be pretty much as it rolled off the assembly line, virginally perfect but for the passage of a few tanks of gas through its unspoiled engine. And, since $1,000 is quite a bit for a Trophy 500, I figured this particular bike might be especially mintlike. So I called the owner.

After a few questions about mileage and the condition of the engine, I got right down to the important stuff and asked him what color it was.

"Black," he said.

"Black? Hmmm. I thought the '68 Trophys were green."

"They were," he said. "I had it repainted after the accident."

"The accident?"

"My carport collapsed on the bike. I guess I had too much lumber piled on the roof. That dented the tank pretty bad, so I had to fill it with Bondo and paint it."

"Any other damage?"

"Just the speedometer and the frame. The speedometer's smashed and the kickstand got bent off the frame. You can weld it back on, though. I loaded it into my truck and took it to a shop and they said they could do it for five bucks."

"Didn't you get it welded while you were there, as long as you had the bike in the truck and everything?"

"No, I just wanted an estimate."

"Does the bike run?"

"It used to, but there's no gas in the tank. I had to have it welded."

No further questions, Your Honor. Your witness. Another long drive saved through the miracle of modern communications.

A short time later, I ran across the following ad: "1973 Norton 850 Commando, stock, $400." Four hundred dollars is pretty cheap for a Commando these days, so I wasn't expecting miracles, but the word "stock" always leaves a nice ring in my ears where British bikes are concerned, so I hazarded a call.

"Is the bike all original?" I asked.

"Everything but the gas tank," the owner told me. "It's a yellow fiberglass tank off an early 750."

"Why did you change the tank?"

"Had to. The old one burned."

"*Burned*?" I'd heard of a lot of weird Norton malfunctions, but tank fires wasn't one of them. "How did it happen to catch on fire?" I asked.

"The wiring harness started smoking while my brother was riding and the gas tank leaked, so the bike kind of burst into flame."

"Ah. What did your brother do?"

"Well, he jumped off. Scraped his arm up pretty good."

"What happened to the bike?"

"Uh, it slid into a curb and bent the forks and front wheel. The only other thing that got hurt was the left side cases, and the pipe and muffler. The seat got torn up, too. So all it really needs is that stuff, plus a wiring harness."

And so ended the Strange Cases of the Mint Trophy and the Stock Norton. But recently, I called about a 1969 Triumph Bonneville in "good original condition." I learned through nimble interrogation that it was "the single-carb version of the Bonneville" with optional hardtail rear end, plus the added glamour of extended forks and improved, updated wiring out of a late-model 750 that got wrecked.

With that, I hung up the phone and recessed for lunch. With my secretary, Della Street.

July 1990

LAST RIDE IN CALIFORNIA

Wistful, I suppose, is the best word to describe our mood in packing for the weekend trip to the USGP at Laguna Seca. This would be our last real ride in California. At least for a while. It seems my wife Barbara and I just signed the papers and bought ourselves a small farm in southern Wisconsin. We are moving there at the end of the month.

"Farm" is actually something of an exaggeration. It's an old farmhouse on a small river, with sixteen acres of woods and pasture, a horse barn, and a reasonably good three-car (twenty-motorcycle?) garage. There's an old iron bridge and a winding country road at the foot of the driveway, which is no small part of the reason we are moving there.

The motorcycle roads in Southern California are great—maybe the best in the world—but it's taking us longer and longer to get to them. The southern coast has become just a bit too crowded for our tastes, and it suddenly feels as though it's time to move on. I'll still be doing this monthly *Leanings* column and the occasional feature story for *Cycle World*, but they will now be beamed from afar through the magic of modem and fax.

Fortunately, this is not a move that calls for the burning of bridges. A decade in California has left us with a great fondness for the place, and if we ever win the lottery, we could easily be convinced to buy a second house here, maybe a place to spend the winter months. I suppose you could say our schizophrenic affinity for both California and the Midwest has left us bicoastal, if you can call our small riverbank a coast, that is.

So, we packed for our third-annual GP run to Laguna with a sort of premature nostalgia, knowing that next year at this time, we might find ourselves in the last snowstorm of a late Wisconsin spring. I'd decided to make this final run on the good old Kawasaki KZ1000 MkII, but the day before we were supposed to leave, I called David Edwards at *CW*, just on the off chance he might have an interesting test bike that hadn't been scarfed up by one of the staff.

"It just so happens," he said, "we have a brand-new Honda ST1100 you could borrow."

Perfect. An 1100 V-four sport-tourer, with real saddlebags, shaft drive, and a fairing. Everything we needed, by all appearances.

As usual, we left for Laguna Seca at 5 a.m., hit the Coast Highway at Santa Monica, and headed north along the ocean under dark coastal clouds. We stopped for our traditional daybreak breakfast at Paradise Cove (where James Garner's trailer used to be parked in *The Rockford Files*), motored through Santa Barbara and San Luis Obispo, then swung back to the ocean past the Hearst Castle and up through God's own fog-shrouded Zen-forest at Big Sur. We got to our hotel late in the afternoon, surprisingly unfatigued.

As a sport-tourer the big Honda worked pretty well, at least for my particular tastes. It has a big, 7.4-gallon fuel tank, for 250-plus miles between fill-ups, a wonderfully comfortable seat for both pilot and passenger, and—best of all—genuinely tall gearing. It purrs along at a relaxed, 3,000 rpm at sixty miles per hour. At a mere 4,000 rpm, it's going eighty.

As for shortcomings, the ST has a windshield that at certain speeds creates helmet-level turbulence, with a whorl that carries cold air down the rider's back and—by extension—down the passenger's front.

The ST is also quite heavy at 700 pounds (with fuel). Though like a lot of big Hondas, it disguises its weight well. Without working too hard, we were able to stay with a gaggle of well-mounted sport bike guys who thought they were dragging their knees in corners. In short, the ST is a nice bike for people whose touring tastes lie somewhere between Gold Wing conservatism and race bike masochism, which is probably a lot of people. In fact, I'm one.

If the Honda had the BMW R100RS fairing and the Boxer's light weight, it would be almost perfect. On the other hand, if the BMW had the Honda's comfortable saddle and suspension, it, too, would be almost perfect. Someone, eventually, will get it exactly right.

As most people know by now, Wayne Rainey won the USGP, riding with a flawless, surgical attack on the course while other riders crashed in his wake. John Kocinski rode a similar race in the 250 class, proving that Kenny Roberts either has a good eye for talent or trains riders very well, or both. (Both, I'm told.) Sadly, it was a weekend with more than its share of injuries, Kevin Magee's being the most serious. Laguna Seca is an unforgiving track for those who leave it at high speed.

We left at relatively low speed ourselves, taking a full, sunlit Monday to ride home through the mountains with our friends Hank Murdoch, Doug Booth, and his dad, Jack, who flew all the way in from Massachusetts to make the ride. Spring rains had made the coastal range brilliantly green, so the cattle ranches looked more like part of Switzerland than the brown hills of the West.

We reached the coast at Malibu on a balmy evening, just in time to witness an almost spectral event. It was a brilliant red sunset, followed immediately by the rising of the largest moon I've ever seen, tinted an unearthly lavender-red. As it came into the darkening sky, the moon threw a shaft of its strange light glittering across the waves through a grove of tall palms. The whole scene was so perfect, so tropically surreal and idealized in its composition of color and form, that I nearly laughed out loud. Nothing looked this good. Not even in the movies.

As we rolled along the beach, it suddenly occurred to me that perhaps California knew we were leaving, and had decided to rub it in. It was showing us, one last time, that its legendary natural beauty still has the power to raise its head and tower over the smog and the gridlock and the shopping malls.

Fair enough, I thought. It deserves to be remembered well. This has been a good ten years.

February 1991

LETTERS FROM THE WORLD

While unpacking the last of our moving containers a few weeks ago, I found an old saltine cracker box made of tin, filled with letters sent to me while I was in Vietnam, twenty-nine years ago. They were addressed to a Sp/4 Egan, MAC V Advisory Team 45, Phan Rang, APO San Francisco, Cal. 96381. Naturally, I stopped unpacking and started rereading the mail, most of which I hadn't looked at since the day it was first opened.

One of the letters was from my old college friend, Todd Saalman, who was still attending the University of Wisconsin the year after I quit and joined the army. Todd wrote funny, bleak, scatological, stream-of-consciousness letters—which almost everyone did at that time—full of disorder, uncertainty about the future, and unpleasant references to Nixon and Agnew. He also mentioned motorcycles in his letters.

Todd was an artist and early computer whiz who could play guitar and sing just like Paul Simon, and he bought the first Suzuki X-6 Hustler I ever saw. He brought it back to the dorms one day and did a smoky burn-out the entire length of the first-floor hallway as we all stood safely back in our doorways and watched. He flew through the open doors of Sullivan Hall at a high rate of speed with the David Crosby–like cape he was wearing fluttering behind him, leaving the hallway filled with acrid two-stroke haze. The handlebar ends cleared the doorway by inches, and everyone was quite impressed with his fearlessness.

This was the sort of thing people did in the 1960s when they were bored, and it probably explains a lot about our involvement in Vietnam. Excessive flamboyance and energy in all things, even self-destruction, was the disease of the decade.

Anyway, Todd would occasionally write me letters while I was stationed in what was then called The Armpit of the World. In retrospect, it was actually quite a beautiful country, a place whose reputation as a vacation spot was somewhat damaged by the stigma of death that clung to its green mountains and rice paddies like so much heavy fog. But back then, we enjoyed calling it The Armpit of the World and sat on sandbags reading our letters from home.

And there I was, in 1969, sitting on my particular sandbag, reading Todd's letter. It rambled on about the usual campus happenings, co-op living problems, politics, and so on, but it ended with a rather key passage. In closing, he said, "Me and a bunch of crazies rode our bikes out to the Mississippi Cliffs last weekend and camped at Wyalusing State Park. Beautiful cold autumn night, huge campfire, guitars, etc. Stayed up all night. Wish you were there. Or here. Or somewhere else. Anywhere."

I could picture firelight reflecting off the spokes and pipes of the gathered motorcycles, see my sleeping bag laid out on the ground near the fire. And then there would be friends around, people with whom you shared beliefs, to talk and drink and smoke with. And girls.

Good Lord, girls. We didn't call them women then. Women were an older species who wore severe business suits and stamped your student registration card with a menopausal vengeance. Women who went on dates and rode motorcycles and camped out were called girls. Even now, it sounds friendlier. We were the boys and they were the girls.

What I felt most of all in Todd's letter, however, were the usual bohemian freedoms we all treasured so much. The freedom to own a sleeping bag of some color other than olive drab, to hike unarmed, to stay up all night or sleep all night, to get up when you pleased, to choose your friends, and let them choose you. Most of all, the freedom to get on a bike and go. That was the key.

I don't think I've ever had a moment where the image of personal freedom was as clearly etched in my mind as it was during the few minutes of reflection I spent with Todd's letter. The whole nighttime autumn camping scene was complete in my imagination, right down to the last detail, like the persistent memory of a landscape seen in a lightning flash. Or a trip flare.

What I also understood, grudgingly, was that without the army and its tiresome discipline, without the vast distance separating me from the Mississippi Valley,

there would have been no vision at all. It was pure contrast that made Todd's weekend ride seem larger than life.

But it did loom large, and it's possible I remember that camping trip better than the people who were on it. I probably had more fun that night than anybody, and I wasn't even there. I was in two places at once, while they were only in one.

Sometimes, however, one is just the right number of places to be. Like last weekend. Barb and I woke up and discovered it was a beautiful golden late-autumn morning, a throwback to the previous month's sunniness and warmth. Indian fall, if not exactly Indian summer.

"Let's load up the Beemer and go camping," I said. "It's probably our last chance of the year."

"Where do you want to go?" Barb asked.

"Wyalusing," I said.

We got out our sleeping bags and tent, packed up, and headed southeast toward the river. Our friends Chris and Dana joined us on their reconstituted $750 Gold Wing, and by sundown we were camped on the cliffs above the mighty Father of the Waters.

It was a cool, rustling autumn night with a diamond-black sky and a million stars, and we built a great big campfire, around which we stood, talking and drinking Jack Daniel's. Firelight reflected off the spokes and pipes of our bikes, and the fire warmed our faces and hands.

It was a very good evening for me, and I drank a silent toast to Todd and his fine letter. And to the little-appreciated, nearly always motorcycle-related luxury of being in just one place at a time, and not wishing to be anywhere else.

March 1991

SHOULD YOU BUY AN ITALIAN BIKE?

Not too long ago, I put together a multiple-choice psychological test to help those without British bikes find out if they had the stuff that long-suffering Anglophiles are made of. This test ("Common threads," *Leanings*, *Cycle World*, February, 1989) was a huge success in weeding out those without the proper qualifications—while encouraging those whose crippling personality disorders made them prime candidates for the ownership of English iron like mine—so I've decided to do another one.

This time the turf is Italian. I've just returned from a week-long trip to Italy, during which I not only visited the Cagiva factory in Varese and the Ducati works in Bologna, but also drank a reasonable amount of chianti. That, along with Italy being my second-favorite country in Europe (right after England, whose main advantage is that the people speak a dialect of my own language), probably makes me some kind of an expert, even if my grandparents were Irish.

Anyway, this should help you decide whether or not an Italian motorcycle is for you. Take your time, choose your answers carefully, and for God's sake don't cheat, or you'll end up with a Kreidler moped. Here's the test:

1) To kill a little time while waiting to go into a movie theater to see Fellini's *Roma* for the fifth time, you wander into a nearby bicycle shop. While browsing around, you find yourself inexplicably drawn toward: *(a)* a sturdy mountain bike with high fat knobby tires; *(b)* a pink folding bicycle with a white wicker basket over the front wheel and a bell on the handlebars; *(c)* a fourteen-speed Colnago roadracing bike with beautifully polished Campagnolo components, an anvil-hard saddle, no fenders, no lights, and high-pressure sew-ups the width of stiletto blades.

2) After the movie, you take your date out for coffee at a small cafe. The waiter asks what kind of coffee you want and you automatically order: *(a)* decaf flavored with almond extract; *(b)* a pot of herbal tea instead of coffee; *(c)* a tiny cup of something called espresso, which resembles two tablespoons of the hot coffee grounds your mom used to dump out of her GE percolator and is made by a huge hissing piece of industrial machinery that looks like the steam boiler on the *Andrea Doria.*

3) Your date orders herbal tea and then offers the opinion that Ingmar Bergman is a much better movie director than Federico Fellini. After packing your date into a taxicab and undertipping the driver in advance, you go out alone for a bite to eat. You gravitate toward a restaurant where the name of the headwaiter is: *(a)* Karl; *(b)* Mohammed; *(c)* Angelo.

4) The best color for a sports car with twelve cylinders or a GP bike with four cylinders is: *(a)* a kind of surfer turquoise with hot pink zigzags and triangles; *(b)* metalflake orange; *(c)* blood red.

5) The most interesting name for a motorcycle is the: *(a)* Exciter; *(b)* Rebel; *(c)* Gilera Saturno Sanremo.

6) The man who, above all others, did the most to advance the cause of Western thinking is: *(a)* Copernicus; *(b)* Isaac Newton; *(c)* Ing. Fabio Taglioni.

7) Of these three famous buildings, the one with the best paint job on the ceiling is: *(a)* Grand Central Station; *(b)* the Houston Astrodome; *(c)* the Sistine Chapel.

8) Having just had a wonderful late-night plate of veal tortellini, served by your favorite headwaiter, Angelo, you head back to your apartment. Feeling a need to relax and gaze at the restored Gilera Saturno Sanremo 500 GP bike parked next to the fireplace and the Campagnolo-equipped Colnago fourteen-speed racing bike hanging on the wall, you open a bottle of: *(a)* schnapps; *(b)* ouzo; *(c)* grappa.

9) Of the following, the most significant sports figure of the twentieth century is: *(a)* Babe Ruth; *(b)* Jack Dempsey; *(c)* Giacomo Agostini.

10) The best nickname for a twentieth-century sports figure is: *(a)* "Babe"; *(b)* "The Manassas Mauler"; *(c)* "Ago."

11) While sitting around your apartment late at night, gazing at your bikes, sipping on grappa, and looking at your framed photo of

Giacomo Agostini cresting Bray Hill on his blood-red MV Augusta Four, you feel the need for some music, so you put on a little: *(a)* Dixieland; *(b)* experimental electronic music; *(c)* Verdi.

12) Opera is best sung in: *(a)* Norwegian; *(b)* a strong Texas accent; *(c)* Italian.

13) The performer with the most powerful voice is: *(a)* Janet Jackson; *(b)* George Michael; *(c)* Luciano Pavarotti.

14) Of the following three great names in motorcycle racing, the one that rolls off the tongue most easily is: *(a)* Mert Lawwill; *(b)* Bart Markel; *(c)* Renzo Pasolini.

15) The one characteristic most important in an older used bike is: *(a)* a really good, logical set of electrical switches that never get hot or go up in smoke; *(b)* flawless paint and fiberglass work without any crooked decals or dead flies or anything trapped in the gel coat; *(c)* beautifully detailed engine that sounds great, never breaks, and wins at Daytona.

16) The best use of wheat flour is in: *(a)* library paste; *(b)* crepes; *(c)* pasta, served with olive oil, red peppers, and a light sprinkling of Parmesan, followed by a little grappa while listening to Pavarotti sing Verdi, with someone who appreciates Fellini, in a room with framed photos of Ago and Ing. Taglioni on the wall and a Gilera Saturno over near the fireplace.

That about does it. The correct answers will be made available *domani*, or possibly the next day.

Arrivederci.

October 1991

DEALERS

The plain truth, I suppose, has been lurking for a long time in the back of my mind, but not until this summer did a fully formed thought shove its way into the frontal lobe, pushing forward like an agitated airline passenger who staggers down the aisle and demands to talk to the pilot.

It happened while I was cruising on my Beemer down County Highway T through southern Wisconsin, heading for a place called C&D BMW in Freeport, Illinois. The shop is a friendly place with a good parts supply, a full machine shop, and real mechanics. It's also about seventy-five miles south of my home. *Why was I going there?* I can't remember the exact pretext. Probably to buy an oil filter.

It was on this trip that truth finally struck: I suddenly realized that at least half of the nontouring riding I do consists exclusively of trips to motorcycle dealerships.

Wait a minute, you say. Is this really possible?

Yes.

Most people, I imagine, buy a bike, ride out of the showroom, and never return unless they need parts or service. The rest of the time they probably take fun rides on back roads or cross-country vacations. It's like buying a loaf of bread. Once you've got it, you don't spend a lot of time hanging around the bakery.

But here I was, riding seventy-five miles (again) to buy something I could easily have ordered by phone. There was a strange behavior pattern here. Why these many trips to bike shops? To what purpose?

Well, some of these rides are actual necessities; I need a headlight bulb or new gloves or something. But more often than not, the trips are made just to look at motorcycles other than the one I'm riding.

Essentially, to gape and gaze, hem and haw, examine closely, and stand back to view from far away. To be in the presence of machinery. To drink coffee that was made six hours ago, to stir sugar lumps and Cremora with a wooden tongue depressor left over from the 1918 flu epidemic while looking at bikes and thinking about them.

While this sort of dealership bumming is a great pastime, it can also be a source of guilt: Your own trusty bike (the one that got you there) sits outside while you stand around ogling new models, talking to salesmen, and reading brochures. It's kind of like leaving your old dog in the pickup while you visit pet shops and admire the puppies in the window. Old Fido has to wonder if he's about to be replaced.

Still, it's hard to stay away from the showrooms. They make a natural destination for short rides, a magnet whose force field penetrates hills and woods and barns, causing the handlebars gradually to turn in the direction of glittering commerce and new technology. Bike dealerships also make a great excuse for taking what would otherwise be considered an unnecessary ride.

"Honey, I'm making a quick run to the Ducati shop."

"Where's that?"

"In northcentral Canada, not far from the Arctic Circle. I'll be back in October."

"What do you need?"

"A can of chain lube."

One of the problems with these excursions is that you eventually feel you should actually buy something, partly to justify your hanging around all afternoon and partly to keep the dealer in business so riffraff such as yourself will continue to have a place to come in out of the rain.

The upshot is that you can end up with a considerable stockpile of redundant stuff. Last time I looked in my garage storage cabinet, I believe I had six cans of chain lube, three spare face shields, a case of contact cleaner, five different brands of oil, and enough bungee cords to build either an Olympic trampoline or a catapult capable of flinging a full-dress Gold Wing over the ramparts of a fairly large castle. Not that I'd want to.

A number of factors seem to determine how long I linger around a given dealership, and how often I return. It seems to me that the most interesting shops have several things in common.

First, they are usually involved in racing—motocross, drag racing, flat-track, roadracing, whatever. If the owner or a few of the employees don't race, they should at least be sponsoring someone or organizing rides and rallies. A dealership without some sort of racing schedule in the window and a counterperson with a knowledge of competition parts always feels a little too quiet. You can sense the lack of excitement when you walk through the door. Some kind of involvement is needed.

Second, I seem to have a predisposition toward dealerships that handle at least one line of non-Japanese bikes. This is not another case of Japan-bashing; it's just that a row of GSX-Rs, CBRs, or YZs always looks better to me if there are a couple of Guzzis parked at the end, or a few Huskys scattered around. It's a matter of contrast, and it also indicates a widened scope of vision on the part of management. And in the case of your slower-selling brands (many now defunct), it shows that the dealer is willing to blow money on perpetual flooring costs in order to have an interesting shop.

A third factor that keeps me coming back is the coffee. I've visited very few dealerships that had a decent cup of java warming on the Mr. Coffee. Maybe I don't get up early enough, when it's still fresh and doesn't resemble creosote. At any rate, a shop that craves my business and wants me hanging around all day wasting their time could do a lot worse than change the filter and grounds every spring.

Donuts are nice, too. The deep-fried, crispy kind with a light sugar glaze. Preferably made within the memory of someone now living.

February 1992

BOOTS AND SADDLES

Just west of Broadus, Montana, on Highway 212, we rode from cheerful sunlight into dark shadow as a large storm moved over the Custer National Forest. In the hills just ahead, pitchfork lightning flung itself out of the black clouds, zapping the hilltops. We could hear thunderclaps, even through the wind and motorcycle noise.

Each time lightning struck nearby, Barb's grip on my waist tightened slightly. This is a silent signal she uses to let me know that I'm *(a)* riding too fast, or *(b)* not paying attention to an obvious hazard. Or *(c)* both. As the storm moved closer, I began to feel like a large squeeze toy, or a prairie dog on its first flight with an eagle.

Barb needn't have worried. At the first drop of rain, I did a 180 and rode back to a nearby hillside. We parked the Beemer by the side of the road, took off our helmets, and sat back to watch the fireworks. A spectacular storm, made more dramatic by the mystical open spaces of Montana.

We were on our way to Custer National Battlefield, taking a lonely two-lane road to the not-so-lonely spot along the Little Bighorn River where General George Armstrong Custer ran smack into the largest convention of teed-off and highly motivated Indians ever to gather on the northern plains. About 9,000 of them. He tried to defeat them with about 600 men of the 7th U.S. Cavalry. This is what's known nowadays as a bad idea.

I'd read a couple of books on the subject and was in the middle of *Son of the Morning Star*, Evan S. Connell's superb narrative of Custer's life and times and the Battle of Little Bighorn. Reading of this type tends to beget motorcycle trips, and we'd been riding for four days on this one. Out of Wisconsin, across Iowa and South Dakota, through the Badlands and Black Hills, north through Deadwood, with a stop at Wild Bill Hickok's grave, and then up into Montana.

When the storm blew over, we mounted up and headed west. Into another storm. Being too lazy to put on rain gear, I decided we should ride it out, toward a patch of blue sky in the west. So we got soaking wet, then rode into sunlight and dried out for the next two hours.

Arriving at the battlefield too late for a tour, we rode to nearby Hardin, where we got the last motel room in town just as another huge storm came crashing in. Morning, however, dawned warm and clear.

At the battlefield, we rode up a long hill to the visitors center, which is only a short walk from the hilltop where Custer and about 225 of his men made their famous last stand. The men were originally buried right where they fell, and a small cluster of gravestones stands near the top of the hill. Others dot the slope. We parked the bike and walked up the path for a look.

All the reading and maps in the world don't have the effect of five minutes standing on that hilltop. You can immediately see the broad valley where the huge Indian encampment once sat; view the end of the valley where Major Reno attacked from the south and was driven back while Custer circled around the back of the ridge to (he thought) cut off the Indians' retreat; see the steep hill where Gall's braves attacked Custer while Crazy Horse and his men flanked them.

You can feel the despair and loneliness of the doomed cavalry, fighting a hopeless battle far from home; feel the fury and indignity of the Indians who had been pushed out of their beloved Black Hills and off the plains in a series of endless treaty violations.

It's a sad place, but it still resonates powerfully with all the passion that was spent in the battle. It would take a jaded person not to feel it. The hill is a place where no one speaks loudly. We toured the battlefield for the morning, then walked down to our bike.

At the visitors center, people were pulling into the parking lot in motor homes and air-conditioned cars, some opening cans of cold soda, walking up to the hilltop in their usual tourist attire—Bermuda shorts, Reeboks, the ubiquitous Hard Rock Cafe sweatshirts, Disneywear, etc.

Suddenly, for reasons more intuitive than rational, I was very glad we'd arrived at the battlefield on a motorcycle.

It seemed somehow more fitting to have ridden four days through cold, heat, and rain to get there; to be wearing boots and leather jackets and clothing with a purpose; to have the soles of our boots still damp from yesterday's downpour; to be wind-burned, saddle sore, and a little dusty.

It didn't seem quite right to step out of a motor home, open a soft drink, and walk 300 feet to the spot where Custer and his men died in the terrible heat and dust on a June morning 115 years ago. The ease of the act was mildly disquieting.

It wasn't realistic or possible to arrive as the cavalry and Indians had, after grueling weeks on horseback, but a motorcycle was at least a semi-legitimate modern counterpart. It made one's arrival seem more sympathetic to the spirit of the place.

As we rode away, it occurred to me that even our own motorcycle was perhaps a little too easy. The seamless, fast, trouble-free BMW R100RS was possibly too civilized and modern to belong in such a place. Was there a "correct" bike for every type of trip? Barb and I discussed this problem later and decided there was.

If we ever came back, we thought it might be better to arrive on an early Harley Panhead, or maybe an Indian Chief or Scout. An unrestored, slightly tired one, with fringed leather saddlebags, a big saddle, and conchos glinting in the sun. An old American bike, colorful, noisy, smoking, and a little unreliable.

I think Custer might approve, and so would Crazy Horse.

March 1992

ROAD MUSIC

While not motorcycling this weekend because of a blinding snowstorm, I decided to reorganize my record collection. Or I should say my record/CD collection, now that I've been replacing old battle-damaged vinyl classics with compact discs. As my brother Brian, who's in the radio business, says, "You have to give the music industry a lot of credit for figuring out how to sell baby boomers the same record collection twice."

Okay, so I'm a sucker. But at least the new CDs don't sound as though I've been skating on them, and their undersized jackets lack that subtle aroma of spilled beer, storage mildew, and cat pee.

Anyway, in the course of this reorganization I came across a couple of vintage Peter, Paul & Mary albums, the first two released. Ah yes, the famous PP&M set. A little cache of history here.

Seems that in 1962, my parents gave me my first guitar for Christmas—a Japanese-made "folk" guitar from Penney's—and it came with these two Peter, Paul & Mary albums literally stuck to the varnish on the back of the guitar, tightly vacuum-wrapped in plastic. The whole package cost about twenty-two dollars, so you can imagine the fine quality of the instrument.

The idea, of course, was that these were the kinds of records the buyer of a folk guitar would want to listen to. They were selling a little piece of lifestyle here (although no one used that dreaded term in 1962), marketing the music that went with the product.

Even then, it struck me as a fun—and funny—idea, and I commented to my family that it would be nice if all important purchases came with a small but spiritually appropriate record collection stuck to them. Cars, books, houses, motorcycles, and airplanes. would all be supplied with their own soundtracks, tailored to the character of the object.

This idea has occurred to me many times since, especially regarding motorcycles. It seems to me that significant bikes, more than any of the other things we buy, suggest their own theme music, a background swell of subliminal sound that follows you down the road.

My 1967 high-pipe Triumph 650, for instance, has always seemed to me a kind of archetypal Woodstock Generation motorcycle. Its dual-purpose nature and semi-knobby tires give it an added goin'-up-the-country counterculture flavor. So if I had to put together a small album package to go with the motorcycle, it would likely be a mixture of Canned Heat, Arlo Guthrie, early Dylan, The Band, and Crosby, Stills, Nash & Young—with the accent on Young.

I've always secretly believed the song "Long May You Run," with its line about a "chrome heart shining in the sun" is Neil's tribute to a Triumph motorcycle, specifically an image of its heart-shaped timing-case cover. If anyone tells me otherwise, I'll be very disappointed.

Nortons call for a harder-core soundtrack, perhaps a little more blues-tinged. The Rolling Stones are more of a Norton group (with considerable spillover into BSA and Harley-Davidson), as are artists like Janis Joplin, John Lee Hooker, J. Geils, or the Allman Brothers. Like the blues, Nortons are simultaneously blatant and subtle.

A cafe-racer Triton or Commando decked out in rearsets and megaphones might have a couple of fairly disparate musical interpretations, possibly from either the Clash or one of Charlie Parker's rapid, staccato sax solos.

Harleys, of course, not only suggest certain albums, but they've actually had music written just for them. Virtually any song from the *Easy Rider* soundtrack will forever summon images of Fonda and Hopper cruising toward disaster in Louisiana. And then there's the classic instrumental, "Blue's Theme," from an earlier Fonda effort in Roger Corman's *Wild Angels*. Other bands and musicians I would put in the Harley camp are Bob Seger, Steve Earle, David Allan Coe, Hank Williams Jr., George Thorogood, and ZZ Top.

Finding the correct album to go with any Harley, however, demands some attention to model and era. Anyone selling an old Knucklehead or a Harley 45 might consider including a selection of Hank Sr. material, or for a

WLA (army) version, a few Glenn Miller 78s. Panheads are Elvis country, but they go well with virtually anyone who ever recorded on Sun Records, such as Carl Perkins and Jerry Lee Lewis. Chuck Berry and Little Richard could be Panhead guys, too, but they also have a Sportster-like leanness about them.

What else? Certain Japanese fours, someone once pointed out, have the character of a Dennis Brain solo on French horn, though some also suggest the fusion guitar of John McLaughlin—seamless and complex at the same time. Italian bikes, as I mentioned in another column, are a natural for a collection of Pavarotti *arias*, but maybe that's a little too obvious. Wagner works just as well for large-bore Italian bikes as he does for big German Boxer Twins.

What about the new Ducati 900s and 851s, or the BMW K-bikes? Horn music, I think; not much guitar. Maybe Red Garland playing piano behind John Coltrane and Donald Byrd on "Soul Junction." Dexter Gordon also comes to mind. Good-natured sophistication with an energetic sense of history.

I'm still waiting for any motorcycle as good as Miles Davis and John Coltrane on *Kind of Blue*, or a touring bike that cruises as serenely as Stan Getz playing "Desafinado."

When these bikes finally show up, they won't have to vacuum-wrap any CDs to the seat cover. I've got them already, standing by. Art occasionally precedes technology, and is then rescued by it. Just when the old vinyl is completely worn out.

August 1992

LIBRARY SCIENCE

Just before we moved from California back to rural Wisconsin a few years ago, Mayflower sent a woman over to the house to estimate our moving costs. "The heaviest things you own," she said, "are all these books and magazines. We charge forty cents a pound to move them, so you might want to get rid of things you'll never read again."

Good advice, and we did just that. While Barb and I are both natural-born book accumulators, we did manage to give away several hundred pounds of volumes whose inner pages would be unlikely ever to see the light of day again; dog-eared spy novels with titles like *The Bridgebourne Conjugation*, Physiology 101 textbooks that predated the discovery of lungs, and all travel books claiming you can see Europe for less than fifty dollars a day.

I even went through my old flying magazines and saved only those featuring old warbirds or classic airplanes such as Stearmans and Cubs, or those with stories by Ernest Gann, Richard Bach, or James Gilbert. Biz-jet issues got the heave-ho.

Motorcycle magazines?

Sorry. No cuts here. I didn't even think about it.

I've been buying and hoarding motorcycle magazines since I reached the age of reason (pinpointed as the moment at which we actually begin to *question* reason, such as that which prevents us from buying a motorcycle) in the early 1960s, and the magazines are, more than anything else I've owned, survivors.

They've lived through a parental move to a new house in high school, through a succession of college dorm rooms and low-rent apartments, survived home-basement storage for two years while I was in the army (which explains that subtle aroma of mildew), been carried up the stairs and filed into the bookshelves of seven different houses after our marriage, been trucked from Wisconsin to California and back again.

They've even survived those periodic but short-lived ascetic moods where I feel overwhelmed by clutter and purge the house of excess objects. All this, and I've never ditched a single issue of any motorcycle magazine.

There are several reasons for this.

Foremost is probably simple consumerism. As I mentioned in a recent column, there are very few motorcycles whose possible ownership I would entirely rule out. I know from long experience that it's perfectly feasible I could wake up tomorrow morning and suddenly find myself in the mood to own, say, a 305 Super Hawk. Or I could look through the motorcycle classifieds in the morning paper and see a sale listing for a Triumph Triple (as if I haven't suffered enough) or a Harley XLCR, two other objects of enduring interest.

And when these moods strike—or the ads appear—there's no substitute for walking over to your friendly sixteen-ton wall of carefully categorized magazines (moved at forty cents per pound) and pulling the issue with that year's road test off the shelf. Then you get yourself a cup of coffee, sit back in a comfortable chair, and soak in another fine piece of motorcycle history.

Once you've read the specific road test, of course, you are forced to pull the file for the entire year, look in the "Advertisers Index" for each issue, and look at all the manufacturer's ads for the bike at hand.

This, in turn, leads to the rereading of dozens of other unconnected road tests, race reports, and articles. "Geez, there's Kenny Roberts at Sacramento, looking like he's about fourteen—and winning. And here's Cal Rayborn at the Anglo-American Match Races. What a rider he was. *Cycle World* goes to the ISDT, and, good Lord, here's the first full road test on the Honda 750 Four. An ad for a helmet that looks like a stroker cap made of Formica, a pathetic idea, created for motorcycle apologists. ("Nice golf hat, Bob, but why the chin strap?") The BSA girls always look a little more like tarts than the Norton girls, but the Bultaco girls looked better. Cool, refined. A history of Velocette . . . maybe I'd better look up a road test on the 500 Thruxton again."

And so on. It can go on for hours. In fact, my wife Barbara can't believe the number of times I've dragged out the road test for the Honda CB550 Four, another bike I wanted at the time and never bought, but will. "Are you reading *that* again?" she asks. Modern stuff, too, gets the treatment. I've read the road tests for the new Ducati 900SS and the Honda VFR750 so many times the print is fading.

What's really sick is that I will read a road test *I wrote*, ten or twelve years ago, to see if the bike is any good and if I still want to buy one. ("Hey, this guy really knows what he's talking about!") Or I'll read my own riding impression of, say, the CBX or GB500, just to remind myself what it was like.

In any case, these magazines, old and new, have remained a part of my regular diet for approximately thirty years, like pizza or Mexican food. There are no cobwebs or dust in this particular corner of the bookshelves, and, as long as my eyesight holds out, there probably never will be.

When my younger relatives finally cart me off to the Golden Age Farm because I can't remember to turn off the stove burner under the oil for the taco shells, I hope they have the presence of mind to bring the entire musty magazine collection along with me, over the probable objections of the white-suited nurses and staff.

That way, while the other patrons are drinking prune juice and making jewelry boxes out of Popsicle sticks, I can sit out on the porch and reread the technical teardown on Buddy Elmore's factory Triumph 500 to see how they got the crazy thing to run for 200 miles at Daytona without blowing its oil all over the back tire.

Also, my room will have that reassuring smell of late-1960s mildew from the basement of some nearly forgotten home.

January 1993

CAMPING PROGRESS

A few weeks ago, editor David Edwards called me and said he was flying into Milwaukee to pick up a new Heritage Softail Nostalgia test bike. The next day, he would join two old friends from Chicago, Tom Daly and Charles Davis, for a six-day trip around Lake Superior. Would I like to come along?

I consulted my calendar and found that, except for work deadlines, family responsibilities, house repair, lawn care, and a couple of weddings, birthdays, and funerals, the week was completely open. "Sure," I said, "I'll go."

We met at the Spring Green, a Frank Lloyd Wright–designed restaurant on the Wisconsin River. Tom was riding his BMW R100RT, Charles rode his just-restored 1975 Honda CB750F, and I took my new Harley FLHS. So, after lunch, we thudded, whirred, and rickety-ticked north through the beautiful hills and hollows of the Coulee Region to a campsite on the Mississippi in Perrot State Park.

Setting up camp early, we rode into the nearby village of Trempealeau for dinner and then cruised back to the campground after dark. Time for a campfire, cheap cigars, and after-dinner drinks.

We bought a bundle of firewood at the park office, and I proceeded to construct my usual teepee-of-wood campfire in the ring of stones at our campsite, scrounging for some small twigs and kindling to get it going. This is the way I've been making campfires since I was a Cub Scout, having been led to believe it was the Indian Way by a long string of Zane Grey novels and campcraft books.

Tom watched me with mild amusement and then said, "Here, let me show you something." He pulled a small hatchet out of his saddlebag, split several of the small logs, and carefully arranged the pieces in a kind of triangular log cabin with an open center, stacking each piece to overlap the last.

"Great," I said, "but how do you light it?"

"With one of these," Tom said, holding up an object that looked like something Cheech and Chong might have invented; a piece of waxed paper twisted at both ends. "There's a small candle in the middle," he explained. "The waxed paper twisted around the candle acts as a large wick and keeps it burning until the wood catches fire."

He lit the thing and tossed it into the center of the wood triangle. In about the time it normally takes me to find my flashlight to look for matches (or vice versa), we had a beautiful, effortless, even-burning campfire.

So simple and effective. How had I missed this technique? And me a former near–Eagle Scout and graduate of the illustrious Fort Polk Infantry School. In fairness, of course, the Scouts taught a more rely-on-your-wits survival camping strategy. ("Out of candles, Bob. Looks like we freeze to death.") And the army was more focused on Night Defensive Positions than camping comfort. Motorcycle touring was not part of the program.

By the time I turned away from the fire, I discovered that Tom had spread a checkered tablecloth on our picnic table, lit a small candle lantern, opened a bottle of wine, and was slicing a large chunk of smoked cheese with his Swiss Army knife.

Remarkable. In five minutes, Tom had transformed our dark, dreary campsite into a little center of civilization with the friendly ambiance of a family-run Italian restaurant. Just by thinking ahead.

A candle lantern. What a good idea. Compact, effective. No flashlight glare. A warm, pleasant glow. I'd have to get one at a camping store. My third camping lesson of the evening.

Wine gone, fire burned down to glowing embers, we all retired to our own tents, me to my battered and patched twenty-one-year-old Eureka Timberline, a lightweight but conventional cabin-shaped tent with a rain fly. Its return from retirement was the result of yet another camping lesson.

After a decade of experimenting with round, igloo-style tents, I had concluded that humans in sleeping bags are essentially rectangular, rather than circular, in shape. If you weren't camping in a 100-mile-per-hour wind on Everest, the classic raised-wall pup tent had a lot going for it. In camping gear, as well as in motorcycles, we sometimes have a tendency to get bored and disinvent the obvious.

And when I climbed into my sleeping bag, I took advantage of yet another hard-earned gem of wisdom from long ago. I slept soundly and comfortably on a great big fat inflatable air mattress.

Too decadent?

Well, as a kid I always slept right on the ground when I camped (Zane Grey again), priding myself on the Spartan logic of a simple ground cloth or an occasional sprinkling of pine needles. Real men—and real kids—slept on the ground.

Then, one fine autumn, I went on a geology field trip with a Dr. Laudon at the University of Wisconsin. Laudon might have been the inspiration for Indiana Jones—an explorer/bush pilot/world traveler and highly regarded oil geologist. He'd hiked and camped everywhere in the world.

On the way home from our field trip, we camped at Wyalusing State Park on the Mississippi. We students laid out our miserable ground cloths, while Dr. Laudon blew up his air mattress.

Looking at our campsite, he chuckled and shook his head. "You greenhorns," he said, "trying to warm the entire Earth with your body heat. Well, I hope you can sleep."

It was cold that autumn night. Very cold. If you go to Wyalusing State Park now, you will find a rectangular patch of ground that is slightly warmer than the surrounding area. It's the spot where I tried to warm the entire Earth with my body heat one night in 1966.

Never again.

As author Verlyn Klinkenborg said in his great novel *The Last Fine Time*, "Progress is so often revenge on the past."

February 1993

THE DUCKS OF AUTUMN

If my typing seems a little shaky this morning, it's because I was up late last night writing out invitations for the monthly meeting of the Slimey Crud Motorcycle Gang, of which I am a member.

The Slimey Cruds are essentially a loosely confederated group of fortysomething hard-core lifelong sport bike–oriented motorcyclists whose motto is "Ride Hard, Ride Short." The club has no formal rules, but hews to an unwritten—indeed, unspoken until this moment—code of honor that might be stated thusly: A Crud never turns down a beer unless he already has one in each hand, or is busy lighting a cigarette recently bummed off another member.

High on the moral fiber content.

Anyway, it was my turn to hold the meeting, so I was typing out the invitations. Each monthly meeting is supposed to have a theme or a purpose, so I wrote:

> *"Eating spaghetti and drinking red Italian wine in preparatory sacramental celebration of a new 900SS Ducati upon which a bank loan was just approved, bike as yet uncollected, still in Pennsylvania."*

Yes, after only two years of hanging around Ducati dealerships, rereading road tests, and boring everyone with endless equivocation, I finally decided it was time to act.

This coming Friday my friend Bruce Finlayson (fellow Crud) and I will drive out to a place called Stahlstown, Pennsylvania, where a friend of Bruce's named Bob Smith has a Ducati shop, there to pick up a red, full-fairing 1992 SS and return, we hope, before the snow flies.

Earlier this year (alert readers will recall) I sold my old 1977 Ducati 900SS to buy a new Harley-Davidson Electra Glide Sport. I've had a great summer with the Harley, but it doesn't take a genius to see that an FLHS is not a direct replacement for a Ducati 900SS, old or new. It's kind of like selling your refrigerator to buy a stove. It's nice to have a stove, but now you have no refrigerator. Owning both would be ideal.

So, I've held on to the Electra Glide but sold my Sportster to help pay for the new Ducati. One Harley is plenty, for my small-time collection, and it's the smooth, torquey eighty-incher that has won my heart over the long run.

The Sportster had a lot of functional overlap with my old Triumph, but the FLHS doesn't really overlap with anything, visually or charismatically. It's an Electra Glide, and—if you like the way it goes down the road in those great clopping Clydesdale hoofbeats, which I do—there ain't no substitute.

Does all this swapping around and horse-trading make sense?

I didn't think so. Nevertheless, it's a done deal. We leave for Pennsylvania, dark and early, next Friday.

To a Ducati bevel-drive traditionalist, replacing an old SS with a new one may seem like a dubious exchange. The old Duck, after all, is a cleaner, simpler, and more elegant design. Each piece of the bike is beautiful in itself, while the new one has a more composite appeal, the sum being more attractive than the individual parts. It's hard to second-guess the future, but I would say that the old SS will probably prove to be the more enduring classic.

So, if I were a determined collector, and—most importantly—could afford it, I would have hung on to my old Ducati. At the time I bought my first 900SS back in 1980, it was the nicest sport bike I'd ever ridden. Brakes, handling, torque, and speed were all marvelous, and that wonderful V-twin sound . . .

But in 1990, ten years later, *Cycle World* sent me to Italy for the introduction of the new 900SS. It was exactly the right venue for the bike: three days of cruising on the high-speed *autostrada*, lapping on Ducati's test track, and riding over twisting Apennine mountain roads, some of them part of the old *Mille Miglia* race route, through villages, farms, and vineyards, all in crisp, clear autumn weather with the whole landscape turning colors of gold and russet.

And over those country roads—my favorite kind—the new SS was simply magical.

As light and spidery feeling as a lean 600, it had tremendous midrange wallop coming off corners, a nice cammy rush at the upper end, quick and agile steering, superb brakes, and that wonderful V-twin sound.

On the afternoon of our ride over Futa Pass, *Cycle*'s Steve Anderson and I stopped at a cafe in a mountain village for a break and a shot of espresso. We sat at an outdoor table, sipping coffee and looking at the red Ducatis parked in the warm afternoon sunshine against an ancient stone wall. As I recall, neither of us could stop grinning. It was that kind of bike.

In the two years since that day, I'd hoped there would be a statute of limitations on the persistence of the romantic aura cast by that fine moment, or on my memory of the bike's speed and general lightness of being.

So far, no relief. In the meantime, I've tried to be practical and hard-headed about the 900SS. For instance, I know that the dry clutches are giving trouble—they squawk and grab after a few thousand miles. There's supposedly a factory fix on the way, but no one seems to have seen it yet. Also, there's the desmo valve adjustment to consider, along with the usual scattered electrical problems with fuses, connectors, and the like. The bikes are not perfect by any means.

So, in the interest of truth and cynicism, I decided to re-examine my enthusiasm for new Ducatis in the cold light of a Wisconsin, rather than Italian, autumn day. Last week, my friend Dan Wilson in Milwaukee kindly let me take his 1991 900SS out for a long ride, just to see if I still wanted one after all this time.

The conclusion?

I have to make some pasta now, and uncork a couple of bottles of Barolo. The Cruds will be here in an hour.

March 1993

BEEMER UPDATE

Those readers with balanced diets and a tendency toward good clean living who haven't killed off too many of their memory cells with a better brand of dark single-malt Scotch, such as Laphroaig or Lagavulin, may recall a column I wrote two years ago about my old BMW R100RS.

No? Neither did I, exactly, but I looked it up.

The gist of the article was that I had just bought a Silver Smoke 1984 R100RS (the Boxer Twin with aerodynamic sport-touring fairing) that had 75,000 miles on the odometer, no less.

I'd seldom seen that many miles on a motorcycle and I confessed to buying the bike at least partly to satisfy my mechanical curiosity, "to see what sort of havoc, if any, 75,000 miles plays on a big Boxer Twin." I promised to report back, and a letter recently came flooding in asking why I hadn't, so here it is.

Ten thousand miles later, the bike has been out to British Columbia and back, two-up with my wife Barbara; it's been on long weekend camping trips; it's taken me the twenty-two miles into Madison when I positively, absolutely had to be there in 15 minutes for a dental appointment; it has also served as an effective Sunday morning sport bike for rides with various manic friends. And yesterday Barb and I returned from a week-long, late-autumn tour of the Ozarks.

As noted, the clutch was slipping slightly when I bought the bike, and this condition gradually got worse, so the pressure plate and disc were replaced shortly after purchase. At this time, I also replaced the grooved rear-brake disc, bead-blasted and painted the wheels, and installed new wheel bearings and a new set of Metzelers.

On our western trip, I did a valve adjust (on Main Street of Jackson Hole, while sitting on the curb and chatting with passersby) and noted that the valves—particularly the exhausts—were tightening up at an accelerated rate, so I suspected valve recession. This is a common problem with BMWs of the early unleaded era; the seats are hard, but the softer valves gradually hammer and curl.

The bike made it home and continued to run fine, but this summer I had a valve job done by my friends at C&D BMW in Freeport, Illinois, and the old exhaust valves looked like a couple of tulips with razor edges. The RS was hardly burning a drop of oil, but we put in new rings, just on principle.

Any other repairs? Let's see, I replaced a worn twistgrip assembly and installed a new O-ring under the seeping brake master reservoir, also replacing a warped reservoir cap. That's about it for the mechanical stuff. All of this has cost about $1,200, spread over two years, but the bike has never been off the road for more than a day or two.

Comfortwise, I've installed a set of heated handgrips (don't laugh until you've tried them) and changed the windshield. The standard RS windscreen is a masterpiece of the aerodynamicist's art, as is the whole fairing—the faster you go, the more stable and planted the bike becomes. But wind flow is also noisy, so for longer trips I use a tall Parabellum Air Balance windscreen. I've tried several alternate screens, and this one seems quietest and calmest.

The Parabellum reduces the top speed on my bike from about 125 to 115 miles per hour and makes it feel a little twitchier above 100 miles per hour, but it's serene enough for eighty- to ninety-mile-per-hour cruising, which is where the Beemer likes to run anyway. The stock windshield, of course, looks better—you lose that Me-109-cockpit look with a taller screen—but long trips are a lot more pleasant.

After two years and 10,000 miles of use, I have to admit I'm impressed with the high-mileage Beemer. It's light, fast, torquey, comfortable, repairable, reliable, thoughtfully engineered, and has a tradition of mechanical continuity that makes parts and service available from people who know what they are doing, and have been doing it for a long time.

Also, the luggage capacity is terrific for touring—the suitcase saddlebags detach in about two seconds—and the fairing keeps you warm when it's cold.

Much has been made of the eccentric handling characteristics of the big Beemers—mostly involving torque reaction from the shaft drive. Quite honestly, this is rather minimal, especially on the late bikes with lighter flywheels, and after a day of riding you don't notice it anymore. With progressive fork springs installed, front-end dive has been reduced under braking, and I can generally ride the Beemer as fast and confidently on a winding road as all but the most steroid-packed sport bikes—and with less drama.

If there is one other accusation that has been leveled at Boxer Twins it is that they lack the charisma of, say, Harleys, Ducati twins, or screaming Japanese fours. I'd agree that the RS is not as soul-stirring in the sound and fury department as some of these bikes, but it has its own special, gray-ghost kind of personality. Call it effectiveness without ostentation.

It's a motorcycle that wears well; the more you ride it, the greater your respect for the thinking that went into its design and evolution. Any number of bikes do one or two things better, louder, or more colorfully, but for all-around, do-everything balance, I would rank the R100RS as one of the best motorcycles I've ever owned. Even at 85,000 miles.

Any regrets in buying the old RS?

No, not really. It's always fun to rescue and refurbish a motorcycle in need, even though costs inevitably exceed the resale value of the bike. But I wouldn't advise anyone to turn down a low-mileage example, either. Miles are miles, even on a BMW.

Nevertheless, the old Beemer passes two of my basic tests for quality and greatness in any piece of machinery, whether it's a motorcycle, an airplane, a drill press, or a toaster: *(a)* you can repair it, and *(b)* after you do, you've still got something worth having, regardless of its age. Or yours.

August 1993

ABSOLUTE POWER

This past weekend I confessed to my friend Tom Quatsoe that I have recently become intrigued with the idea of someday owning a Kawasaki ZX-11, partly just for the fun of having a really quick two-up sport-tourer, and partly to cast my vote for any motorcycle that can crank out 132 rear-wheel horsepower and a top speed of 176 miles per hour while remaining civilized and rideable around town.

"This is probably a good time to do it," Tom said. "We might not ever be able to buy a motorcycle that fast and powerful again."

No? Well, maybe not. Still, I couldn't help but smile, hearing this familiar old refrain. An echo from the past.

Thirteen years ago, when I first came to work at *Cycle World*, then-Executive Editor John Ulrich had just bought himself the last of the slide throttle–carbureted Suzuki GS1000s. He was leaving it in the crate and storing it away in his garage because motorcycles would probably never be so fast and powerful again, so unfettered by smog controls.

I suppose a case could be made that few performance motorcycles made since have been as versatile and comfortable as that old Suzuki, but there have been many, many bikes made since 1979 that are faster, smog controls or no. John realized very quickly after buying the Suzuki that the horsepower race had not peaked after all, and sold the bike a year or two later.

Now, of course, there is a real threat of future horsepower restrictions. Germany and other European countries have a voluntary 100-horsepower limit on motorcycle engines, partly as a response to the Greens and partly, I suppose, as a sop to the professionally indignant safety-fixated nonmotorcyclist who needs three times that horsepower to make his Mercedes get out of its own way.

This limit has always seemed slightly amusing to me, as there is nothing magical about 100 horsepower, except in the minds of people who don't understand its arbitrary nature. It is a measurement of work, based on the force required to raise an arbitrary unit of weight an arbitrary distance in an arbitrary amount of time. If horses had been extinct before the Industrial Revolution, it could just as easily have ended up as dogpower, in which case 100 horsepower might equal 479.6 dogpower.

So would there be a public outcry to limit our bikes to 479.6 dogpower? No. I imagine 500 dogpower would become the very image of dreaded excess. We like our numbers tidy, our packages neatly wrapped.

Essentially, what the public does not like is fast bikes, and 100 horsepower has become the bogey, the place in the mind where others begin having too much fun or behaving too dangerously.

Never mind that there has never been any link made between horsepower and motorcycle accidents. In fact, some insurance studies have shown an inverse relationship, probably because young, inexperienced motorcyclists can seldom afford big, powerful bikes. I've been riding for twenty-nine years, and the causes of near accidents have always been the same: sand on corners, wet leaves, car turning left, following too closely, passing too late. None of my close calls had anything to do with horsepower. I had exactly the same threats to good health on my Honda CB160 as I have now on my Ducati 900SS. More, in fact, because I was less experienced.

In fact, the only danger I see in powerful sport bikes is that the owner of one is more likely to think of himself as Wayne Rainey, when, of course, he's generally not. And the main danger with the old CB160 was a tendency to think of oneself as Mike Hailwood, who the owner also usually was not. In any case, you could crash just as effectively on twenty-eight horsepower then as on 132 horsepower now. Let's face it—the source of nearly all accidents is the human brain. Horsepower doesn't know poor judgment from Shinola. It is indifferent.

Why am I saying all this?

Well, to paraphrase Will Rogers, I never met a horsepower I didn't like.

Horsepower gets us around trucks right now, livens acceleration in uphill sweepers, allows us to carry a passenger and luggage without diminished elan, tugs (or, better yet, yanks) gratifyingly on the arms when we pass the city limits sign. Horsepower is fun.

And it has not escaped my notice over the years that, within my own small, ever-changing motorcycle stable, I have tended to favor those bikes with power over those that were lacking it. Once I bought my KZ1000, my CB750 Honda went almost unridden. One weekend on a BMW R100RS test bike caused me to trade in my sweet-running but docile R80 for the bigger Boxer. The new generation of more powerful Ducatis quickly seduced me away from my favorite bevel-drive Duck. The new BMW K1100RS I rode last week is much nicer than the old K100RS, and people are constantly trading in their 883 Sportsters on 1200s or big twins. They almost never, ever, go the other direction.

This is not to say big bikes are better than small bikes, only that a small bike with power is more fun than a small bike without power. I have never seen the riding experience on a motorcycle within any size, weight, or utility category diminished by the addition of extra ponies—except in a few screwed-up nonfactory tuning projects.

The way power is delivered, of course, has a lot to do with its appeal. In any streetbike, I generally prefer immense torque and strong midrange acceleration to a peaky, high-end whoop that blasts out another twenty-mile-per-hour rush just as you are entering the next corner. This is probably why I've owned a few more big twins than cammy inline fours over the years.

On the other hand, there's nothing wrong with immense torque, strong midrange acceleration, *and* high-end whoop. Which the guys at the magazine tell me may be found in abundance with the ZX-11.

Good for Kawasaki. And may the day never come when they have to make the last really powerful bike for collectors to store away in crates.

September 1993

DO LOUD PIPES SAVE LIVES?

In Daytona this year I saw two interesting T-shirts, both bearing messages that left me scratching my head and pondering.

The first one said, "Live every day as if it were the last day of your life."

Now there's a bad piece of advice if I ever saw one. Can you imagine how we would conduct ourselves?

"What did you do today, dear?"

"Well, I got up late, skipped work, and rode my Ducati through town at about 120 miles per hour and had three McDonald's chocolate shakes and large fries for breakfast, then I sold our house and car to a guy on the street for a quick $10,000, and invited the Dallas Cowboy cheerleaders out for dinner . . ."

And so on. Three days of that and you'd be broke or in jail.

The other T-shirt that attracted my attention said, "Loud Pipes Save Lives."

Do they really, now?

I've yet to see any scientific data one way or the other on this question, but I've also noticed a curious lack of safety legislation requiring the use of loud pipes to reduce the accident rate on our highways. ". . . All riders below the age of eighteen shall be required to have very loud pipes unless accompanied by an adult, and shall not be exempt unless they can show financial hardship . . ."

Let's face it; the safety establishment in America and elsewhere has been distinctly slow to embrace the loud pipe concept. Even the statistics-happy insurance industry has overlooked this adjunct to public health. They give me a discount for advanced age and a clean accident record, but have yet to offer a loud pipe discount for riders over forty.

There are times, I suppose, when loud pipes do notify car drivers of your presence—during a pass, for instance, or in those states where you are allowed to split lanes. But it has been my observation that a sudden, loud exhaust note usually just causes an unaware driver to swerve or make some other erratic maneuver, and leaves that hapless individual with a vague sense of having been mugged. I don't know if sonic shock waves make a pass any safer.

What loud pipes mostly do is make the public madder than an overturned anthill on a hot day.

When a motorcycle annoys or shocks them, they compose imaginary (or real) letters to their senators and representatives and daily newspapers demanding that motorcycles obey the same noise laws as cars. Eventually, this legislation gets passed, and our new motorcycles are so quiet we can't hear them at all.

Meanwhile, manufacturers are forced to develop water-cooled, heavily shrouded engines so they can eliminate the last audible trace of piston slap, gear whine, intake noise, and valve clatter from a bike that may soon be roaring around with its mufflers off. Logic and good sense are once more defeated.

I bring this up only because I am in the market for some louder pipes.

I own a Ducati 900SS with extremely quiet stock mufflers (thanks to all those angry letters), and would like to find some canisters that make genuine mellow big-twin nonlawnmower ear music, yet don't offend the neighbors or provoke even more letters.

It's a shame, really, that I have to waste this money and that Ducati was not allowed to put some nice euphonious (but nonbelligerent) pipes on in the first place. I have a 1967 Triumph and a 1974 Norton with dead stock mufflers that sound, well, like motorcycles, yet don't seem to offend anyone. Pedestrians, if they are aware of my passing at all, turn, look, and give me the thumbs up.

Big twins, with just the right level of muffling, make one of the more pleasant sounds of the industrial age, as do Continental 220 radial aircraft engines, steam locomotives, and Gibson ES335 electric guitars played at moderate volume through tweed Fender tube amps. You'd have to be pretty hostile to all forms of technology not to like at least one of these sounds.

Everyone has a different threshold, of course. I thought the Conti pipes on my old 1977 Ducati 900SS SP sounded beautiful, but a neighbor tactfully told me as gently as possible that he'd kill me and murder my whole family if I ever started the bike again early on a Sunday morning. So I used to get up for my 6 a.m. Sunday ride, *push* the bike to the end of our block, and point the pipes out at the local golf course before leaping on the kick starter. Golfers, I reasoned, cannot be offended. Look at the way they dress.

Anyway, I've been looking for some larger caliber but nonlethal mufflers for the Duck, and the search continues. My riding pal Randy has some stainless tapered mufflers on his 851 that sound great out in the country, especially if you are following his bike. I took his bike for a ride around town, however, and gauged from the reactions of bystanders that they were not universally popular. If looks could kill, I'd be deader than Franco. I'd like something a little quieter so I could rev the engine more in town without drawing much attention to my rate of acceleration.

I've always liked a little sound and fury out of my bikes, but as time goes on it seems more enjoyable to have more fury with a little less sound. Not exactly a stealth bike, but something with just enough exhaust bellow and clout to create a halo of aural pleasure for those who appreciate life's finer things, while passing through town essentially unnoticed by those who couldn't care less but have typewriters and a full drawer of stationery.

One person's music is another's noise, and finding a tolerable compromise between the two might be seen as a kind of minor litmus test for civilization. Barbarians, whether they write letters or ride bikes, are always loud and they always want others to keep quiet.

I need to find some mufflers that fall about halfway between the personal tastes of Attila the Hun and Torquemada the Grand Inquisitor.

December 1993

TRIUMPH MOTORCYCLES IN AMERICA

At long last, a book about Triumph motorcycles that does not come from England.

I thought I was going to have to write one myself, but fortunately a guy named Lindsay Brooke has done it, thereby saving me years of research and dozens of missed Triumph rides on summer afternoons.

The book, *Triumph Motorcycles in America*, arrived last week by mail, sent to me by the author with a note of thanks for my editing help. Brooke sent me a manuscript of the book about a year ago and asked if I would check it over, a task I gladly accepted. This is like being asked to eat cookie dough with a large spoon, with the understanding that you will later tell the cook if it was any good. My kind of job.

In all honesty, however, my editing help was modest at best. Though I have owned four Triumphs and followed the news of company fortunes since the early 1960s, I am no trained Triumph historian. Just an attentive fan of the marque. In researching his book, Brooke learned (and now reveals) more about Triumphs than the random owner could hope to discover in a lifetime.

With or without my help, this is the Triumph book I always wanted to read.

Why?

Because nearly all my other British bike books come from England. Which is fine, except that most of them naturally tell the story from an English point of view and tend to immerse themselves in the politics of factory life, while ignoring the fact that North America was generally Triumph's biggest market. The huge American competition scene is usually mentioned only in passing, as is the considerable impact of Triumphs on American culture.

So Brooke's 224-page book is quite a relief. Here's the story of Triumph's growth in America, with Johnson Motors on the West Coast and TriCor in the East; of racing with Ed Kretz, Bill Baird, Gary Nixon, and Gene Romero; of Hollywood's love affair with Triumphs (Brando, Robert Taylor, Lee Marvin, Keenan Wynn, Steve McQueen, and Ann-Margret, no less); of Bonneville speed records, warranty claims, corporate fumbling, and wrong turns. It's all here, nicely written, with lots of good photos.

While the book is naturally a celebration of Triumphs, it also has another side. Careful reading can leave the involved reader with an undeniable sense of sadness and frustration.

In the late 1960s, Triumph was absolutely on top of the world. The motorcycles had style, racing victories, speed records, social cachet, and an on-road/off-road versatility that has not been seen since—at least not in any motorcycle with a claim to aesthetic excellence. Triumph was on a roll.

So what did Triumph's managers do with this resounding success?

They threw it away in a few short years, that's what.

Instead of figuring out ways to reduce vibration in the world's most popular vertical twin, they spent millions on a "think tank" where overpaid nonmotorcyclists could ponder the future of design. Instead of investing in simple O-rings and good gaskets to keep the oil inside their engines, they "modernized" with ugly plastic sidecovers and tall oil-in-frame models that sent welding slag straight to the engine innards. Instead of buying new machine tools at the factory, they took big stock dividends and long lunches. Instead of listening to their American dealers' cries for better quality, they designed Buck Rogers mufflers.

While Japanese workers built the oil-tight CB750, British workers went on strike. Or casually dropped the random handful of screws into the crankcase, just to teach capitalism a lesson.

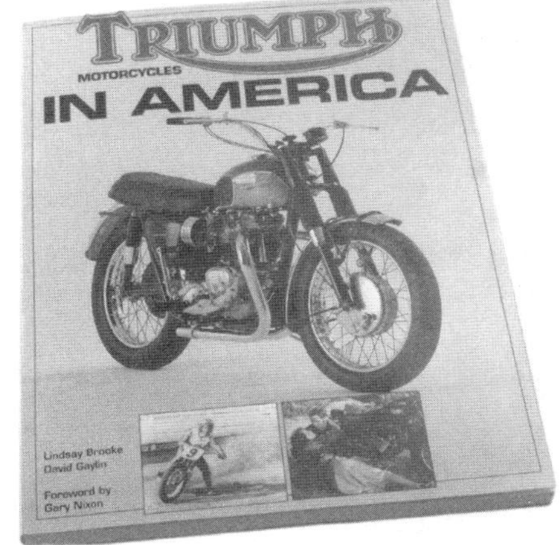

How a successful company could have made so many boneheaded decisions and fatal errors in such a short period of time is hard to comprehend, though I suspect a sociologist might attribute it at least partly to the Swinging London Syndrome. The late 1960s and early 1970s were a time when everyone wanted to be a Beatle and smoke dope in Chelsea, but no one wanted to study metallurgy or drill-bit technology. Specificity and real knowledge were out of fashion. Bell bottoms got caught in the drive chain of quality.

Reading Brooke's book now, a paraphrase of Brando's famous line from *On the Waterfront* kept going through my mind: "They could have been a contender."

By concentrating on the simple things that really mattered to people—smoothness, oil tightness, build quality, and long-legged stamina for the road—Triumph could now be England's version of Harley-Davidson. It turns out there were a lot of people who wanted Harleys, once the company could prove the bikes wouldn't fall apart, and I suspect the same might have been true of Triumph Twins.

The Triumph name, of course, is alive and well in the hands of John Bloor, with his perfectly modern fours and triples. By all accounts, these are excellent bikes (I haven't ridden one yet), and they certainly look good. No complaints here.

But the old Bonnevilles and Trophies are gone, and I'm not sure they really had to go, despite the well-known limitations of the large-displacement vertical twin. With cleverly integrated counterbalancers and other internal improvements, their lightness and striking good looks (circa 1967) might have put them in the same class as Harley, Ducati and Guzzi V-twins, or BMW's Boxer, classic designs that never die because they work.

Every time I ride my 1967 TR6C, it occurs to me that there is no satisfactory modern substitute. I'd still love to buy a brand-new, 380-pound, big-bore road bike (with 1990s reliability) that can successfully handle cow trails, deserts and continents; win at dirt tracks, enduros, TTs, and Daytona; be ridden solo or two-up; and have chrome an inch deep, beautiful paint, and timeless styling.

If someone made such a thing today, I'd probably own just one motorcycle.

April 1994

SHOULD YOU BUY A GERMAN BIKE?

Well here we go again—another complex and difficult psychological exam. Some readers may remember a couple of previous columns from recent years, provocatively titled "Should You Buy a British Bike?" and "Should You Buy an Italian Bike?"

Both were short, one-page tests cleverly designed by yours truly (a Psych 101 dropout from 1967 and occasional smoker of fine cigars) to determine whether undecided readers should take the plunge and purchase motorcycles produced in either of these two famous countries. The bikes have their peculiarities, after all, and not everybody is cut out to own one.

And so it is with German bikes. Until recently I would not have felt confident tackling this subject, but five years of German-bike ownership, a grandfather from Stuttgart, and a fondness for Spaten Dark have given me courage.

Remember, only one answer is correct. Here goes:

1) The best way to adjust the valves on a motorcycle is to: *(a)* remove the body panels, gas tank, air plenum, fairing ducts, ignition coils, and cam covers to measure and/or replace up to sixteen shims; *(b)* take the bike into a shop because the job is so complicated it's better if someone else screws it up so you don't negate your warranty; *(c)* remove two aluminum valve covers that stick out in midair and adjust four rocker arms while you sit on a mechanic's stool listening to Beethoven's Symphony No. 6 (*Pastorale*) on the garage boom box and sip a heavy Bavarian beer that seems to have been brewed from dark honey found in the Black Forest.

2) A motorcycle, before it wears out and is no longer worth rebuilding, should be able to go: *(a)* about 18,000 miles; *(b)* about

50,000 miles; *(c)* at least 250,000 miles, and then be rebuilt anyway.

3) The famous maxim, "Without music life would be a mistake," was written by a cynical critic of public morals named: *(a)* Ross Perot; *(b)* the Reverend Jim Bakker; *(c)* Friedrich Nietzsche.

4) You are having some friends over for venison sauerbraten with potato dumplings and *Ganseleberpastete*. A good wine to serve with dinner would be: *(a)* Night Train; *(b)* a "blush" wine that looks like someone poured cherry juice into a perfectly good batch of peach syrup; *(c)* Schloss Vollrads.

5) Halfway through dinner, one of your guests says, "What's that terrible music on the stereo?" You: *(a)* smile politely and explain it's Wagner's "Das Rheinegold" from *Der Ring Des Nibelungen* and politely offer to turn it down; *(b)* put on any album from the Windham Hill catalog; *(c)* begin to clear the table and turn lights off in the house, helping your guests into their coats and explaining that you have to get up early, after which you listen to the entire four-CD boxed set of the *Ring* until 4 a.m., while polishing off the Schloss Vollrads yourself.

6) Motorcycle luggage should be carried: *(a)* under an elastic cargo net stretched over the rear seat and clipped to the protruding body side panels in such a way that it does not scratch the plastic; *(b)* inside your jacket; *(c)* in a pair of waterproof suitcases that were designed for your bike and clip on and off in about ten seconds.

7) Ideally, a dog should look as much as possible like: *(a)* a small piece of sculpted shrubbery from the gardens of Versailles; *(b)* a dust mop; *(c)* a wolf.

8) The best name for a dog is: *(a)* Fifi; *(b)* Mopsie; *(c)* Wolf.

9) The best name for a rocket scientist is: *(a)* Al; *(b)* Jimmy; *(c)* Werner.

10) Confronted at a cocktail party by a person with "way out" opinions, the best response is to: *(a)* shake your head and smile quietly at the strange diversity of humankind; *(b)* tactfully change the subject; *(c)* straighten the person out with crushing precision of logic and lucid Hegelian dialectic.

11) The most confidence-inspiring name for a general commanding huge numbers of troops is: *(a)* Gamelin; *(b)* Graziani; *(c)* Eisenhower.

12) A good length for a motorcycle ride is: *(a)* over to the 7-Eleven store; *(b)* up and down Main Street about six times; *(c)* down to Tierra del Fuego and back on opposite coasts.

13) A dual-purpose bike for serious exploration should hold: *(a)* 1.2 gallons of fuel; *(b)* 2.3 gallons of fuel; *(c)* 9.3 gallons.

14) The most inviting commercial description of a malt beverage is: *(a)* Lite; *(b)* Dry; *(c)* Clear; *(d)* Dark.

15) Dark Bavarian beer should be drunk: *(a)* in standard six-ounce bar glasses; *(b)* in thin plastic cups with the names and helmet designs of famous NFL football teams on them; *(c)* in huge one-liter steins depicting folk scenes of castles, stag hunts, and happy peasants eating an entire wild boar and falling down drunk.

16) Huge one-liter steins of dark Bavarian beer should be served by: *(a)* a guy named Brad who will be your server tonight; *(b)* a vending machine; *(c)* a great big healthy blonde woman who can carry four steins in each hand.

17) The best part of every touring day is: *(a)* when you get to oil your chain; *(b)* when you forget to oil your chain; *(c)* neither of the above.

18) If you were shooting a helicopter-assault scene in the movie *Apocalypse Now*, the best choice of sound-track music might be: *(a)* a Glenn Miller dance tune; *(b)* Gary Lewis & the Playboys Greatest Hits; *(c)* "The Ride of the Valkyries."

19) Motorcycles: *(a)* are fun to ride around sometimes when it's nice out; *(b)* really look radical with some of those wild colors they got; *(c)* are a lifetime passion whose enjoyment can be enhanced through exacting craftsmanship and the thoughtful application of technology; *(d)* all of the above.

That should do it. No need to reveal the correct answers. Like the handlebar switches on my old Beemer, they are logical and obvious.

July 1994

YEARS OF GEAR

Last week I finally bought myself a pair of leather riding pants—street leather bottoms, I guess you'd call them. They have plastic inserts for knee and shin protection and closed-cell foam where the hip bones meet the ground. Or could.

The incentive came during a recent three-day comparison test ride in the California mountains with U.S. twins roadracing ace Nigel Gale and two other fearless types. I looked down at my blue jeans after a fast ride one slidey wet morning and suddenly pondered the protective capacity of a single layer of denim twixt flesh and tarmac versus, say, padded and reinforced leather.

Perhaps it was time to unlimber the old checkbook and buy myself a little protection of the lower extremities.

So I bought these extremely svelte-looking Euro-pants that have some fantastic name, like Stealth Death Ray Rocket Ship Pilot Pants or something, but they feel good and look good. (Try to imagine Jim Morrison if he'd lived another twenty-three years, and you've got the picture.)

The only problem, of course, was that I brought them home last week and now there's no place to hang them up.

Okay, I can't say there's literally *no* place—you can always get one more thing in a closet, creating a kind of riding-gear laminate. But the inescapable fact (I just realized) is that we now have an astounding amount of riding equipment lurking in the dark recesses of our home.

Why so much?

The problem seems to be cumulative. I bought my first bike in 1963 and have since owned a grand total of thirty motorcycles. All but four of these bikes have come and gone, yet I've hardly ever deep-sixed a piece of riding gear.

In the beginning, life was simple. During the 1960s and early 1970s, I had only a Bell 500TX helmet, a black leather jacket, a pair of work boots, and some gloves. Period. There was nothing else in those early student apartments that could be construed as riding gear, except maybe my Bob Dylan–edition Triumph T-shirt, which finally fell apart in the wash. All of this stuff could easily be packed in a single box the size of one Pioneer stereo speaker—and it was, when I went in the army.

So far, so good. Years passed, and only one other item was added: I bought a new Norton Commando in 1975 and naturally had to have a genuine waxed-cotton Belstaff Trialmaster jacket. I still have it, of course, but it's faded and worn. This year, I bought a new one, so there are now two Belstaff jackets in my closet.

Then, with roadracing, things began to pick up steam. In 1978 I bought a used set of Lewis leathers, along with two sets of boots, two sets of gloves, and a new full-face Bell Star helmet. Within minutes, a virtual doubling of gear mass, and then some.

Things got worse when *Cycle World* hired me in 1980. Desert riding, with its rocks, cactus spines, and high speeds, demanded real off-road riding gear, so boots, shoulder pads, pants, socks, goggles, and a Bell Moto III helmet were added.

This dirt-riding stuff alone now occupies an entire, oversized Hondaline duffel bag that sits upright in the closet of our guest room and sometimes falls on visitors who open the door, like a stiff body in an Abbott & Costello comedy. It also imparts to the guest room a delightful *je ne sais quoi* aroma of desert flowers, fear-induced sweat, and spilled beer from Mike's Sky Ranch and the Slash X Bar. One deep breath and you're there.

Cycle World also bought me a new set of Bates leathers for roadracing and photography, along with matching boots and gloves. These leathers don't fit me any more, but how can I give them away? They still have a pavement smear from Riverside's Turn 7 across the thigh and knee. Historic stuff. They are also a pungent reminder (literally) that by dieting and running four miles per day, a person with my skeleton can weigh as little as 162 pounds. And once did.

I've since acquired a newer set of Z leathers, as well as a yellow Dry-Rider rain suit, an Aerostitch touring suit, newer helmets—oh Lord, the helmets. I also have an antique wooden box in the back corner of our den that contains nothing but visors of different shades for different helmets. Most of them are badly scratched "spares."

Boots? Yes. Boots of many lands. Roadracing boots, touring boots, cowboy boots, work boots, motocross boots, engineer boots . . .

All right. So we have way too much stuff in our closets. This would not be so bad, except that my wife Barbara has also been riding since the mid-1960s, so you can double all the road gear. She even has a Belstaff Trialmaster suit—bought in 1982 at the Isle of Man, no less. Our closet under the stairs looks like the Birmingham Waxed Cotton Exhibition of 1939.

Considering that our house is of only average size, I have to admit, however, that careful sorting, folding, and packing have allowed us to keep most of this stuff pretty well hidden from public view. Visitors, for instance, are not immediately aware that the house around them is virtually insulated with leather, Kevlar, Gore-Tex, nylon, Vibram, waxed cotton, and closed-cell foam, tightly packed and spring-loaded for action.

It is only after looking for a couple of aspirin, a bath towel, or a place to hang their clothes that guests gradually come to realize things are not quite normal in this household. Some of them stay a few days. Others don't.

So the new pants are a problem. But the real crunch will come if I decide to buy the Death Star Space Invader Jacket that goes with them. Right now the pants are a serious mismatch with my faded old Buco riding jacket. I look like a Frankenstein creation stitched together from different riders who once lived in widely separated decades.

Which, of course, is exactly what so many of us have become. And we have the closets to prove it.

August 1994

DOES YOUR BIKE HAVE CHARACTER?

Last week I went out and bought a great big brand-new Japanese bike, black in color, that is reputed to be the fastest production bike on Earth, according to all magazines and the kid at the gas station.

A Japanese bike? *Moi?*

Yes. I have decided to dip once more into those deep eastern waters of technology, and in my mind I have already named this magnificent beast "The Land Shark." No doubt some kind of column will come out of this ownership experience, but I want to withhold judgment until I've broken it in and ridden it more.

In the meantime, my many Europhile friends have expressed both concern and trepidation. They worry for my sanity, yes. But more than that, they want to know if the bike has "character."

There is no easy answer to this question. There are only symptoms and signs, some obvious, some cryptic, that collectively add up to either a motorcycle with genuine character or a bike that should be sold to someone else as soon as possible, lest you lose your immortal soul.

With so much hanging in the balance, I have decided to help others, as well as myself, by putting together a simple guide to character. Under this scientifically correct system, a bike with complete, fully formed character will score 100 points. Maybe more. A bike without character can go hundreds of points into the red. Here goes:

- If your bike is now, or was at any time in history, the fastest production bike on Earth, give yourself fifty points. (Ha!)
- If your bike, or one very much like it, has ever won its class at the Isle of Man, score fifty points. Ten more if Hailwood, Surtees, Woods, or Duke were riding.

• If the workers who built your bike drink espresso or grappa during their lunch break at a small trattoria across the street from the factory, add ten points.

• If your bike has a fake gas tank, or false air scoops, subtract forty points. Sixty points off for chromed plastic anywhere on the bike.

• If your bike's name uses any three initials of one or more dead Englishmen or any defunct British arms company that made military rifles during the Boer War, give yourself seventy-five points.

• Fifty points for springer or girder front forks.

• If the girder fork on your bike is made of aluminum from melted-down war surplus P-51 wing spars and Spitfire propellers, give yourself ninety-five points.

• If your bike was designed by a nonmotorcyclist car designer who thought he would step in and "revolutionize the look and concept of motorcycles forever," knock off thirty points. Then take back ten for sheer weirdness.

• Twenty-five points for any two-stroke triple. Ten more if it wheelies out of control and hits things with no particular provocation.

• Forty points for any V-twin, any four that revs beyond 13,000 rpm and all sixes.

• If Lawrence of Arabia owned a bike like yours, give yourself 100 points.

• If Lawrence of Arabia actually owned your very bike, give yourself 700 points and feel free to buy six other bikes with no character at all.

• If your engine was originally designed for a light Italian military vehicle, award yourself forty points.

• If you died tomorrow and no one else would ever be able to start your motorcycle, add fifty points.

• Subtract forty points for any motorcycle that appears to have been designed by a cartoonist who saw a Harley once, but then forgot the exact details.

• If the ad-taker in the classified department of your newspaper never heard of your brand of bike and you have to spell it out more than twice before he or she gets it right, award yourself forty points.

Then subtract forty-five for selling the bike.

• If your insurance agent absolutely refuses to consider insuring your bike, even though you are forty-six and have never had an accident, add sixty points.

• If the owner's manual specifies either bean oil or mineral oil of a viscosity higher than sixty-weight in the crankcase, add ten points.

• Add ten more if most of it leaks onto the floor.

• Ninety points if the bike is so difficult and cranky to start and operate that you almost never ride it. Ten more if the seat causes actual prostate damage.

• Twenty points for hairpin springs or any external oil line to the cylinder head; five more if it has banjo fittings with copper washers that "mist."

• Forty points if Steve McQueen rode your bike in a movie.

• Ten points for each square inch of visible engine surface.

• Fifty-five points for magneto ignition. Fifty more if it has a sticky advance mechanism that causes the engine to kick back, nearly breaking your leg.

• Seventy-five points for a broken leg.

• Thirty-five points if your bike runs noticeably better on miserable, damp days with pockets of thick fog, as seen in *The Hound of the Baskervilles,* with Peter Cushing as Holmes.

• Fifty points if your clutch adjustment procedure is so arcane and complex that only a taciturn hermit machinist and former RAF Gloster Gladiator mechanic named Alistaire who lives on a farm in Vermont is able to make it work correctly.

• Twenty more points if Alistaire requires a "gift" of strong Stilton cheese and Isle of Islay single-malt Scotch before he will even consider working on your bike.

• Ten more if Alistaire is said to have murdered a man who brought the wrong kind of cheese.

• One hundred points if you think your bike has character and no one else does, except other owners who are in on the secret.

January 1995

ANOTHER SUMMER IN REVIEW

Most of us have probably seen those inspirational gift-shop tracts (usually affixed to a piece of varnished knotty pine and hung on a wall) in which the anonymous writer tells us what he or she would do if given this life to live over again: "I would laugh more, make more friends, be kinder, learn to dance, take more chances, sing out loud, chew tobacco, learn Swahili . . . ," that sort of thing.

Well, that's always how I feel at the end of summer, when the first Canadian winds and purple-blue clouds come rolling down from the north, reminding me that my riding days, for this year at least, are numbered.

I always look back at the summer and wonder why I didn't ride more, take better advantage of those perfect summer days, block out time on the calendar for weekend trips, or just think ahead and call my riding pals *before* 6 a.m. on Saturday morning ("Gee, Pete, I'd love to go for a ride, but I promised I'd disinfect the back of the Caravan where our dog threw up and take the kids to a nine-hour soccer game . . .").

Anyway, with the frost now securely gripping the pumpkin, it's too late for regrets, but it may be a good time for what W. Somerset Maugham called the Summing Up.

'Tis the season to sit in the garage, peering through coffee steam at your bike—or bikes, if you are so disposed—thinking about what you did and didn't do and what you may do in the future. The motorcycles, and their odometers, tell the story. Here's how my own summer shaped up, mileage-wise:

For some reason, I didn't ride my Norton 850 Commando nearly as much as in past years, just over 800 miles in total. Maybe it was because each time I rode the bike for any distance, exactly two things went wrong, which is also the reason I didn't get to the British Biker Rally this summer.

On my last ride, for instance, the brake-light switch broke off and the speedometer suddenly quit working, stuck in time (or space) at 18,000.8 miles. Looks like the rear-wheel speedo drive gear has packed up again. Or maybe it's another case of Smith's Revenge. Could be the drive cable. All three components work in unison to give each other bad reputations, so you never know which to blame.

Ah, but the sound of that vertical twin, and its midrange torque. Smooth on the highway, lovely to the ear, good to look at in the garage. There were about three good rides this summer, but they were short ones.

Perhaps it's time for an all-out, new-everything rebuild, to restore faith and dependability. It is a fine thing to leave on a Norton; a finer thing still to arrive.

Next summer, I'll try to do more arriving.

My BMW R100RS reflects another failure of personal planning. The Beemer, despite its comfort and sport-touring capabilities, never had a chance to open up and strike cross-country this summer. Barb and I took our Big Tour this year in the Alps on a rented R100GS, while the poor RS sat home, draining its battery with the slow tick-tick of its electric clock—which quit ticking in July, hands frozen at exactly 8:17.

I did put about 1,100 miles on the bike, just batting around the countryside and running into town. No fault of the bike's; after four summers of use, this high-mileage wonder (now 87,000 miles) is still the best all-around motorcycle I have ever owned. It goes fast, carries stuff, tours well, handles fine, and keeps the weather off. Every ride ends with a quiet glow of respect for the old Beemer and a sense that it was built to be real, long-lasting transportation for actual adults.

Next year, I hope to do some long-distance touring on the RS, with tent.

The Honda CB550-K is what everybody needs one of: a user-friendly bike that may properly be ridden in an open-face helmet, work boots, and a denim jacket. Sportsters and Triumph 500s have this quality, and so does the old Honda four. Casual fun, no girding yourself for battle or anointing of the forehead before each ride.

Another mere 1,000-plus miles here, none very fast or far, but all of them comfortable, heads-up, taking in the sky and scenery. And not a single mechanical or electrical problem. Mr. Honda, rest his soul, may be proud of this little beauty. It lit up the errand-running part of my summer, revived the concept of the random, spur-of-the-moment ride.

I've already written quite a bit about my ZX-11, the newest of the brood. If there is a mood for every motorcycle, this is the one I rode when I wanted to feel like a cat on 2,000 volts. Hair standing straight up, wired.

Besides being an espresso machine for the nervous system, it also handled the civilized in-town mode pretty well, so I put 3,000 trouble-free miles on the ZX this summer.

I guess my best rides of the year were on this bike—those few special free-roaming days where small towns, farms, hills, and winding asphalt disappear in your rearview mirror from dawn to long-shadow time and home. I managed a memorable few of these, but not nearly enough. Every summer has its main bike, its defining spirit, and this was it for 1994.

And now I need a new rear tire.

It's gone, like the season and the scenery, in the rearview mirror.

Next year I'd like to do better. At the end of the season I'd like to look back on at least one big tour. (Greece? Mexico? Isle of Man?) But more than that, I'd like to plan ahead, get my work done, and take many more short rides, so those sunlit weekends don't keep slipping through my fingers.

The clock may be stopped on my BMW and the odometer frozen on the Norton, but I have the terrible feeling that, somewhere in the universe, gears are still turning and the hands are still ticking away. In an ideal summer, correctly lived, every motorcycle should age more than its owner.

May 1995

GLOWING INSPIRATIONAL RESTORATION MESSAGES

As I climbed into my salt-spattered van and headed down our driveway yesterday afternoon, I almost had to laugh (but not quite) at the sheer dismalness of the winter day: dark and wet with heavy fog and big snow clumps flopping out of trees (Fap!). The radio said all major midwestern airports were closed down with pea-soup fog.

Not exactly riding weather, but a good motorcycle day of another kind, nonetheless.

I was a man with a mission. In my pocket was a shopping list of unlikely items that would probably have confused the layman: fifty-pound Grainger glass polishing beads, #610G98; one gallon DuPont Kwik Prep metal primer 244S; p/u bronze swingarm bushings at Wisconsin Bearing; one tube Tripoli buffing compound, Farm & Fleet.

If you haven't guessed already, I have just dived into my first full motorcycle restoration since I did my Triumph TR6C, six years ago. This time the subject is a 1964 Mach 1 Ducati 250 Single.

How I came to own this bike is a long story, but I'll keep it simple.

I recently confessed to my friend Bruce Finlayson that I was thinking of building a Ducati Single cafe racer—or possible vintage racer—and he told me he knew of a Mach 1 for sale in the Chicago area. He'd almost bought it himself, but being deep in the throes of a Motobi 250 restoration, decided that one red Italian cafe-racer project was enough for anybody, simultaneously speaking.

So we drove down to the Chicago suburb of Batavia to look at this Ducati, which belonged to a Moto Guzzi/BMW–owning former roadracer named Steve Isleib.

For those not immersed in such things, the Mach 1 is one of the sportier Ducatis of the 1960s, a genuine 100-mile-per-hour-plus 250cc cafe racer with a lumpy cam, 10:1 compression, five-speed gearbox, red frame, tach, and (usually) with clip-ons and a racing-style bum-stop seat.

This one, as accurately represented over the telephone by Steve, was a mostly complete restoration project of loosely bolted-together parts: correct frame and motor, broom-painted tank and fenders, mildly rusted rims, headlight, and rebuilt tach in a box, etc. All there, except for the original factory clip-ons and the sidecover toolboxes.

After inhaling deeply at the magnitude of the project, I forked out a reasonable wad of green stuff (thank you, Mastercard) and trucked the little Ducati home.

You haven't lived, incidentally, until you've had the exquisite pleasure of rolling a mere 255-pound streetbike up a ramp into your van. It's ridiculously easy, like bench-pressing a papier-maché barbell set.

Anyway, the past few weeks have been spent disassembling, degreasing, bead blasting, inhaling paint-stripper fumes, reading Mick Walker's *Ducati Singles Restoration*, and gradually tuning in to that vast underground and overground network of collectors, racers, parts suppliers, and enthusiasts who have chosen to concentrate their attention on these remarkable Taglioni-designed creations.

I've also been running back and forth to a nearby German car restoration shop called Brooklyn Motoren Werke, Inc., where a painter and body man named Gary Elmer transforms my stripped, bead-blasted parts of bare steel into Italian red.

And, of course, every few hours the UPS man shows up at my door, with a set of chromed San Remo wheel rims, a fender decal, or an Aprilia-made headlight rim. Things are jumping.

As they have to be.

I have discovered in thirty years of restoring bikes, cars, and airplanes that finishing a restoration is kind of like pushing a Sherman tank or a Gold Wing to a distant gas station: Momentum is everything.

The random injection of money helps, too, of course, but it's really just another component of momentum, along with faith, vision, and pure restlessness. If any one of these is missing, the whole project can quickly grind to a halt.

This most commonly happens, I think, when the restorer takes on too much of the project at one time. If the entire bike is disassembled down to the last nut and bolt, scattered around your garage on shelves and in aluminum cake pans, it can lead to that dreaded state some sociologist recently defined as "Option Paralysis."

For me, it's best to leave a few things (like the engine, or fork assembly) bolted together until you can attack them with your full attention. If nothing else, they are a partial reminder of what the bike used to look like.

While this little subterfuge helps, I have discovered that my best tool for maintaining momentum is probably derived from the well-worn Confucian analect, "The longest journey begins with a single step."

Restorations begin, and end, with a thousand single steps, one directly after the other.

So every day I do at least one thing to further the cause. One step.

I order a part, sandblast a chain guard, clean a set of bearings, pick up some paint, drop off the swingarm bushings at the machine shop, whatever. Even if it's a hectic day of work, family disorder, veterinary emergency, stock market collapse, or nuclear war and national chaos, I still try to get at least one thing done, however minor.

Then, when retiring for the evening, I always stop and ask myself this simple question: "What have you done for your Ducati today?"

Or Triumph or Norton or Lotus or Piper Cub . . . fill in the blank.

It's a cheap trick, but it seems to work on a wide range of exhausted machinery upon which the previous and possibly more intelligent owner has folded his cards, walking away and shaking his head.

July 1995

NORTON GOES TO FLORIDA

I am reminded of the old joke about the two buffalo hunters riding across the prairie in a wagon pulled by a mule. The mule stops suddenly and refuses to budge, so one of the buffalo hunters gets down from the wagon, looks the mule right in the eye and says, "That's once!"

He climbs back in the wagon and the mule slowly, reluctantly, starts moving again.

A few miles down the road the same thing happens. Dead stop, mule won't budge. The hunter climbs down, looks the mule in the eye, and says, "That's twice!"

Gradually, the mule starts plodding along. But, a few miles later it stops again and will not move. This time the hunter calmly gets down from the wagon, looks the mule in the eye, and says quietly, "That's three times." Then he pulls out his big hogleg pistol and shoots the mule dead, right on the spot.

His partner can't believe it. "You stupid idiot!" he shouts. "Here we are in the middle of Indian country with a wagonload of hides, and you've shot our only mule! You must be out of your mind. That's the stupidest thing I've ever seen!"

The buffalo hunter who shot the mule slowly turns toward his partner, looks him right in the eye, and says, "That's once!"

So, why am I reminded of this particular joke? Let me explain.

I drove down to Daytona Bike Week in my blue Ford van again this year, hauling along my new Ducati 900SS SP. My friend Pat Donnelly went with me. Pat, who has owned many Triumphs and Hondas, is "between bikes," as we say, so we brought my Norton 850 Commando along for him to ride.

We did the usual coffee-and-sandwiches thing, driving straight through the night and arriving at the track early in the morning, just in time to watch a full day of vintage races through a fog of uncomprehending fatigue.

On the way down, of course, the Norton managed to radiate gas fumes the way a Voice of America transmitter gives off radio waves. Only this was the Voice of England. Pat asked, "What's wrong with that thing?"

"It's the petcocks," I said. "They're only a year old, but they leak anyway. We'll just have to keep the windows cracked open. Don't smoke."

It was somewhat chilly riding weather in Daytona this year, but we nevertheless unloaded our bikes at the house a bunch of us rented and did some riding around town and to the track.

The Ducati ran great. The Norton, however, began dying every time the brake lights came on. Last time it did this it was a shorted brake light switch, but I checked out the switch, wires, and lights, and everything looked okay. That evening, I put the battery on a trickle charger for a few hours.

The next day, the Norton seemed to have partially recovered from the brake light problem, but would die instantly when the main headlight beam was switched on. I told Pat to ride with only the small pilot light on, which helped, but we had to quit riding at night. Also, Pat informed me the speedometer had stopped working.

"The rear drive must have gone out again," I said. "I've already replaced it twice." Another fine English replacement part, by way of India. Home of the Bangalore torpedo.

After bike week, we headed down to Sebring, for the famous twelve-hour sports car endurance race. Arriving a day early, we decided to unload the bikes at our hotel and take a ride down to the shores of Lake Okeechobee and back up through the Seminole Indian Reservation.

About seventy miles from Sebring, the Norton started running intermittently on one cylinder. I traded bikes with Pat so I could try some diagnostic listening and riding. Sounded like a plug loading up. "We better forget the rest of the ride and head back to the fort," I said. "I don't have an extra plug."

As we rode along, the Norton ran worse, so I switched to reserve, just to make sure the main fuel line wasn't clogged. The petcock lever broke off in my hand and fuel started spewing onto the engine. I got out some pliers to shut it off and the whole petcock disintegrated. Luckily, it plugged itself with its own debris. I looked around. It was mighty lonely out there on the Seminole Reservation, and we were a long way from home.

By the time we got to Sebring, the Norton was running on just the right cylinder, with an occasional BANG from the left pipe. We limped into the hotel, bucking, surging, and popping.

I took off my helmet, looked at Pat wearily, and said, "I have an Excedrin Headache No. 9. It's a special tension headache you get from riding a malfunctioning English bike through the middle of nowhere."

Pat looked at the Norton and shook his head. "I don't know, Egan. There are so many interesting bikes out there now that really *work* . . . I like old English bikes, too, but I just wouldn't put up with it anymore."

We loaded the bikes into the van, and I took one last look at the Norton before slamming the rear door.

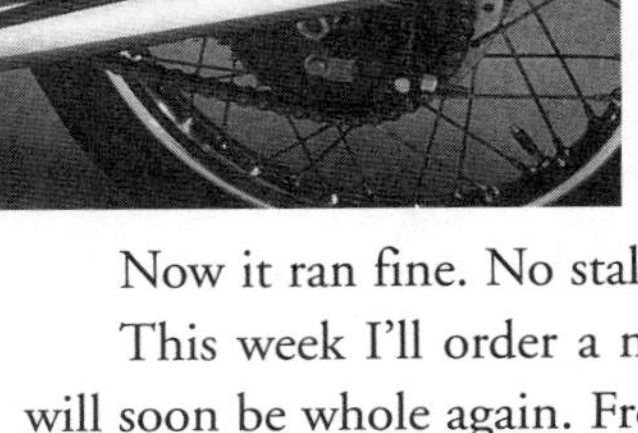

"That's three," I said quietly.

Not being armed, I didn't actually shoot the bike. I just turned to Pat and said, "That's it. I'm selling this thing."

When we got home, I cleaned the bike, replaced the plugs and the slightly weak battery, then fine-sanded all the electrical connections on the Zenier diode and the lighting system.

Now it ran fine. No stalling. Perfect idle, lights on or off.

This week I'll order a new petcock and speedometer drive, so the bike will soon be whole again. From three back to zero known problems.

It looks quite beautiful, all cleaned up and polished, sitting there in my garage.

Seems a shame to sell it now, just when everything's perfect.

August 1995

GOOD COMPANY

Let's face it: Motorcycling does not have a tremendous number of historically famous persons to call its own.

I don't mean legendary insiders, such as motorcycle racers. We've got plenty of those. I'm thinking more of people who are world famous for accomplishments outside the motorcycle world—writers, statesmen, etc.

Aviation seems to have attracted the lion's share of colorful and literate public figures in this century. The romance of flying has been pretty well documented by such luminaries as Cecil Lewis, Antoine de Saint-Exupery, Charles and Anne Morrow Lindbergh, Richard Hillary, Richard Bach, Ernest K. Gann, Roald Dahl, Beryle Markham, and many others.

Car enthusiasm, too, has produced many famous exponents, though they are distributed through such a wide range of general interest (touring, rallying, racing, collecting) that the focus is rather watered down. You have to concentrate mostly on the higher levels of racing to find evidence of passion and philosophical speculation. Everybody drives.

But not everybody rides a motorcycle. There's a finer focus here; thousands are eliminated from the sport by timidity, incompetence, or—most often—simple lack of interest. So those who participate automatically become members of a relatively small club.

Probably the best known historical figure to have been a motorcycle buff is T. E. Lawrence. He had the unfortunate distinction, of course, of being killed on his Brough Superior, but it was not such a bad end to a dashing life.

Though he was also an avid bicyclist and an aviation devotee, Lawrence's most impassioned descriptions of machinery and the joy of speed are dedicated to motorcycling, mostly in a few great passages from his oft-quoted book, *The Mint*.

Who else can we think of?

Novelist Thomas McGuane has written a nice essay on motorcycle racing, and poet James Dickey has caught the essence of a lone bike on a country road. Gonzo journalist Hunter S. Thompson, of course, has written all kinds of lively stuff about bikes (recently right here in *CW*, I am pleased to say). My own need to be out on the road was fueled by an early reading of Peter S. Beagle's fine book, *I See by My Outfit*.

In terms of wide public appreciation for the aesthetics and pleasures of bike ownership and riding, however, probably nothing has had as much influence as Robert M. Pirsig's *Zen and the Art of Motorcycle Maintenance*. When the book came out, you could almost hear the reading public of America say to itself, "If anyone this smart likes motorcycles, they must be good."

Besides writers, and the random anomalous capitalist such as Malcolm Forbes, most of motorcycling's celebrity exponents seem to have come from showbiz. We've had Clark Gable, Robert Young, Keenan Wynn, Marlon Brando, James Dean, Lee Marvin, Elvis, Bob Dylan, Arlo Guthrie, Duane Allman, Peter Fonda, Dennis Hopper, the Carradine brothers, and many others revealed to the public as riders whose enthusiasm goes beyond the movie screen or the recording studio. And then there's Steve McQueen. When I was in high school, McQueen made bike ownership seem almost a requirement, like breathing.

Currently, Jay Leno is probably the celebrity best known to the general public as a motorcycle nut. As such, he may have done more good than the Honda 50 to convince the American population that motorcycling is fun and enjoyable ("If Jay likes bikes . . . ").

Okay, I retract my premise. There are quite a few famous motorcyclists, and we are in good company. Still, we can always use one more.

Which is why I was happy to learn, in a recent reading of Thomas Keneally's remarkable book, *Schindler's List*, that Schindler himself was a motorcyclist.

Yes, Oskar Schindler, the businessman with a heart, the fellow who brewed up a dangerously clever mixture of camaraderie, daring, intrigue, economics, and outright bribery to save his Jewish employees from the Nazi death camps, was one of us.

Not just a motorcyclist, but an enthusiast and hard-core racer. Born to an Austrian family living in Czechoslovakia, he spent his teen years zipping around the Moravian hills on a red Italian 500cc Galloni, which Keneally says was probably the only one in the country.

In 1928, he bought one of only four Moto Guzzi 250 race bikes sold outside Italy and rode the bike to a third-place finish in a mountain roadrace between Brno and Slobeslav, against tough international competition. At the Altvater circuit, he beat the Moto Guzzi, BMW, and DKW teams across the finish line, only to be relegated to fourth place over a flagging error on the last lap. A personal triumph nonetheless.

When I finished the book, I set it aside and said to myself, "Well, I should have known."

It follows a pet theory I have long nurtured that enthusiasm for something real (motorcycles, for instance) is a great displacer of hate, which is imaginary yet has terrible consequences in the real world.

It has been my general observation, as an avid reader of history, that religious and political fanatics are usually people who don't actually know how to *do* much. Except maybe fret about the conduct of others.

In other words, they are people in need of a good hobby. They need, more than anything, some passion outside themselves and the dark whirring of their own mental gears.

Schindler was a man who was incapable of organizing a death camp. Or of blowing up a federal office building. He had better and more important things to do. He loved life.

He was a motorcyclist.

Proud to have him aboard.

November 1995

CAFE RACING

I can't remember when I first heard the term "cafe racer," but I think it was during my high school years in the early 1960s. My first reaction was to laugh, thinking it was a term of derision, like "sunshine patriot" or "drugstore cowboy."

Just as a drugstore cowboy is one who dresses like a cowboy but hangs around in town and never gets near a horse or a cow, I figured a cafe racer was a motorcycle rider who dressed like a roadracer and prepared his bike to look like a race bike, but hung around the cafe, drinking coffee and swapping lies rather than taking himself and his bike to the racetrack for a true test of riding ability.

There may, in fact, have been a note of put-down in the origin of the term, but by the time I got out of high school, the cafe racer, as both lifestyle and type of motorcycle, had been elevated to something of an art form. It turned out some of the bikes were beautifully rendered and some of their riders, though they might consume a great deal of coffee, took their riding quite seriously.

I finally quit snickering when I saw photos of some of the creations coming out of England, such as the exquisite Tritons: Norton Featherbed frame (usually Atlas) paired with highly tuned Triumph Bonneville engine, generally with long, polished alloy tank, bum-stop race seat, clip-ons, rearsets, etc. Lean, clean, and elegant.

There were also other hybrids with unlikely pairings of half-names, such as the Norvin, a Vincent V-twin whipped-and-chaired into (again) the Norton Featherbed frame. These were supposed to be best-of-both-world combinations, and I always wondered if the folks at Norton were troubled to observe that everyone kept their frames and threw the engines away. Or if Triumph engineers wondered why everyone liked their engines but replaced the frames with something from Norton, or a specialized frame builder like Seely or Rickman.

You'd think, like chefs who notice the fish always comes back to the kitchen untouched, they might have sniffed the provisions now and then.

While cafe racing was slow to catch on in the United States, it became a big thing in England. (Do yourself a favor and buy Mike Clay's marvelous book, *Cafe Racers*, a priceless bit of history.) The cult thrived in Italy and other parts of the continent, too.

I lived in Paris one winter, after I came home from Vietnam in the autumn of 1970, and this was the first place I observed the cafe-racer movement first-hand. British twins were waning, but Paris was full of heavily racerized Honda 750 Fours, many of them done by Japauto, a Paris Honda dealership that built 989cc, eighty-horsepower street-racer conversions.

I used to hang out in such Hemingway-redolent bistros as La Chope and Coupole, and up would howl a group of riders in full black leathers, expensive sheepskin aviator boots, soupbowl helmets, and goggles, usually with colorful scarves or the popular checkered Arab *kaffiyeh* worn around the neck. They would tramp into the cafe, rubbing their hands together for warmth and ordering large amounts of hot coffee, all of them charged with that special energy that comes from a sense of being a romantic figure in the right place at the right time.

Their bikes almost always had tank bags, rearsets, and clip-ons. The clip-ons, I thought, were not ideal for guiding a heavy, wide motorcycle around the shiny damp cobblestones of Paris, but they looked neat.

Back home, a few of the faithful began similar transformations on Honda 750s and 500s, then Kawasaki Z-1s when they came out. And for those who didn't want to send away to England for parts from Paul Dunstall, there were at least a few bikes around that could be considered cafe racers at birth.

Leftover from the 1960s were Ducati Singles, Bultaco Metrallas, Velocette Thruxtons, Royal Enfield 250 GTs, and Honda CB92s and Superhawks. Actually, most twin-carb Hondas of the era were really cafe racers at their core, no matter what dirt-inspired bars or pipes you might slap on them. Soichiro Honda himself, I think, was pure cafe racer at heart.

The 1970s brought more factory cafe bikes: Ducati 750 GT, SS, and 900SS; Harley XLCR; Honda 400F; Guzzi V-7 Sport; Laverda Jota; BMW R90S; John Player Norton; Kawasaki Z1-R; Yamaha SR500; Suzuki GS1000-S; Yamaha RDs; the Euro-equipped CBX Six, and others.

Later cafe hall of famers would have to include the various GPzs, Interceptors, and Katanas, the SRX600, GB500, R100S, most Guzzis, Hailwood Replicas, and nearly all other Ducatis except for the really dumb-looking ones aimed at American bad taste as imagined by misled Italians. And now, of course, we are absolutely awash in bikes that could be considered cafe racers. The Japanese make them in every displacement category, Ducati is thriving, and Harley has picked up an interest in Buell. The new Triumph Speed Triple is the very avatar of the tradition. They are all around us, these nonstandard, noncruiser, non-luxo-tourer bikes whose performance and good looks beg discussion in your better bistros and cafes everywhere.

I may have laughed at the concept when I first heard it in high school, but looking back now on the thirty-some streetbikes I've owned, it seems nearly all would qualify under that elusive know-one-when-you-see-it banner of cafe racer.

I've strayed here and there, in the search for long-range comfort, charm, or relaxation, but I've always come back to the type. Perhaps there is an association in my mind between motorcycles, cafes, and strong coffee. I like bikes that are nervous by nature and slightly on edge, as if they themselves might have consumed a little too much caffeine.

Also, I live in a climate where racing to the next cafe has always made a lot of sense.

January 1996

THE LONG WAY HOME

About fourteen years ago, when I first got my pilot's license, I used to regularly rent a beat-up old Cessna 150 from the Orange County airport, near the *Cycle World* offices in California.

One day when I was at the airport, signing out the 150 for a weekend flight, my former flying instructor asked where I was going.

"San Francisco area," I said, "Palo Alto airport."

"In a 150? You must like to suffer," he said "Why don't you take something faster, like a 182. You could get there two hours sooner, without stopping for fuel."

I thought about that for a minute and then said, "Well, if I get there two hours earlier, I'll just be back on the ground again, which is where I've been all week. Frankly, I'd rather be up in the air. I don't fly just to get it over with."

He just grinned and shook his head.

The instructor was right, of course, in the logical sense. But he was taking the professional view, and I was a mere hobbyist. I certainly don't object to speed in an airplane, but neither do I wish myself elsewhere when it's a clear day and I have plenty of time.

It was just another version of a basic travel conflict we often face: County road or interstate? Biplane or retractable twin? Time versus sensation. Both have their points. Sometimes you have to slow down and think for a minute to pick the right one.

Like last weekend, when I went to Michigan to retrieve my Ducati 900SS.

It was at Greg Rammel's shop in Northville, near Detroit. Northville is not exactly freeway close—it's 400 miles from where I live—but I go there because I trust Greg more than myself to fiddle the desmo valvetrain and get it right. While the bike was there, he also rejetted the carbs and bolted on a set of Fast-by-Ferracci carbon fiber mufflers. Last week, he phoned to say the Ducati was ready. "You're going to love this thing," he said.

So I hitched a ride to Detroit with my pal Bruce Finlayson, picked up the bike, strapped on my tank bag, and hit the road.

It was a crisp Friday evening in suburban Detroit, with an autumn bite to the air. Long shadows, headlights just coming on. I rode down to nearby Saline, to stay overnight with my friends Larry and Tracy Crane.

Greg was right about the Ducati: I did love this thing. The pipes had a mellifluous basso rumble without being overly loud, and the Dynojet kit had replaced the Ducati's lean, hunting condition at part throttle with smooth and instantaneous response.

At last, the bike was exactly the way I wanted it. I'd installed a Corbin seat and a larger, thirty-nine-tooth sprocket, and now the jetting was spot-on, so it sounded like a Ducati, rather than a Lawn-Boy. Comfortable, quick, light, and beautiful to hear.

After an early breakfast with the Cranes, I walked out into one of those autumn mornings for which we live—a warming sun, deep blue high-pressure sky, the first red tinge on the maples, and air that smells like the dry, clean dust of harvested corn. Days like this are achingly beautiful for their very transitory quality—we know there won't be many more like them. Not this year. Maybe not in a lifetime.

Leaving the driveway, I was faced with a choice. Left toward I-94, or right toward the two-lane Highway 12? The interstate would get me home faster, in seven hours, while Highway 12, winding through all those little towns and villages, would take . . . what? Eight hours? Ten?

Had any human ever spent ten hours on a 900SS, even with a Corbin seat?

I looked at my watch. It was only eight in the morning. Plenty of daylight left. Hmmm.

What was the big hurry? This was the kind of day I dreamed of all winter, all week while working. Good weather, no promises to keep, and a favorite motorcycle, reborn and working better than ever.

"Don't fly to get it over with . . ." I mumbled to myself. I turned right, on Highway 12.

What a day: A fine twisty road; Michigan football fans streaming into Ann Arbor; people raking their yards; garage sales; antique shoppers in minivans; kids in letter jackets; pumpkins and Indian corn for sale in farmyards; a million Harleys rolling into Sturgis (Michigan) for a toy run.

I passed a state historical site—two odd, lighthouse-like towers along the road. Pat Donnelly and I had ridden this route twenty-seven years ago, almost to the week, on our trip to Canada and stopped at that very spot. Me on a Honda CB160, Pat on a 305 Dream. An involuntary shudder. Like Phaedrus, we were here. Smoked a cigarette on that lawn over there, hadn't been back since.

Approaching Chicago, I opted for the interstate and the Chicago Skyway. A wonderful elevated view of steel mills, the lake, and one of the world's great skylines. I pulled off at the Arlington Heights Guitar Center, fell in love with a black Les Paul Standard I don't need, then got off the interstate again and rode into Wisconsin through Beloit. Past Blackhawk Farms Raceway (bike races!), through Brodhead, where the air was filled with biplanes from an antique fly-in.

Up County T, with rolling green hills, red barns, silos, and forty miles of crystalline visibility. A yellow Piper Cub flew over the road. Just like our old one. Maybe it was our old one.

I pulled into our driveway early in the evening and shut off the engine.

Deafening silence. Wind noise ringing in the eardrums. Back among the mortals. I looked at my watch. It was almost 6 p.m.

By taking Highway 12, I'd given up two hours of time—in exchange for scenery, sensations, curves, memories, bridges, skyways, steel mills, guitars, hills, upshifts, downshifts, biplanes, and the harvest smells of a thousand farms.

It seemed like a reasonable trade. I've got all winter to be on the ground.

February 1996

THE SAME GUY

Last month I flew into Sedona, Arizona, for the introduction of Yamaha's new luxo-cruiser/tourer, the Royal Star.

Beautiful place, good ride, nice bike. Not precisely my kind of motorcycle, but a fine example of the type nevertheless. If Yamaha's marketing people are correct in their assessment of the motorcycle-buying public, I suspect the bike will do quite well.

We were given a flood of information on the Royal Star and its development, but there was one particular point that really caught my attention during the slide-and-pointer session that preceded the bike's unveiling.

Yamaha's marketing staff gave us a brief history of the ups and downs of the motorcycle biz from the 1950s onward: the growth of the motor culture in the late 1950s through the 1960s; the all-time sales peak of 1973, when an explosion of dirt-biking coincided with the popularity of exciting new streetbikes; a '70s downturn in off-roading with public-land closures and the loss of two-strokes; a renewed peak of street riding (six million active riders) in the late 1970s; a long slide downward through the 1980s as baby boomers had children and an increasing percentage of young people metamorphosed into passive video zombies who never go outdoors except to a mall.

Yamaha credits Harley-Davidson with arresting this big slide, catching the attention of those aging, money-earning boomers and giving them something they want to buy: cruisers. Low-key, highly styled motorcycles that suggest rebellion but are actually just fun to ride around on.

Not only has the downward slide been arrested, says Yamaha, but the boomers are exhibiting a trend that apparently has never before been seen in the entire history of the whole world: They are becoming more active as they get older, rather than less.

Traditionally, fifty- to sixty-year-olds have slowed down, growing more comfortable and complacent, not to say doddering, buying cardigan sweaters, baggy pants with a scosh more room, etc.

But not the boomers. No way.

We (I am one, after all) are apparently behaving like agitated air molecules in an overheated laboratory flask, bouncing off the walls. As a group we are getting fitter, spending more time outdoors, and blowing more of our income on canoes, parachutes, mountain bikes, skis, and motorcycles. For the time being, at least, it appears we are going to boogie 'til we drop.

Good for us, I say.

But obviously there's also a dark side in all this.

Yamaha's Ed Burke pointed out that all of the ups and downs of the motorcycle business, from the early 1960s to the present, have been caused by exactly the same bunch of people. He waved his pointer over a four-decade sales graph and said, "All the way through, this is the *same guy*."

Okay, not exactly the same guy. Naturally, some of us bought dirt bikes when others got Z-1 Kawasakis, and others will buy Ducatis instead of Harleys or Royal Stars. But we are the same generation, with a similar slant on life and a shared notion of how it is well lived.

And, obviously, there are thousands of younger motorcyclists (some of them sitting in study hall right now) who are every bit as enthusiastic as we overstimulated, aging boomers—about whom they are no doubt sick to death of hearing.

Every generation has its special, curious breed who somehow escape television or computer screens to go outdoors and do something real.

What worries me, however, is there may not be enough of these inspired youthful types getting into motorcycling any more. And I've been wondering all week why that is.

Money?

Could be a big part of it. Bikes were cheap when I got into this sport. I paid off the loan on my first bike in one summer with two part-time jobs.

Can a sixteen-year-old buy any new bike now on one summer's unskilled labor?

I doubt it.

On the other hand, my first bike was a Bridgestone Sport 50, so maybe my expectations were lower. You can probably buy a Honda Spree on one summer's minimum wage, but I'm not sure these small scooters have the same social meaning my first motorcycle had. I suspect they are often just transportation rather than a foothold on a way of life.

There are, of course, lots of larger-displacement used bikes out there at very low prices, but a used 600 is harder to slide past parental consent than a new Bridgestone 50, which I portrayed to my parents as a harmless little device—which it almost was. The 50 got them accustomed to the idea that I could ride and survive. The used Honda Super 90 and CB160 that came later were a much easier sell.

Maybe that's what the motorcycle market needs: an inexpensive foot-in-the-door bike for sixteen-year-olds who have to do battle with their parents to have a bike at all.

The hard part, of course, is making a small bike that is not perceived as dorky. Whatever it is, it has to have substance and a certain cachet. It can't pander.

That was the beauty of the small-bore bikes of the 1960s—they were not just aimed at kids. They were made for everyone, and everyone wanted them—movie stars, athletes, etc. They were a hot social commodity.

If I were Yamaha, I would take care of those bucks-up aging boomers, to be sure, but I would also be scratching hard to come up with an inexpensive bike that a 16-year-old would be proud to own.

Not a diminutive baby chopper or a bad imitation of a much larger sport bike, but something desirable for itself, as so many small-bore bikes were in the 1960s. A bike to get this thing rolling again, to start another revolution.

We Same Guys are getting pretty old. We are all a lot closer to our last motorcycle than we are to our first.

March 1996

OUR BROTHER'S KEEPER

A few years ago, while doing my periodic cruise of record shops in search of blues CDs I don't already have but should (*Little Walter: The Intentionally Lost Chess Sessions*), I ran into an old college acquaintance on State Street in Madison, Wisconsin. He asked what I'd been doing and I told him I'd just come back from the Oshkosh Fly-In.

"When are they going to shut that thing down?" he asked, blithely.

I looked at him and blinked. "Shut it down? Why would they shut it down? It's the biggest, most popular fly-in in the world . . ."

"Well, I see they killed four more people this year. The thing's gotten too big."

Maybe it was the indiscriminate use of the word "they." Maybe it was the whole attitude, or the three cups of double espresso I'd just had at Victor Allen's coffee bar while vainly searching for a cheap Vincent in the new *Hemmings*. Whatever it was, I felt my blood pressure rising, adrenaline kicking in.

"Are you a private pilot?" I asked.

"No," he said quickly.

"Well then what do you care if four more people got killed flying into Oshkosh? You weren't even there. Thousands of people fly in every year, and they love doing it. Sometimes there are a couple of accidents, but you'd have more fatalities if the same number of people drove their cars to a football game. Or stayed home and took a shower."

He shrugged and said, "Well, I see your point. Seems like a dangerous event, though."

Through the miracle of subject change, we parted amicably, neither of us probably convinced of the other's wisdom. In any case, my friend had walked into it; he'd hit one of my few (okay, multitudinous) hot buttons.

All my life I have observed with interest and amazement the general human need to eliminate pleasurable risk in the lives of others whose diversions we do not share. The first time I noticed it was in school. The subject was football.

Every time a kid got injured in a game there was a general outcry to ban high school football. The outcry, of course, never came from football coaches, players, cheerleaders, managers, fans, or parents who loved the game. It came from people who had never played football and didn't care to watch.

All through grade school, I was worried the game would be eliminated before I had a chance to play. Never mind that I eventually turned out to be a perfectly mediocre football player. At least I was given the opportunity to try.

In my lifetime I've seen the same pressures brought upon boxing, mountain climbing, auto racing, and dozens of other activities. In some cases these sports have gotten out of hand and reform has been needed to keep them civilized (we can't be feeding Christians to lions just because it sells tickets, I suppose), but all these risky pastimes have fortunately sidestepped extinction through reasonable compromise.

I don't need to tell you that motorcycling is among those sports over which nonparticipants constantly agonize. We've had many public suggestions over the years (some from our own transportation officials, such as the redoubtable Joan Claybrook) that motorcycling should be eliminated entirely. Veteran riders of the 1950s' anti–*Wild One* hysteria tell me we have no idea how close we came to being swept off the road forever.

None of this lively opinion or pending legislation—need I mention—ever comes from anyone who ever threw a leg over a motorcycle.

Strangely, we have some of this same conflict right within the bounds of our own sport. Almost every year some racing insider opines that the Isle of Man TT should be eliminated because it's too dangerous. While I feel it should not be a required World Championship event—no one should be forced to ride there to keep a job—I don't see why willing and brave riders should not be allowed to compete in the last honest-to-God road race on Earth.

Once again, criticism of this event seldom comes from the people who still ride it, the dedicated organizers, or the thousands of fans who love to attend. Condemnation always comes from afar. My standing advice to those who don't like the TT is that they should stay home. Don't go.

Helmets are another battlefield, both outside of and within our sport.

Those who would not ride to the corner mailbox without a helmet seem to spend a great deal of time worrying about riders who would.

My own take on this complicated question is *(a)* I almost always wear a helmet; *(b)* new riders should be required to wear them during their vulnerable novice years, largely because it removes economic and peer pressure not to; and *(c)* if consenting adults want to ride to Sturgis with their hair flying in the wind, more power to 'em.

Yes, I know. The old social cost argument: The rest of us have to pay for their medical care. Swell. Let's get rid of everything with a social cost: football, rock concerts, skydiving, boating, sex, airplanes, racing, bathtubs, cars, electricity, uphill golf fairways, snow shoveling, Christmas tree lights, and fettuccine alfredo—yes, the dreaded "heart attack on a plate."

The bad news, friends, is that nearly all of us are going to get sick and die. Or fall down or crash into something. Gravity always wins.

I know. I am forty-eight years old, and I would guess at least sixty-five percent of the people who were on this planet when I was born are now gone. And of those once-teeming millions, only a very few died at Oshkosh, the Isle of Man, or on the road to Sturgis.

Some people enjoyed these things a lot when they were alive. Others didn't, but that's no concern of mine.

April 1996

SHOULD YOU BUY AN AMERICAN BIKE?

Okay, you knew it was coming. In the past few years, I've concocted several complex psychological tests to determine whether or not readers had the right stuff to own British, Italian, and German bikes. The response has been virtually—if not literally—overwhelming.

Dozens of people who once thought they were mentally unfit to own British bikes are, at this very moment, standing along a roadside somewhere in the dark, peering at the Lucas dual-points setup in a big vertical-twin with a flashlight, if they remembered to bring one along.

Others, who worried that perhaps they didn't have the right flair and high sense of personal style to master Italian machinery, are now married to opera stars and downing one cappuccino after another as they attempt to master the famous desmo valve adjust from instructions written in oddly translated English.

Many closet Germanophiles, who wondered if a flat-twin was right for them, are, even as you read this, thriving on bratwurst and schnapps, and struggling to snake a skinny little BMW two-piece hinged oil filter past the exhaust pipes on an old R100RS, or wondering why the clock in the instrument panel has suddenly stopped running, just before summer.

Now it's time for American bikes. Are they right for you? Or, more to the point, are you right for them?

Read the questions, take your time, and remember, there is only one right answer per question:

1) A real low point in Western Civilization occurred during: *(a)* the sack of Rome in 410 AD by the Visigoths; *(b)* the decline of secular scholasticism in the Middle Ages; *(c)* the AMF years.

2) The actor whose film roles best personify the modern anti-hero would be: *(a)* Sal Mineo; *(b)* Anthony Perkins; *(c)* Lee Marvin.

3) You are trying to decide on a career after high school. The best choice is: *(a)* professional home-care pet groomer; *(b)* Washington lobbyist for a consortium of motorcycle helmet importers; *(c)* the Marine Corps or Army Airborne.

4) The guitar player you would ride across several state lines to hear is: *(a)* Julian Bream; *(b)* John McLaughlin; *(c)* Billy Gibbons.

5) You drop into a bar and ask for a shot and a beer. The bartender says, "A shot of what?" Your answer should be: *(a)* Amaretto; *(b)* Baileys Irish Cream; *(c)* "You're kidding, right?"

6) The proper displacement of a motorcycle engine should be determined by: *(a)* nervous insurance agents; *(b)* the arbitrary division of racing classes as developed by fuel-starved Europeans just after World War I; *(c)* the pleasure center of the brain.

7) Motorcycle boots should be worn: *(a)* on Sunday morning rides; *(b)* after work; *(c)* any time you aren't sleeping in a bed with clean sheets.

8) The best place to sleep is: *(a)* in a bed with clean sheets; *(b)* on a pool table; *(c)* beside your bike in some field in South Dakota.

9) If you could fly any airplane you wanted, it would be: *(a)* a Beech Bonanza; *(b)* a Gulfstream V biz-jet; *(c)* a P-47 Thunderbolt.

10) The best-looking design for an aircraft engine is: *(a)* a fuel-injected Lycoming flat-six; *(b)* a BMW/Rolls-Royce turbofan; *(c)* a Pratt & Whitney Double Wasp air-cooled radial.

11) The best chase vehicle for following a pack of bikes on a weekend motorcycle run is: *(a)* an extended-bed minivan; *(b)* a Mercedes 190E sedan with a trailer; *(c)* a restored 1946 Dodge pickup.

12) Legislation that restricts smoking in public places is good because it: *(a)* protects your health by reducing exposure to secondary smoke; *(b)* prevents your designer sweater from smelling stale the next morning; *(c)* keeps the riff-raff out of the smoking section.

13) The main purpose of a motorcycle gas tank should be: *(a)* to cover up the electrical system so the real gas tank can be hidden somewhere under the seat; *(b)* to make the bike look as much as possible like someone else's design; *(c)* to hold gasoline and look good.

14) The best thing about light beer is: *(a)* you can drink and stay thin; *(b)* it's less filling; *(c)* you don't have any in the refrigerator.

15) A properly designed motorcycle engine should idle as smoothly as a blender filled with: *(a)* piña colada mix; *(b)* banana daiquiris; *(c)* black-strap molasses and hand grenades.

16) The person with whom you would most like to have a beer and a shot of Jack Daniel's while listening to ZZ Top on the jukebox of a smoky bar would be: *(a)* Newt Gingrich; *(b)* Roseanne Barr; *(c)* Willie G. Davidson.

17) Historically, the people with the best sense of design and personal style were the: *(a)* Vatican Swiss Guard; *(b)* court of Louis XIV; *(c)* Indians of the American Great Plains.

18) The main purpose of the "peanut" tank on the Sportster is: *(a)* to provide fresh air and exercise for those walking to the next gas station; *(b)* to enhance the relative largeness of the engine beneath; *(c)* no one now living can remember.

19) During winter, a restored Panhead should be kept: *(a)* under a carport; *(b)* in the garage with the lawn mower; *(c)* along the living room wall, between the fireplace and the full-stack Marshall JCM 900 and your black 1959 Les Paul Custom.

20) The most significant film director of the 1960s is: *(a)* Russ Meyer; *(b)* Blake Edwards; *(c)* Dennis Hopper.

21) If motorcycles could sing, your bike would sound most like: *(a)* Michael Jackson; *(b)* the Vienna Boys Choir; *(c)* Bob Seger harmonizing with Gregg Allman.

22) A motorcycle should look good: *(a)* for five years; *(b)* until next year's model comes out; *(c)* until you go blind or die of old age.

There. That should do it. The answers, once again, are self-evident. If you got any wrong, you can at least take some consolation in knowing you won't find yourself on a three-year waiting list for a new motorcycle.

May 1996

BROCHURES

In the corner of one of our upstairs bedrooms is an old steel file cabinet that is neither green nor brown, but one of those indeterminate colors that suggests it was invented by the government sometime before World War II for use by the FBI. I keep expecting to find the Alger Hiss files every time I open it. That, or more dirt on J. Edgar Hoover: "Look here, Barb. A photo of Hoover and Jack Ruby at some kind of stag party. . . . Do you still have Oliver Stone's phone number?"

No such dark intrigue here, however. The top drawers are mostly old tax returns, and the bottom drawer is filled entirely with sales brochures, about 35 years' worth. The back half is dedicated to guitars and amplifiers and contains such gems as "Harmony Guitars for 1966" and about fifty pounds of other slack-jawed drool inspiration, mostly from the Gibson, Fender, Guild, Gretsch, Rickenbacker, and Marshall schools of material lust.

Dusty, forgotten memorabilia?

Would that they were. These things are exhumed and examined weekly, depending upon the shifting breezes of the collector instinct, which repeatedly cause me to raise sail and run aground.

The front half of the cabinet drawer contains motorcycle brochures, of course.

These are segregated by brand, with brown manila dividers. The thickest one is Triumph, with Norton and Honda following a close second, backed up by slightly slimmer sections for Harley, Kawasaki, and one catchall file marked "Eye-talian," in honor of Ezra Pound's inspired misspelling. There is also a pretty good Yamaha section from the RD350 and RD400 era, as well as a small cache of Suzuki info from the GS1000, early GSX-R, and recent dual-purpose periods.

I suppose the relative thickness of these files pretty well reflects the storage content of their owner's brain. The first Triumph brochure I collected and toted home is from 1964, and I've been gathering them ever since, with the usual lapses that reflect the company's own production gaps in the 1970s and 1980s. But it's the mid-to-late 1960s stuff that's most worn and dog-eared. If mere eye contact could wear out paper, my 1966–1970 Triumph brochures would look like the Dead Sea Scrolls. And they almost do.

The Norton file is a little thinner, mostly because I wasn't as powerfully attracted to Nortons—except for the superb Manx racing bikes—until the Commando models came along. So there's lots of Commando stuff, with emphasis on the 1973–1975 bikes, leading up to my purchase of a brand-new 1975 850.

Hondas, I note, show a remarkable concentration from the Superhawk years, followed by another surge in the mid-1970s. By choice and chance I have owned five 1975 Hondas—a 750 Four, a 550 Four, two CB400Fs, and an XL350—all purchases preceded and followed by lots of brochure gazing. From there, the literature skips from CBX to GB500 to VFR, with a solid clump of XL and XR info from nearly every year since their inception. I always own—or feel I am about to own at any moment—a dual-purpose bike; it's a state of mind.

Why is the "Eye-talian" file so thin? I've had five Ducatis and have long admired Moto Guzzis, so what's the deal? The deal is the Italians have historically been somewhat stingy with brochures. Or else their postal system doesn't work. I've been trying to get a brochure for my current 900SS SP ever since I bought the bike last year, and the dealer still can't lay his hands on one.

It's probably the language barrier. Fortunately, the Italians are able to communicate quite clearly in steel, polished aluminum, and red paint, so the lack of sales literature has never slowed me down much. You don't have to speak Italian, after all, to enjoy a Sophia Loren movie. Also, the Italians tend to produce classy magazine ads, suitable for framing, which compensates somewhat for the empty sales literature rack.

I often wonder, however, if motorcycle manufacturers have any idea how many hundreds of hours a prospective buyer can spend staring at the pictures in a sales brochure, or reading the usually all-too-brief description, general puffery, and model specifications, looking for clues and nuances of clues as to the personal rightness of the bike.

Some obviously do. Modern Triumph brochures for the new triples and fours are small masterpieces of photography and description. They draw you into their world and make you want to live there ("Sell the farm, Barb, we're moving to the Cotswolds!").

Harley-Davidson, too, has done a bang-up job with sales literature; they make all the right connections between history, physical sensation, wide-open American spaces, and big V-twins. And, like Triumph, they make their brochures BIG, on nice thick glossy paper.

I would encourage this lavishness in any company that wants to sell me—or those poor impressionable souls who are like me—a motorcycle.

The very act of going to a dealership and bringing home a big color brochure is like a preview of the day when you go to that same shop and bring your new bike home. Good practice, all around.

Brochures are simply a mobile version of the nose against the display window. They allow us to bring the window home and ponder the view at our leisure, preferably while sipping a drink or eating popcorn in a large, comfortable chair.

I've spent entire evenings doing just that, staring at the pictures of a new bike and letting the image sink into my very bones, like radiant heat from a fireplace. Warms the skull and makes the nerve ends crackle and glow.

To the casual observer of such a scene, nothing would seem to be going on, but it's these episodes of quiet, transfixed silence that are the true source of all motion in the universe.

October 1996

OBSERVATIONS ON RAIN GEAR

It was not a day upon which even the great Sherlock Holmes would have been out and about. Rather than tramping around the Grimpen Mire or spying on the Stapletons of Merripit House, he would probably have looked out his window at the solid, steady rain and retired to the fireside at Baskerville Hall, sipping tea with Watson.

Which is probably what we should have been doing, but were not.

Instead, my riding pals from the Slimey Crud Motorcycle Gang and I were hopping around on one foot and then the other, donning rain suits, Totes, and waterproof gloves, steaming up our visors and generally steeling ourselves for our traditional ride to the superbike races at Elkhart Lake, Wisconsin, some 150 twisting back road miles away, as the crow never flies.

A lot of trouble, but there was not much grumbling. We were getting used to this rain gear routine. Had to.

For those who have been fortunate enough this year to find themselves in one of the nation's sun-drenched microclimates, I should mention that the spring and summer of 1996 have so far been about the worst riding season in the Midwest since the invention of the twistgrip.

Months and days of cold, blowing, driving rain. Flooded roads, flooded fields. Darkness at noon, freezing fog. The kind of weather that has stopped whole armored divisions in their tracks and ruined grade-school class picnics from time immemorial.

Anyway, you'd think that with all this rain—and our advanced years—we might have figured out by now what to wear. And yet the four of us who were riding to Elkhart Lake together mutually agreed to delay our departure by well over an hour, just so we would have time to dig the appropriate gear out of our closets. Indecision time, again. What to take?

Essentially, when it rains I have three options, other than staying home: *(a)* a lightweight two-piece PVC-coated nylon Harley-Davidson rain suit; *(b)* a bulkier but much warmer two-piece Gore-Tex Aerostich suit; or *(c)* a waxed-cotton Belstaff jacket and pants, now made in Australia by a company called "Driza-Bone," replacing the old English-made one I finally wore out in only twenty-five years.

They all have their advantages, and which one I take depends mostly on temperature.

The Harley rain suit goes along in hot weather because I can wear it over my regular leather jacket and store the whole suit in a small envelope in my tank bag when I don't want it.

Aerostich gets the nod when it's cold out, because if it's too cold for this suit you shouldn't be riding anyway, but should be indoors brooding. The disadvantage here is that the pants are bulky to store if the weather turns warm. Also, the breathable Gore-Tex will gradually wick in some moisture in a really driving all-day rainstorm.

It has been my lifelong observation that only shiny materials resembling a child's cheap wading pool seem to keep out all water—assuming the seams are sealed. If they aren't, the leaked water will automatically run straight to your crotch and stay there all day. Rainwater, like spilled coffee, is drawn magnetically to the human crotch, as any scientist will tell you.

Basically, if you wouldn't make a life raft out of it, it ain't waterproof. On the other hand, shiny, nonbreathable fabrics suffer from Turkish Bath Effect—you drown in your own sweat—so you get a little damp either way. Nothing is perfect.

My third choice, the Belstaff suit, is for intermediate temperatures. A Belstaff will also wick a little water in eventually, but the pants are slightly more compact to store than the Aerostich's, and the jacket is somewhat lighter for formal evening pubwear, making those elbow bends easier with a pint in hand.

A hard call, but I decided to go with the Belstaff because the weekend weather forecast called for (and would duly receive) drizzle, rain, and cool overcast, just like England, and I could wear the jacket all weekend and laugh at the weather without having to run for my rain suit in the Ducati's tank bag.

Boots? I packed rubber Totes overboots. These used to be the cheeziest rain boots on Earth, tearing at the slightest tug, but my local dealer assured me they are of a new, stronger material (in response to numerous death threats), so I bought another pair, mostly because they are compact and fit in a tank bag.

The finishing touch was my prized pair of kidney-red rubberized canvas gloves, with cotton liners, bought in a hardware store in New Zealand, where veterinarians apparently use them to check for prostate problems in livestock. These gloves are so ugly they tend to make people nervous—especially men over forty—but they really work, unlike those tight-fitting "overmitts," which make your hands feel like lobster claws and offer so little control sensitivity that you risk missing the turnoff to your hotel, or Sturgis.

Thus equipped, I rode all weekend in varying degrees of pouring rain, fog, and mist in complete comfort. The Totes didn't rip and the rain never soaked through my waxed-cotton jacket. Maybe Belstaff is using a new, improved grade of wax.

Also, a young rider named Alessandro Gramigni won the superbike race, stunningly, on a Ducati in the pouring rain.

And I must confess that I genuinely enjoyed our group ride despite the weather. If you have adequate rain gear, there is something pleasant about riding through the elements untroubled, that feeling of both observing and being immersed in nature at the same time, like a scuba diver, or Dante touring Purgatory.

Once you accept the fact that a rain-soaked road is a sort of parallel universe with its own rules of traction and physics, the rhythm of rain riding can be quite pleasant.

Has to be. So far this summer we ride in the rain or almost not at all.

January 1997

THE FINE ART OF CARRYING STUFF

Last week I finally put a clutch in my old Triumph 500, after enduring half a summer of vague slippage somewhat on the order of my dad's 1956 Buick DynaFlow slush box transmission.

Amazing transformation with those new clutch plates and springs in there; speed is now directly related to engine rpm. What a concept.

Anyway, while I was crouched gorilla-like beside the bike, I couldn't help but notice that the rear-seat loop of the frame was slightly crunched and dimpled, just behind the rear shocks.

Ah, yes. The telltale sign of an aftermarket luggage rack having been installed and overtightened. A long and glorious tradition.

In our period-perfect restorations of classic old motorcycles, we sometimes forget that during the historic period roughly between the Spanish-American War and about 1983 nearly every fool who bought a new motorcycle immediately plunked down twenty-nine dollars for a big, heavy, chromed JC Whitney–class luggage rack.

These things generally clamped to the rear-seat loop of the frame and were supported at the back by a bracket sandwiched between the taillight and rear fender. And they always left their mark on the frame tubes.

I installed one of these racks on the Honda CB160 I bought in 1967 so I could carry a tent and my official Boy Scout knapsack on a road trip through Canada, and then put an almost identical rack on the Honda CB350 I bought new in 1973.

In fact, I used to visit distant friends with my Gretsch guitar case bungeed along the seat and rack lengthwise. I actually put red reflector tape on the end of the guitar case, to ward off destruction of my second-most valuable possession, which was strapped to my first. Guitar and bike: My whole material world in one vulnerable package.

Come to think of it, I also had luggage racks on my Norton Commando, 400F Honda, and CB750. These things were remarkably sturdy and useful, but they look a little nerdy these days, evoking images of commuter bikes with red plastic milk crates strapped on the back. But in the 1960s and 1970s, they could be found on nearly every real-world bike. Only racers and the aesthetically pure of heart avoided them.

They are mostly gone now, except on true touring rigs, and even these are usually integrated factory racks. The one-size-fits-all luggage rack on sporty, small-displacement bikes is almost a thing of the past. We are in the age of tank bags, cargo nets, and seat packs. Two of which I bought last summer, just before my friend Pat Donnelly and I rode our two 900SS Ducatis out to Sturgis.

As I mentioned last month, Pat had found himself a nice, low-mileage 1995 900SS SP right before we left, so he had to hustle around to local bike shops, trying to figure out some way to heap rain gear, a toothbrush, and a week's road clothing onto the Ducati's lean, plastic-covered flanks. And so did I.

The tank bag was no problem. I have an Eclipse bag that stays more or less permanently on the bike. On a road trip, of course, it's taken up mostly with rain gear, extra gloves, glasses, etc., so there's almost no room left for clothing.

I already had a pair of soft saddlebags (with holes ground through them by the rear wheel of a Buell Thunderbolt), but ruled those out because modern monoshock bikes have no structure to prevent them from rubbing on the rear fender or tire. They do, however, allow you to carry a passenger, which seat packs do not.

My first solution was to buy a simple cargo net, which I would theoretically use to strap a small duffel bag down to the rear seat. I tried this, however, and it was a little unwieldy. The bag wanted to slide off its narrow perch and damage the paint. I finally went back to the store and bought a reasonably roomy (ninety-seven dollars) seat pack with built-in bungees that grip the sides of the fiberglass seat panels. Pat bought a similar seat pack, but with those small, built-in side panniers that allow you to carry two socks, or two Italian sausages, or one of each.

All in all, this motley luggage combo worked out okay on our five-day road trip, though both our seat packs shifted constantly from one side to the other and looked from the rear like an Apache warrior trying to shoot underneath his own horse at a wagon train. Untidy. Also, my seat-pack rain cover blew off in a thunderstorm. Pat caught it and showed up at the next stop sign with the cover clenched in his teeth. Good man.

In other words, we both spent several hundred dollars on luggage solutions that were nearly satisfactory, but hardly ideal.

I guess what amazes me in all this is the unrealized or lost opportunity presented to Ducati, and the makers of many other sport bikes. They could be doing what BMW has done forever—and Buell and Triumph recently began doing: selling their customers hard saddlebags that are specifically built to fit the bike.

Click on, click off. Waterproof, theft-proof. Narrow, tucked into that stylish bulging bodywork. Solidly mounted so you don't have to keep feeling behind you to see if they're still there. Basic stuff. I keep hearing that Ducati is building a sport-tourer with built-in luggage, so maybe there's hope.

In the meantime, I may have to find one of those big dumb chrome aftermarket luggage racks and graft it onto the svelte, aerodynamic tail of my 900SS. Maybe strap my Boy Scout knapsack on there—or a red plastic milk crate. If that doesn't get me kicked out of the Ducati Owners Club—and polite society in general—nothing will.

Still, good ideas never really die. Like bell-bottoms, they only sleep.

May 1997

CLASSICISM AND THE MODERN BIKE

My friend Jim, who used to ride bikes and doesn't anymore, stopped by with his family for a visit last weekend and took the mandatory after-dinner drink-sipping tour of my humble workshop and garage.

He carefully looked over my Ducati 900SS SP, felt its carbon fiber parts, examined the monoshock rear suspension, stood up, and said, "Well, that's a pretty bike. I have to be honest, though, and tell you I don't think it's as good looking as your old silver and blue bevel-drive 900SS."

I considered that comment for a moment and smiled. "No, you're right," I said. "It works better than my old one, but it's not as handsome."

A strange conclusion coming from me, the bike's owner. I happen to think the current Ducati 900SS SP is one of the best-looking bikes around. I have a large color picture of it on the wall of my office and I look at it often, with great satisfaction. I love the flow of the full fairing, the low narrowness of the front perspective, the depth of its red paint, and its suggestion of birdcage lightness.

But my friend is right. I don't think—and have never thought—it is as classically handsome a bike as the old bevel-drive 900SS, or the 750SS before that.

How can you compare a riveted aluminum exhaust canister (or its carbon fiber replacement) with the seamless, tapered chrome beauty of an upswept Conti with its bell-curved tip?

Can black plastic over a toothed-belt cam drive ever replace the finned, polished tower and triangular bevel gear cover of a shaft-driven cam? Are downdraft Mikunis, buried in hoses and wires, a substitute for a pair of backswept Dell'Ortos with velocity stacks?

Of course not. If God is in the details, the old Ducati 900SS sits near the right hand of the Father and the new 900SS is a mere messenger angel of the middle kingdom. There's no comparison.

The new bike succeeds as the sum of its parts, but the old one has better-looking parts, even when they are held separately in your hands. And when you put them back on the motorcycle, the sum is better still. The old bike is simple, clean, and purposeful in a way that technology, federal regulations, and fashion do not allow the new one to be; it's high-tech industrial utility versus artisanship.

I should say quickly here that this is not necessarily a tome to the good old days, so much as a wistful observation from one who is in the gradual process of shifting mounts as we near the end of the millennium. Out with the old and in with the new.

For instance: I sold my old, high-mileage BMW R100RS last year to my friend Barry Mirkin, despite my belief that the old RS is one of the great classic shapes. Why did I sell it? Because I was planning to buy a new-generation R1100RS. Haven't yet, but probably will eventually. More power, better brakes, better handling, a real alternator, and I like the way the new bike looks. A lot.

But is it as classic in form as the old R100RS?

Not in my book. Actually, I believe the Silver Smoke R90S of the mid-1970s was probably the most beautiful bike BMW ever made (if the Earles-fork buffs in the crowd will excuse a little heresy). It was to BMW what the Series I E-Type was to Jaguar, and I despair of either company ever repeating the feat. I think someday in the future when children go skipping through the BMW museum, it's the R90S that'll stop them in their tracks. Does me.

Triumphs?

Same thing. The new bikes work better, last longer, go faster, and a few models are quite handsome. The Speed Triple is one of my favorites, and the new T595 Daytona is a piece of work. But has anyone ever suggested that any new Triumph is the aesthetic equal of a 1967 Bonneville?

Not within my hearing.

Seems to me that every branch of design goes through a phase of development that leads up to its own small golden age, a period of irreducibly classic form. After that, people add on, embellish, and progress technologically, but end up either gilding the lily or putting the petals on crooked.

And I happen to think the mid-1960s through the mid-1970s was one of those small golden eras for motorcycling.

Is this just age speaking? Could be, but I'm skeptical of the "my generation" theory.

Fighter aircraft, for instance, got continually better after World War II, yet I would trade you several F-104s for a Supermarine Spitfire, a P-38 Lightning, or a P-51. And I wasn't even there at the time they were made.

Lots of examples here: The M-1 Garand of World War II looks better to me than either the M-14 or the M-16 of my own army years; the handsomest buildings on the nearby university campus were built before the Civil War, while those built after World War II are—by popular vote of almost everyone who uses them—largely dreadful.

And Lauren Bacall, who's old enough to be my mother, still has more class in reruns of *To Have and Have Not* (1944) than any actress I've seen recently.

So age alone doesn't explain it. Nearly all of us recognize some high point in art, music, movies, literature, etc. that occurred before we were born. We seem drawn to even the most ancient periods of proportion and quality quite naturally, with just a little exposure.

Could it be mere perspective, then?

Don't think so. When I saw my first BMW R90S, Ducati 750SS, or Triumph Bonneville, they set off an almost audible humming of pleasure in my brain, and I knew instantly they were classics.

Didn't have to ask anyone or discuss it; I just knew. Everyone did.

Maybe that's what a classic bike is: The complete absence of doubt, done in metal.

June 1997

TANK ARCHAEOLOGY

There was an item on the news last night about brain-tissue shrinkage in teens who sniff glue, nail polish, and various inhalants to get high. After hearing a few of these supposedly brain-damaged kids interviewed, I couldn't help wondering how smart they'd been *before* acquiring the inhalant habit. I mean, what kind of brain instructs a healthy body to inhale nail polish? I can't picture Einstein suddenly rising from his desk and saying, "Jeez, I really need to breathe in some poisonous chemicals to see if my brain will shrink and render me useless to myself and society."

Still, who am I to criticize?

There I was in my green garage coveralls, eating leftover Paul Newman spaghetti, watching the 5:30 news, and reeking of professional-strength paint stripper and acrylic lacquer thinner while drinking "burgundy" out of a box with a collapsible plastic bladder. Which was cheaper per gallon, incidentally, than either the paint stripper or the lacquer thinner. Hardly a poster boy for nontoxic, vibrant good health.

But at least I wasn't rotting my brain as an end in itself. I'd been out in the garage, kneeling on old newspapers, and stripping paint from the tank and sidecovers of my 1968 Triumph T100C. At last.

When I bought this bike last year, the tank and sidecovers were encrusted in a remarkably thick coat of gold metalflake paint that had aged and yellowed to a kind of burnt bronze tone. You know the look—it's the same color you see on twenty-year-old snowmobile helmets at garage sales, a purist, low-key alternative to the popular "Captain America" theme.

I should have painted this bike last summer. Every time I turned on the garage lights it was like getting hit across the eye sockets with a baseball bat dipped in glitter. Still, I did nothing about it because I couldn't bring myself to take the bike off the road long enough to paint it. I put several thousand miles on the Triumph last summer, just noodling around the countryside, and saw no reason to cease and desist simply for the cause of good taste and ordinary decency.

Also, truth be told, I kind of got to like that ugly old metalflake paint. For one thing, it seemed to make the bike virtually theft-proof, at least in my own imagination. Lock the Triumph up? Who'd want to steal it? The bad paint also allowed me to be absolutely careless of the bike in the garage. No fear of bumping that tank with a Weber grill or leaning a bicycle against it, no vain compulsion about zipper scratches or friends lifting their children into the saddle so they could hold the handlebars and make engine noises.

"Go ahead and drool there, Junior. What do I care?"

The Triumph had that friendly, utilitarian invulnerability you find in old, unrestored pickup trucks, the kind you can use to haul fertilizer without a bed liner, or carry cans of drain oil to the recycling center. Maybe we all need one vehicle like this, the motorcycle equivalent of what, in cars, we used to call a "deer hunter special," before the invention of Eddie Bauer interiors.

Then too, one friend of mine actually suggested I leave the bike gold because it was "more historically correct." His reasoning was that everybody has now restored old Triumphs back to original showroom colors and condition, when, in fact, many people repainted them some offbeat hue the first time they got a dent or a scratch in the tank. By the early 1970s, he pointed out, most Triumphs looked like mine rather than the versions we now see in museums. "It's a perfect Age of Aquarius paint job," he said, "and fifty years from now no one will know they looked like this. Your bike is actually more 'authentic,' more of an endangered species, than a perfectly restored one."

That's an interesting point I'm willing to concede, but not for long. If I'm going to have a bike that's in bad taste, it has to be my own bad taste, and I have never really liked anything the color of gold but gold itself—other than the lettering on a black or red motorcycle.

So there I was the other night, soaking up paint-stripper fumes like a sponge and pushing gobs of gold paint off my tank with a putty knife. Interestingly, I have noticed that paint stripper seems to "sense" the division between coats of paint, taking off just one color at a time. When I stripped the paint off my old 1967 Bonneville in 1979, I had to descend through five distinct layers of paint, one at a time. Beneath the flat-black outer paint I found strata of metalflake blue, metalflake white, Candy Apple Red with green trapezoidal pinstripes, and then, finally, the original "Aubergine/Gold" two-tone.

On the T100C I stripped last night, the layers were a little simpler. Beneath the very thick gold (it must have been put on with a trowel) was a coat of plain glossy black, and under that I found the original "Hi-Fi Aquamarine" with silver center stripe. The sidecovers were the original black underneath, but the decals had been sanded off to make room for a pair of huge Triumph logos done in fish scale reflective splendor.

With my rubber gloves on, I Scotch-Brited my way down to the metal on the sidecovers, but I left most of the original aquamarine paint on the tank. I want to look at the color (however dull and patchy) and ponder it for a few days. Also, the original silver stripe is still visible, with its highlighted edge stripes, and I want to measure it before I destroy the evidence.

In the meantime, I have reached the point of quandary. What color to paint the Triumph?

Conscience and the weight of history tell me I should simply paint it the original aquamarine with silver stripe. It's not a bad color, sort of a mixture of Mediterranean seawater green and Aqua Velva blue, with bluebottle-fly overtones. I liked it when it was new, and still do, when I see a restored bike.

But.

Twenty-some years ago, when my friend Pat Donnelly needed to paint *his* Triumph T100C (a 1966 version), he borrowed from me a leftover quart of British Racing Green enamel that I'd used to paint my old Lola T-204 Formula Ford racing car. And I have to tell you, the bike looked stunning in green. Especially with that black, chrome, and white Triumph emblem and black knee pads on the tank. The sidecovers, of course, were painted black on Pat's bike, as they should be, and mine will be, too. Brightly colored sidecovers on Triumphs (to my eye) detract from the shape of the tank, which is one of the most beautifully shaped containers ever to hold 2 3/8 gallons of gasoline.

In struggle with the morality of this important issue, I called up my friend and aesthetic conscience on difficult problems such as this, Bruce Finlayson, interrupting an important coffee break and stream of consciousness about white cadmium plating. Nevertheless, he found time to talk about Triumph colors.

Perhaps sensing that I wanted to paint my bike British Racing Green, Bruce graciously assured me that, once you have done a perfect, original, and correct factory-stock restoration on a motorcycle (as I have on four or five bikes), you have paid your debt to society and earned the right to paint your vintage motorcycle any damned color you want.

Thank you, Bruce. Later today, for further encouragement, I may call *Cycle World* Editor David Edwards, who has a fine disregard for purity and paints flames or scallops on nearly everything he owns. I think he'll go for the British Racing Green idea, too.

This could be fun. I've always done restorations with the phantom of some nameless, faceless museum curator hanging over my shoulder, passing judgment on each phase of the job. Essentially, I've done restorations for History, or for some future owner I've never met.

Maybe this time I'll just do one for myself. Paint the tank BRG, make the bike look nice, but not too nice. Build a runner instead of an heirloom; make it good-looking, but not so good-looking it makes you nervous to have people walk through the garage. Or move the Weber grill or park a bicycle nearby.

And if parents want to set their kids on the seat, that's okay too. If they scratch the tank, who cares? It's just green paint, which is not the same thing as History.

Besides, we have to leave something for the next generation of restorers to complain about, and something to do. Otherwise they'll just end up sitting around, watching television, and sniffing paint stripper, with no understanding of its proper role in a fully lived and well-rounded life.

December 1997

TRIUMPH AND THE FATES

You'd think by now it would be axiomatic never to compliment a British bike on its reliability, even in the mind, much less with the spoken or written word. But sometimes one forgets.

Last year, for instance, I was riding my 1968 Triumph (high-pipe T100C version) from our deeply rural home into the city of Madison, thinking to myself how beautifully the bike was running—as it had been all summer.

Yes, with hardly a turn of the wrench, the old girl had given me a full season of enjoyable short trips. Late-afternoon meanderings through the green hills, nighttime runs to book and coffee shops with that surprisingly adequate Lucas headlight illuminating the dark tunnnels of trees on the back roads to town.

Pure joy. And, as anyone will tell you, nothing feels as good as a British bike "when it's running right." (Always that final caveat, the specter of imminent failure perched on your shoulder like a parrot. Or albatross, perhaps.) I speak here of old bikes, of course, not the vastly more durable new-generation Triumphs.

Anyway, there I was, making one of my twenty-five-mile runs to the city, thinking how fine the Triumph was running and mentally composing a column for this magazine in which I would explain to you, the reader, that the troublesome reputation of these serviceable old bikes was badly overstated.

At that moment, of course, the Triumph stopped running. Coasted to the side of the road, dead as a doornail. A short investigation revealed nothing more serious than a loose connection on the back side of the ignition switch. I clapped the space connector between two rocks (having inexplicably left my 600-piece professional tool chest at home) to tighten it up and was on my way. Another great moment in Stone Age roadside repair. A few more minutes and I might have figured out how to fashion a Clovis point, or start a fire with flint.

This summer saw almost a repeat performance. Did a little maintenance on the bike—changed all oils, adjusted valves, etc.—but no major mechanical work. I did, however, repaint the dreadful metalflake-orange tank and side-covers. Despite my avowed resolve to personalize the bike (stated right on this 'ere page) with a British Racing Green paint scheme, I genuflected to history and returned the tank to its original 1968 "Hi-Fi Aquamarine" and silver, with proper black sidecovers. I sent them out to a company called Cycle Colors, in North Carolina, who did a stunning job at a reasonable price. I can hardly keep my eyes on the road because I keep looking down at the tank.

So, with those minor mechanical and cosmetic tweaks, the Triumph and its original, untouched 1968 engine unreeled yet another fine summer of batting around the locale, nearly 1,000 miles worth. Until yesterday.

I'd just finished cleaning the garage and decided to reward myself with a fifty-mile back road run to the country home of my old buddy, Pat Donnelly. It was a sunny, early-autumn day with a hint of moisture in the air, the kind of day British bikes love, when combustion feels akin to honeyed clockwork. The bike never felt better.

Naturally, at the exact moment when I was heaping mental praise, kudos, and laurel wreaths on the Triumph's forthright stamina, the engine went into a sudden loud bellow, almost as if I'd hit a toggle switch marked "Deafening Mechanical Racket."

The timing was flawless: simultaneous praise and retribution, like being socked in the mouth by someone to whom you are handing an Academy Award.

Being an old Norton man, I leaned forward to see if an exhaust pipe collar had fallen off. Nope. Hole in the exhaust pipe? I put my hand down to feel for pressure pulses. Nothing there, either, so I pulled over and got off the bike.

Ah, so. One of my two side-swept mufflers had fallen off. I roared back along the shoulder and finally found it in the ditch among the faded beer cans, dented on its exhaust tip but otherwise undamaged. Clamp intact, but rear bracket bolt missing. I slipped the muffler back on,

then motored slowly along the road, looking for a scrap of wire. I finally found a home construction site and fished a charred piece of copper wire out of a fire pit full of old building scrap. Wrapped the wire around the muffler, secured it back to the frame, and made it home with no further drama.

Obviously, it's time for a little bolt-checking and preventive maintenance. I may even succumb to a full restoration on the bike this winter. We'll see. In the meantime, I have relearned an elemental lesson of British bike ownership: Don't ever shower approval on your bike.

I know this sounds ridiculously superstitious, and I am not trying to imbue simple nuts and bolts with some kind of foggy New Age mysticism. But just as some dogs can sense fear in their adversaries, I swear an old British bike can sense patronizing approval. Especially if it's not backed up with the required hours of meticulous maintenance. Even a trace of sloppy sentiment turns the bike instantly into a lightning rod for trouble.

We call them British bikes, but in a sense they aren't British at all. They are Greek, in the classic dramatic sense, like the men and gods in Homer. Beautiful, spirited, heroic, flawed, and full of fateful games that measure hubris against honor and seek to test our tenacity and sense of adventure. They are here to see what we are made of, not to be our friends.

An early Guzzi or BMW Boxer might be your good old pal on the road, but an old Triumph, Norton, or BSA is not. It's as indifferent to your fate as Zeus or Poseidon might be of Odysseus' efforts to return home after the Trojan War. You may plan a trip with an old Triumph, but what you more often get instead is an odyssey, full of detours, unexpected contests, new acquaintances, and strange turns of fate.

It's what keeps some of us coming back to British bikes, and others from ever reaching Ithaca. Some, perhaps, find themselves delayed by the lovely sea nymph, Calypso. Others are looking for their mufflers.

January 1998

SLIMEY CRUD CAFE RACER RUN

It started four years ago as an idea kicked around at one of our casual monthly Slimey Crud Motorcycle Gang meetings. And by "casual" I mean these meetings are nothing more than a bunch of guys in leather jackets standing around in someone's garage or driveway, alternately gazing at motorcycles and examining the labels of the beer bottles they're holding.

Conversation is deep: "Wow! This Sprecher Black Bavarian is good. Say, is your Norton leaking oil again, or was that spot already there?" And so on.

Anyway, at one of these casual meetings someone suggested that Madison, Wisconsin, and the surrounding hills—which extend, roughly, from Detroit to the center of Iowa—were teeming with odd, interesting, beautiful, and eccentric bikes, most of which we knew only from rumor or a flash of noise and color passing on the highway.

Why not, this same person suggested, lure them out of their lairs with a spring and autumn cafe-racer ride? We could start at, say, Jake's Bar and Grill in the nearby village of Pine Bluff with a ride over curving country roads, across the Wisconsin River, and north to a bar called the Sprecher Tap at the little crossroads village of Leland, about sixty miles away.

The two people in the club who actually Get Things Done (not me) somehow found time to post some clever fliers at bike dealerships and to put a small, cryptic ad in the paper. "SCMG Cafe Run, 12 noon this Sunday. Vintage limes, spaghetti, pork, rice . . ."

Big success, by our standards. Probably sixty bikes showed up—virtually every Ducati, Norton, BMW, Triumph, Laverda, and Harley XLCR we'd ever seen in the area, along with a good helping of new and old Japanese bikes and a few classic old crocks.

That first run was great, but we made two mistakes: First, we had a prescribed route, and second, we all left at once. Some people thought they were in a race. Others didn't. A guy with a Ducati 900SS just like mine dogged my back wheel for thirty miles then suddenly decided he had to stuff me going into a fast corner, nearly taking us both out.

No good.

The next year we simply handed out maps showing all the county and state highways between Pine Bluff and Leland and said, "See you there."

Much better. People left in small groups of like-minded riders, going as fast or slow as they pleased over a dozen different routes. No one had that left-behind feeling. Since then, the event has evolved into simply a nice excuse for a ride combined with a communion of interesting motorcycles owned by everyone and anyone who has a loose understanding of the cafe-racer tradition, with accent on cafe. Sunday morning High Mass at the Church of Mutual Admiration.

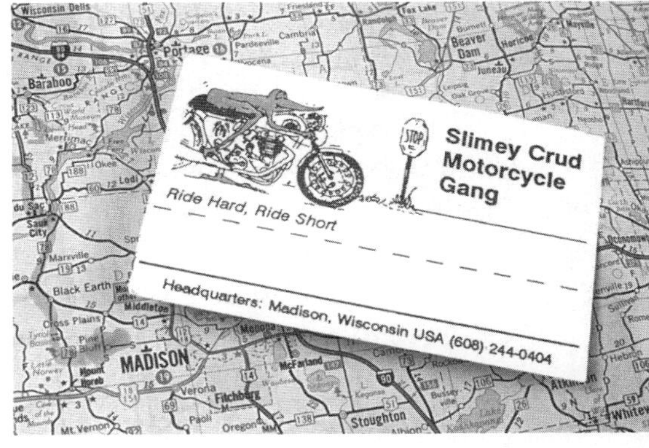

This fall's ride, which took place yesterday, was all-time perfect. Perfect warm autumn weather, trees in full color, golden corn shocks in the fields, pumpkins in farmyards, and orange leaves swirling across the road in small, benevolent cyclones. I took no official count, but one member who attempted it said there were around 450 motorcycles.

We had riders from Detroit, the Twin Cities, Chicago, and small towns all over the Midwest. Couples, old people, college kids, guys in full leathers, and guys with garage-sale helmets. And I noticed a wonderfully democratic trend: In this cycle-mad crowd, a clean old CB550 is appreciated as much as a genuine blue-chip classic. The mood is, "Nice 916, but look at this X-6 Hustler!"

I rode my Norton Commando two years ago, the Ducati 900SS last year, and this year decided to go with my '68 Triumph Trophy 500. I put about 200 miles on the old girl yesterday, and it was simply one of the finest days of riding—and being around other motorcycles—I've ever had.

So: A late-1960s Triumph scrambler on a cafe ride?

Yes. And this leads me to a couple of observations on the changing nature of the ride itself, an evolutionary trend, if you will.

That first year we had all kinds of bikes, but the majority, I would say, were serious sport bikes—Ducatis, FZRs, CBRs, etc. But the last few rides have seen an ever-growing number of freshly restored vintage bikes, faded old classics, eccentric and oddball survivors, and genuine modified cafe racers that I almost believed had disappeared from our garages and roads.

Follow me down this row, if you please: We got a pair of Bultaco Metrallas, one stock, one not; a dead-original BSA Thunderbolt with an oversized touring tank; a Buck Rogers Rocket III; an orange Laverda SFC; a Yoshimura 400F Honda; a Suzuki Water Buffalo; a Ducati 750SS in its original duck-egg green paint; a pair of Earles-fork BMWs; a Honda CL350 scrambler; an eye-watering perfect '67 Bonneville; a Yamaha SRX; and so on.

Want to know what I think is happening here? I think people are reconsidering the wealth of great old bikes we have moldering in the woodwork and saying to themselves, "Wouldn't it be fun to fix that thing up and take it out on the SCMG Cafe Racer Run, where someone can *see* it and hear it run, or just stand around and admire and enjoy it?"

It's working on me: I've been cleaning up my old Triumph all summer with the subliminal notion of bringing it out for the run. And I'm already beginning to frame an image of my nearly completed 1964 Ducati Mach 1 rolling down the road in next spring's ride. If nothing else, it's a deadline, a reason to get this stuff done that goes beyond our own personal satisfaction.

Architect Frank Lloyd Wright once said that creativity seldom exists in isolation, but feeds off the energy and excitement of a movement where like-minded people are striving to please one another and show what they can do.

I'd like to think that our little run, started so casually, is turning into one of those centers of energy. Organize one in your own area, keep it going for a few years, and see if I'm not right. Around here, it's the best thing that ever happened to motorcycling.

March 1998

WINTER STORAGE

Snow fell again last night, silently, and in large flakes, like an airborne invasion coming off the Great Plains. This morning, I made a lone trail through the snow to the workshop with my coffee (Triumph mug), turned the heat up a notch, and sat down to look at my bikes.

Did I say, "Turned the heat up a notch?" Yes.

One of my non-negotiable, self-imposed conditions for moving back to the Midwest from California seven years ago was that I would buy, rent, or build a large heated workshop that would be as warm and comfortable as the living room in my house. Period.

No more sockets frozen to the toolbox, I vowed. No more paint cans too cold to spray, no more frozen feet, blue hands, or visible breath between me and the bike I'm working on, no blown fuses because the air compressor oil is thick as taffy. Been there, done that.

As it turned out, I built a shop in a clearing in the apple orchard near our house, a thirty-by-forty-foot structure with a Kentucky-cabin roofline and a raised front porch to sit on while looking at bikes, observing rain, watching geese fly south (or, preferably, north), reading a shop manual, or drinking coffee. Or beer from the garage refrigerator. The shop also has skylights, lots of fluorescent fixtures—and a furnace.

Not just a feeble electric heater in a losing battle against nature, but a genuine ceiling-suspended gas furnace with forced air vents running the length of the garage and a liquid propane tank the size of a small submarine out back. I leave the thermostat set at fifty degrees Fahrenheit, and then kick it up to seventy when I enter the shop. Within three minutes, it's warm enough to work in a T-shirt.

Barb occasionally shakes her head at the heating bills, but I defend it as part of the cost of being alive, like blood transfusions for a hemophiliac or insulin for a diabetic. We all have our own ideas of health care, and the heated workshop is mine. When I can no longer afford it, I'll bring the bikes into the house. Or move south. I can't stand being cold while I try to do mechanical work. Can't concentrate, and don't want to.

So, where was I?

Ah yes, sitting in my heated garage, drinking coffee, and looking at the bikes. I was thinking about "winterizing" them.

Now, I've read at least fifty articles on how to winterize your bike, and I probably even *wrote* one in the early 1980s, when I was technical editor at this magazine. But I've always been incredibly lazy and slack about this stuff myself. Last winter, for instance, I never got around to taking the battery out of my Ducati 900SS, and in the spring it just barely started. Then I rode it all summer and the battery never recovered a full charge. Now the battery is coming out (also the Harley's and Triumph's) and going on the automatic trickle charger for the winter to see if it can be saved. Better late . . .

I did, however, put some fuel stabilizer in all three bikes (I hate looking for gum in carburetors), and I'll start them all a few times with the pipes sticking out the door, just to circulate oil and move the piston rings. This heat cycle may do more harm than good, condensation-wise, but I've always been amazed at how fast rings can form a band of rust inside the cylinder barrel of a stationary bike. Unused airplanes do it, too. The air above a piston seems to make its own weather, like a small terrarium.

What else? I usually pump the brakes a bit, move the bikes around, and change any disgusting-looking brake fluid during the winter. That's about it.

All useful stuff, but I still think the best way to winterize a bike is to treat it as you would a dog or cat: Bring it inside. My theory is, if you are warm and comfortable, so is the bike. Fortunately, you don't have to build a big fancy heated workshop to do this.

My friend Joe Deane, for instance, rents a commercial/industrial space with an actual trucking dock out front and shares it with two other motorcyclists. Among them, they have a couple dozen bikes, with plenty of room to work on them, store parts, and so on. The rent, when shared, is reasonable.

Fellow Slimey Crud Bruce Finlayson is fortunate in having one of those garages where you drive in underneath the house. I've always thought that this is the best combination of all because you can get to the bike(s) without dressing up like a deer hunter and the heating bills are unaffected. If you can't sleep, you can fix yourself a drink, go down, and bike-gaze in your bedroom slippers. If we ever build a house, it will probably have a ride-in basement garage.

You can also carry a bike down basement stairs, of course, but this is not exactly a spur-of-the-moment deal, and later you'll need disc surgery or hernia repair. Or four strong friends to get the motorcycle off your chest. Still, it's a good place to keep a bike.

Another ideal winter-storage solution is to put your bike dead center in the middle of your living room. My friend Jeff Weaver does this, and it works out splendidly. He does full engine rebuilds, just feet from the sofa. Jeff, however, is a bachelor, as you might expect. Married guys will find this strategy slightly tougher than importing a French maid with big eyelashes to do "light dusting."

However you do it, I heartily recommend bringing a bike indoors during the winter, just as a sympathetic and preservative gesture. I am always amazed, when I drive into the city or past nearby farms, how often I see a bike left out in the snow and rain, or only partially covered. Even from a distance, you can see the chrome turning ashen-white, the bolt recesses holding small wells of water. And yet a motorcycle is such a small thing to move and to store properly, hardly bigger than a bicycle. Or three bicycles, in the case of my Harley.

Still, it takes so little effort to bring them in under a warm roof. And, unlike those cats and dogs I mentioned, they don't demand much, except maybe a light battery charge and a moderate amount of admiration. Also, they are more realistic than a poster—or a photograph taken last summer—and a lot more fun to watch than television.

June 1998

REAL VERSUS TOY BIKES

I had my fiftieth birthday a couple of weeks ago, and we threw a big party in my palatial garage/workshop. I got the cars out of there, parked my four bikes in relatively safe nooks and corners where nobody could drink one too many Sprecher Ambers from the half-barrel and fall into them, and then I put down a large piece of carpet for a "stage," so our blues band could play.

It turned out pretty nice, I think, and about sixty-five people showed up to eat, drink, dance, etc., all bathed in the romantic yellow bug lights I screwed into the overhead sockets for atmosphere so our garage would look more like an ersatz nightclub and less like Kmart.

After our band quit playing, I was wandering around the party when an old college buddy of mine came up. Sweeping his hand at the motorcycles parked about the garage, he said, "Okay, I can understand the two Ducatis and the Triumph 500. But why the *Harley*?" He was staring at my green Road King as if I'd hung a black velvet Elvis portrait in the Louvre.

I thought about the question for a moment and said, "The Harley? I guess I have it because I *use* it all the time. At present, it's my only real bike. The others are toys."

Seemingly satisfied with this answer, he shrugged amiably and went off in search of another beer.

Sometimes your own words catch you by surprise and continue to ring in your mind long after you've spoken them. The effect, in my case, is much like a handclap in an empty room.

A *real* bike? And the others *toys*? Was this true? The more I thought about it, the truer it seemed. But what was the distinction?

I guess I'd always known, without pinning it down, that some of the bikes I'd owned were more practical than others, but what would cause me to deem one machine "real," while characterizing others as frivolous? Was it the ability to travel long distances comfortably? Carlike reliability? Ease of maintenance? Luggage capacity?

Maybe all of these together, uniting to form a concept called utility.

Thinking back on the bikes I've owned or ridden, it occurred to me that the distinction has always been there, the boundaries clear, for whatever subtle reasons. You simply *know* which bikes are which, just as you know which friends can be counted on to pick you up at the airport.

Nearly all the BMWs I've ridden, for instance, have been "real" bikes. They were conceived and made by responsible adults who expected you to use them, possibly every day and all the time, and to go anywhere. To work or to the ends of the Earth. And, as an article of faith, you could fully expect to find parts or repair shops in New Delhi, Boston, or Nairobi. They were made for transportation, and any sporting qualities are just icing on the cake.

Just the opposite of Ducatis—they are made for sport, and any utility is just an accident. Probably the only Ducati qualified as a "real" bike would be the 750 GT (and maybe the new ST2 and the Darmah, slightly), but the rest are toys. You make a Faustian pact when you buy one, trading anvil-like longevity, comfort, and low maintenance for lightness, beauty, and performance. You go out on a limb a little. No real bike ever came with desmodromic valve actuation. How would you adjust them on the road from Katmandu to Gorakhpur?

All Bimotas, it goes without saying, are toys.

Moto Guzzis have always been 100 percent real bike, but a few of their more recent models, such as the Sport 1100 and the Daytona 1000, have made a stab at toylike impracticality.

Hondas? Nearly all Hondas used to be real bikes, but now I would limit it to the Gold Wing and ST1100, with a half vote for the luggageless VFRs. (We'll leave dirt bikes out of this discussion to keep it simple. Dual-purpose bikes qualify as that oddest of hybrids, "the real toy.")

Some Harleys are getting to be more like expensive jewelry than useful motorcycles, but any number of models still qualify as real, particularly the Electra Glide family. Beneath whatever chrome and conchos may festoon the object beats the heart of a bike that intends to take you somewhere every day and keep doing it for years, with the tune-up schedule of a Buick. Hydraulic valve lifters, you know. And when it's finally worn out, it expects to be rebuilt—and can be. Another key attribute of the real bike, perhaps. If you won't be able to rebuild it (or won't want to) twenty years from now, it's probably a toy.

Some of the new Japanese cruisers, I think, are metamorphosing into real bikes, which is why they are selling well. At least those with a comfortable seat, windshield, and saddlebags are real. The rest are toys, as are all Japanese sport bikes, no matter how comfortable or durable. They just are.

Triumph now makes a few real bikes, but old Triumphs, those perennial favorites of mine, are toys, and so are Nortons. They were built by people who were amazed to get from Meriden to Wolverhampton without major trouble. When I wanted to ride to Watkins Glen in 1979 with my pal John Jaeger and his BMW R90S, I traded my 1967 Triumph Bonneville straight across for a 1975 Honda CB750 Four. I needed a real bike for the job.

Looking back on it, most of my favorite motorcycles have been toys, as are three-fourths of the bikes I now own. But I've always liked having at least one real bike in the garage. Here at the half-century mark, in fact, I don't think I could get along without one. Must be getting old.

August 1998

ONLY SLEEPING

Naturally, on the first really good day of spring riding weather this year—a record seventy-eight degrees and sunny—I was not riding one of the bikes I actually *own*, but driving all day to look at a bike I don't own. Nothing ever changes.

Windows open, elbow on door, I was cruising through downtown Chicago in my blue Ford van, headed for Indianapolis where a 1979 Moto Guzzi 1000SP lurked in the back of a man's garage. Yes, the very bike whose attractions I mentioned in last month's column.

"Lurked" is perhaps the wrong word, as it suggests a certain readiness. This bike was "located" in the garage, as Grant's Tomb is located in New York City. It had been, according to its owner, absolutely stationary since 1986. Twelve years. I wondered if centerstand steel could form a molecular bond with concrete, and moving it would be like pulling King Arthur's sword out of the stone. We'd see. "How," my friends would later ask, "did you ever find out about an old Guzzi in Indianapolis, 350 miles from home?"

The owner, I explained, sent an e-mail to my friends at the nearby Moto Guzzi Cycle shop in Brooklyn, Wisconsin, saying he had a silver-blue 1000SP he'd bought brand-new in Denver in 1979, but it had been sitting for a long time and needed a battery, carb cleaning, brake work, etc. Did they know anyone who wanted to buy an SP, cheap, with only 7,700 miles on the odometer? A few days later I was on my way.

And breaking one of my own rules. I had vowed some time ago that I would never, ever, buy another motorcycle that could not be started up and ridden. There's too much mystery in a nonrunning machine. A motorcycle that starts, runs, and shifts is worth twice as much, in my book, even if it needs rebuilding. At least you can assess the extent of work needed. With a nonrunner, everything is unknown.

Still . . . a Guzzi with 7,700 miles on it. These bikes are notoriously overengineered and reliable. What could go wrong, unless the guy had run it out of oil? I decided to place an $1,800 bet that the bike could be brought back to life.

It was the shortest transaction in the history of commerce. I found the owner's tidy suburban home, he lifted a blanket off the bike in the corner of his eerily uncluttered garage, and I saw a dusty, unrusted, and fairly straight SP. There were a few minor flaws. The centerstand had its side peg broken off, and some minor fairing damage had been repaired around the right handgrip, as if the bike had tipped into a wall. A small dent in the tank had been painted over with a slight wave in the filler material.

Otherwise, the bike was clean and straight, and the engine turned over when pushed in gear. All the gears worked. The rear master cylinder (which controls both the rear caliper and the left front on Guzzi's integrated braking system) was mush, but the front master and right front caliper worked. The carb slides were stuck solid.

"Why did you quit riding it?" I asked the owner.

"I took up golf," he said.

Fifteen minutes after my arrival, we loaded the SP and I headed home.

It took about one week of evenings and $120 in parts to get the Guzzi back to perfect running condition. I removed and rebuilt the Dell'Orto carbs, which were full of red granules of rust and fuel precipitate, checked the valve adjust (still perfect), installed an eighteen-dollar garden tractor battery (which fits right in older Guzzis), cranked it for oil pressure, added gas, and put the plugs back in. It started right up and ran fine. I also rebuilt the rear master cylinder and bled the brakes, changed all the fluids, and gave the bike a thorough cleaning.

I've put 600 miles on the Guzzi the past two weeks, and it feels like a brand-new, just-broken-in 1979 motorcycle.

This is the first Guzzi I've ever owned, and I confess to being pretty taken with it. The bike has a strangely seductive mechanical presence, with a great relaxed rhythm and heartbeat going down the road. It also handles remarkably well, turning-in effortlessly and falling through corners like a fighter plane peeling off into an attack. It has a very low center of gravity and a low saddle, so you sit *in* the bike rather than on it.

The 1000SP was Guzzi's answer to the BMW R100RS, a sport-touring take on the G5 with a wind tunnel–developed upper fairing and short bars. It's nowhere near as fast or smooth as my old 1984 R100RS, nor as long and roomy for two-up touring. Nor did it come with built-in luggage. On the plus side, the SP is easier to work on, has slightly better handling (or at least more reassuring), and is a little nimbler and more fun to ride around town. The Guzzi also emits nicer exhaust sounds and has a harder, more direct and charming mechanical essence. Italian, you know.

It's a fun, honest motorcycle, and I'm glad now I used up a perfectly good spring day to go get it. Two or three times on that trip I almost turned around and came home, imagining all the things that could be wrong with a motorcycle whose crank had not turned a single revolution since the year (according to my almanac) *Platoon* won Best Picture and Chernobyl melted down.

I was thirty-eight when those pistons stopped in their bores, and now I'm fifty. But with a battery and a splash of gas, the engine turned over and started running instantly, rocking itself gently in that measured, even beat that only Guzzis have. The abiding patience of forgotten motorcycles always amazes me.

September 1998

PASSING TEMPTATIONS

Deep summer has arrived in the Midwest, and the want ads are finally in full bloom. They came out in the spring like lilacs or black locust blossoms, and, at this writing, fill nearly two full columns in the newspaper. I count 89 bikes for sale this week.

A nice change from winter. Had you looked under "Motorcycles for Sale" in, say, February, you'd have found the section slightly shorter in length than "Livestock Removal Services." I've never quite figured out why dead farm animals are called "livestock," but there you go.

Peruse the want-ad section in midwinter and you'll typically see only three or four entries: a couple of ATVs, maybe, a Honda Mini-Trail for sale, and one guy trying to get $22,500 for a Softail Custom he bought for $16,000 just three months earlier, perhaps because he's added "much chrome." Hope springs eternal.

But now the ads are back, in force. Garages are being cleaned out, trades are being made, estates are being settled, and people are getting into motorcycling, out of motorcycling, or moving up or down a rung on the motorcycle food chain of cost, speed, and sophistication. It's musical chairs time in the world of bikes. After six months of frozen tundra and pent-up supply and demand, it's as if somebody poured gasoline on the anthill. Stuff's happening.

Which is fine with me, of course, as I am a motorcycle classifieds junkie. I begin virtually every morning of my life with a ritual that involves a large cup of coffee with a little chicory in it, the Fred Ramsey Memorial La-Z-Boy on the front porch (named in honor of my late father-in-law, who knew a good chair when he saw one), and the motorcycle classifieds in that day's paper. I admit to checking on cars and musical instruments as well, which can help compensate for a thin day in the motorcycle market and ease the disappointment, like a good closing ramp on a camshaft lobe.

What is it, I sometimes ask myself, *that I am looking for? Don't I already have a couple of perfectly good bikes to ride? Why don't I just read a good book instead of the motorcycle classifieds? Or go for a ride?*

The answer, it seems, is that I am looking for temptation. Preferably cheap temptation.

Let's look at last Sunday's paper, just as an example. There were lots of bikes in which I am not very interested, but hidden among them I found a Honda 550 Four, "All original, $475 rides it away." The hair naturally stood up on the back of my neck, so I called and found the guy had already sold the Honda to a buddy who bought it on the spot when he heard how cheap it was.

Elsewhere in the Honda section was a low-mileage 1979 CBX for $2,200. A legendary motorcycle for about the cost of a new 50cc campus motor scooter. Intriguing, but I decided not to call. I don't have $2,200 and don't need a CBX right now, but someday I probably will. The chemicals in my brain will tell me when.

Or how about a 1969 BSA 441 Victor, "stored for 5 years, $1,950, incl. some tools." A beautiful bike, but troublesome by reputation, the "441 Victim" has always been right on the edge of my lifetime wish list. Lovely alloy and yellow tank, great-looking pipe and muffler, a classic big single.

I jumped up and dug out my 1969 hardbound *Cycle World* volume and found an ad for this bike with a picture on page thirty-seven of the February issue. "BEEZA, The Bold Way to Make Time," it proclaimed. Bold indeed. Sultry British model in skimpy dress, nice side shot of bike. Only in 1969. I circled the ad, but did not call. My Triumph 500 is presently keeping me supplied with all the strange electrical problems I need for true happiness.

Not too far down, a Moto Guzzi T-3 with a sidecar for $3,200. Neat chance for somebody to have a classic standard Guzzi *and* enter the strange world of sidecars, at a reasonable price. But not me. Not this week, anyway. Still, I circled the ad because it qualified as circleable.

A seller with a BSA Spitfire was looking for "serious offers only." Whenever I see this phrase, I am tempted to call up and do my Daffy Duck imitation

("Whaddaya mean, a B-Eth-A THPIT-fire!") or show up to look at the bike in a clown suit. Serious, schmerious.

Two different Nortons, a 1971 750 Commando project bike for $2,000/offer (wince), and a 1975 Commando in "beautiful condition" for $3,950. I've had three Commandos, and am currently "between Nortons," i.e., still at least a year of healing away from my next one. Nonetheless, I was commanded by instinct and honor to circle both ads.

"Ducati 900 Monster, black, $6,800." Hooo, they are nice in black. Agile and light, like a Triumph 500 that goes fast. All-day back road fun. Circle ad. No call. No bucks.

When the coffee was gone and I'd combed the ads, I grabbed my jacket and went out for a Sunday ride on my own Guzzi, down along the Rock River. It was still early in the day, but it felt almost like my second motorcycle trip of the morning.

The first one took me backward and forward in time, past landmarks of engineering, blunders in marketing, evolutionary dead ends, shining moments in design, the romance of my own past bikes, and deep into the pages of a magazine I bought when I was only twenty-one. All from an easy chair, and it didn't cost a dime.

Not this week, anyway. I got off easy. The Honda 550 was gone, and with only $827 in checking I couldn't make any serious offers. Barb got off easy, too. She makes an audible sigh of relief whenever I put the paper away and say the magic word, "Nothing."

November 1998

BUYING A SHADOW

Can't say I haven't been warned. A few years ago, when I wrote a column called "Saving for a Vincent," my friend Jeff Craig called from Pennsylvania and said, "I had to call you. Four or five of my friends have phoned in the past two days and said, 'Hey Jeff, you know Egan. Why don't you tell him not to buy a Vincent?'"

"Why would they say that?" I asked naively.

"Because we belong to a club called Vincent Owners Anonymous. We've all owned Vincents and sold them."

"Why is that?"

"Well, a couple of the guys have crashed, inexplicably, from sudden speed wobbles, and others of us have just had lots of . . . mechanical problems. Forget Vincents. They are more trouble than they're worth."

I took this under friendly advisement, but I did not forget Vincents.

Since long before and after this call, I have continued to collect books, literature, and pictures of Rapides and Black Shadows from the little factory in Stevenage, England. In my garage I have a large calendar photo of a Black Shadow, and my office wall has an embossed tin sign advertising the Series C Black Shadow: "The World's Fastest Standard Motorcycle. This is a Fact, Not a Slogan." I even have three Vincent T-shirts in my T-shirt drawer.

Easy for Jeff to say, "Forget Vincents." This is like an older man, weary from a troubled marriage, telling a teenager to forget women. Sometimes good advice is not wanted, even when we know it has a core of wisdom. We like to make our own mistakes. An active life, as nearly as I can tell, is nothing but a long series of errors and overcorrections.

So, having amended the Lord's Prayer to read, "Lead us not into temptation—unless it's something we really want," I accepted a *CW* assignment two months ago to fly down to Austin, Texas, and ride a 1951 Vincent Black Shadow for a full day and to report on its virtues, or lack of same. The bike belonged to a lawyer and Vincent collector named Herb Harris.

It was a Series C model, with Girdraulic forks, engine No. 5708, and frame No. 7608 (frame numbers are normally 1900 greater than engine numbers), which means it was made in late 1950, though sent to the United States and titled as a 1951. In other words, some full-fledged adult was riding around on this bike about the time I was struggling with tricycle dynamics and listening to *The Lone Ranger* on the radio.

Those who read the story in the September 1998 issue may recall that I was quite pleased with the bike. It went fast, stopped well, and handled beautifully. Also, it sounded good and looked stunning. I was not, in other words, deflected from my desires. When I got on the plane to fly home, I said to Herb and his partner in restoration, Stan Gillis, "I am going to go home and sell a couple of my bikes and start a Vincent fund tomorrow. I don't suppose you'd want to sell your Shadow, would you?"

"No," Herb said, "we just got this one restored and dialed-in. But we'll help you find one. They're out there."

I made many phone calls to Vincent people, such as the legendary Vincent exponent and locator Summer Hooker of Nashville, and Dick Busby, the California Vincent specialist who'd done such a nice job building Herb's engine. Phone calls flew back and forth, the long-distance bill blossomed.

Meanwhile, I gritted my teeth, girded my loins, tossed logic out the window, and sold two of the best bikes I've ever owned, my Harley-Davidson Road King and my Ducati 900SS SP. I also sold my full-stack Marshall guitar amplifier. I believe this is called throwing furniture into the flames of desire. All proceeds went straight into the Vincent fund.

Two weeks later, I got a call from Herb. "Would you like to buy my Black Shadow?" he asked.

"Yes," I said. "I would."

Seems in searching for a bike for me, Herb had run across a Black Shadow basketcase with a famous Texas drag-racing history—the legendary Mel Thompson nudist bike. (Mel, I was told, had been a member of that smallest of minority groups, Vincent drag racers who live at nudist colonies.) Herb, being more interested in bikes with racing history than in having a restored "runner," decided to sell the bike I rode and start yet another restoration.

So, a couple of weeks ago, I cleaned and washed my blue Ford van (as if to make a good first impression on an inanimate object) and drove out to the

AHRMA vintage race weekend at Mid-Ohio, where Vincent happened to be the featured marque. My friend Bruce Finlayson went with me. We crashed in a motel room with my pal Mike Cecchini, who rode his BMW R100RS from Maryland, and three buddies on Vincents.

At least eighty-one Vincents showed up, including "my" bike and the partially disassembled Mel Thompson dragbike. I got to shake hands with Summer Hooker and Dick Busby, whom I'd only met by phone, and lifelong Vincent expert and author "Big Sid" Biberman. Restorer Scott Dell let me and others take his Series A Rapide for a ride. I had dinner with the Vincent Owner's Club. Total immersion.

Herb and I sat in his car and traded bank check for Vincent title, and then we loaded the Shadow securely into my van and Bruce and I headed for home. Just before we left Mid-Ohio, Dick Busby shook my hand and said, "Welcome to the Masochists' Club."

"Ha, ha!" I laughed, trying to take this comment as lightly as possible.

Masochists' Club? A joke or another friendly warning?

No matter. I've been warned against everything in life that has ever turned out to be worth doing. And, of course, a couple of things that haven't. There's only one way to find out which is which.

January 1999

PAPERWEIGHTS OF THE GODS

Sitting up late in the garage the other night, I was having a beer and gazing at the evening's handiwork. I'd just installed a newly rebuilt Miller generator in the Vincent and was basking in that warm glow of satisfaction one always feels when such a task is completed without breaking off a cooling fin, dropping the gas tank upside down on the floor, or stabbing yourself in the center of the forehead with a screwdriver.

The first tenet of the Hippocratic Oath, "Do no harm," works for mechanics as well as doctors.

Anyway, there I was, looking around the garage, when my eye fell upon a large cardboard box of spare Triumph parts donated to me last year by my friend Dan Wilson. The box has a mid-1960s Bonneville oil tank sticking out of it, and I was admiring the neat contours of the tank—certainly one of the greatest shapes in all motorcycling—when I experienced one of those strange depth-of-field changes and the box itself suddenly snapped into focus.

Printed in bold type on the side was the legend, "CENTURY TOILET TRAINER." Below that it said "Customer approved for fast, realistic toilet training," with the added appeal of a "Snap-in deflector" and "Vinyl safety belt." Was this a little joke on Dan's part? I doubted it. Like me, he probably never even saw the box. He was looking at the Triumph parts.

There's nothing quite like the power of well-designed motorcycle parts to mesmerize and distract us from the mundane things in life. Totality of design means a lot in a motorcycle, but the fact remains much of the beauty in the bikes we admire comes from their individual pieces. Motorcycles, perhaps more than any other machines we use, are, at their best, a collection of wonderful places for the eye to rest.

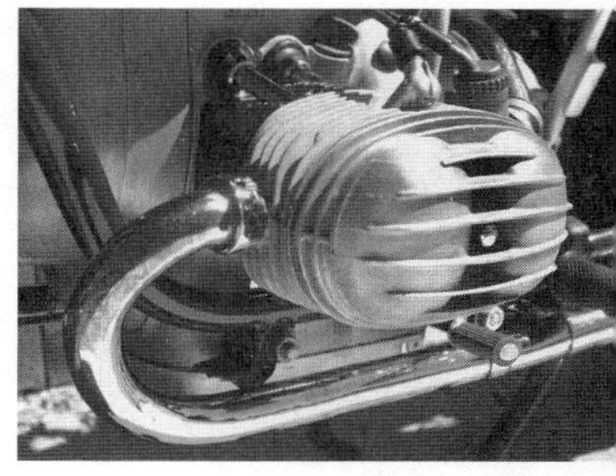

That Bonneville oil tank is just one of many harmonious designs to grace this past century of motorcycling. It blends in nicely with the rest of the bike, but it also successfully stands alone and reflects the basic quality of the whole machine, the way a briefly heard riff from a Beatles tune on the radio suggests the whole song. Not to mention a whole era. Your memory and imagination fill in the blanks.

Along these lines, I've often thought that a perfectly good—and lower maintenance—substitute for a motorcycle collection might be a glass display case with a few famous pieces of your favorite bikes on view. (Think of the savings on oil changes and insurance alone.)

What would go into this component hall of fame?

Everybody has his or her own favorites, of course, but my own nominations would have to include some of the following:

• The heart-shaped Triumph timing chest cover from the right side of the 500 and 650 twins, and one each of the "garden gate" and wing-style tank emblems.

• The old-style rounded valve covers from both BMW and Moto Guzzi twins.

• Right-side engine and gearbox castings from the Norton Commandos, and maybe a set of "pea-shooter" mufflers. The walnut-shell valve covers are pretty nice, too, as are the polished footpeg/muffler brackets. And all levers. Okay, Nortons are nothing but a gathering place for gorgeous pieces. Might as well buy the whole bike and leave it together.

• The shield-shaped gear cover on the rear cylinder head of Ducati bevel-drive twins. In the case of Ducati singles, the whole engine would have to go in the display case.

• Conti mufflers.

• The iron cylinder barrels and external oil lines on Harley Shovelheads. They have a hard, lean mechanical look the later ones lack.

• Panhead "pans" and pushrod tubes.

• The 4-into-1 exhaust headers and muffler from a 400F Honda.

• Both styles of "tombstone" gas tank on the Z-1R Kawasakis. The Harley XLCR cafe-racer tank also goes into my hall of famous parts.

• Head and barrel from a Manx Norton.

• Dell'Orto pumper carburetors.

• The twin handlebar-mounted choke levers from a Vincent, and at least one HRD or Vincent-embossed valve-adjuster cover. And . . .

Okay, I can already see this list could go on and on. Most of the great or noteworthy motorcycles are fairly rich in nice castings, unique forgings, and other small monuments to quality.

Nice pieces, of course, do not a great motorcycle make. A case might be made, in fact, that there is either an inverse relationship or none at all between finely wrought fiddly bits and engineering quality. BMWs, for instance, are generally well engineered, yet they are often a mixture of handsome, well-crafted pieces and mundane-looking parts that are designed to be strong and light, effective rather than beautiful.

Nevertheless, it's in the artisanship of these future paperweights that we glimpse a little of the bike's soul and read the signature of the people who made it. They are the means by which the designers tell us whether the bike was built to be kept and treasured or used up and thrown away. Or, to put it another way, whether our seduction was meant to be permanent or only temporary.

Great parts also have a Darwinian function; they save the bike itself from extinction. More than one semi-useless or functionally treacherous old motorcycle has been restored at lavish expense just because someone liked the look of its tank badges or the polished, dental-tool exquisiteness of its shift and brake levers.

Believe me, I know.

March 1999

WASTED MILES

A few years ago, when I was on a motorcycle trip around Lake Superior with our editor, David Edwards, and two friends named Tom Daley and Chuck Davis, we wrapped up a week on the road by shooting diagonally across Wisconsin to my place, where everyone planned to stay the night before heading home.

Suddenly, while we were cruising through the town of Fort Atkinson, only about eighteen miles from home, Tom waved us all over to the side of the road. "That corner back there looked like a nice spot," he said. "What say we stop for a beer or some coffee?"

I looked back over my shoulder at the bar and then at the road ahead. I was struck absolutely speechless for a moment. Finally my brain and jaw kicked in. "Sure," I said reluctantly, "why not?"

The problem was, I'd never done such a thing. One of my longtime bad habits as a touring motorcyclist has been to get "homing instinct" toward the end of a long trip. This is where you put the hammer down and blow off the last day (or two) of your ride so you can get back to the old homestead. No long lunches, scenic overlooks, or detours on side roads. Just twist that grip and go.

I have no idea why I do this. After a long midwestern winter spent dreaming about long rides, you'd expect a person to savor every mile and delay the end of a trip as long as possible, but it seldom works that way for me. Or at least it didn't until Tom brought me to my senses. I sat in the bar that day and vowed to do better, and since then I've been at least partially successful, if not fully reformed.

Late last year, for instance, the *CW* office called and asked if I could return the long-term yellow BMW R1100S, which I'd had through the summer and into fall. Could I ride it back from Wisconsin to California?

Swiveling my office chair around, I gazed at my large Rand McNally wall map of the United States and felt that odd, almost electrical current of elation that runs down my spine when I contemplate any map depicting wide open spaces and wrinkled mountain ranges. “Yes,” I said, “I surely can.”

You can make it from Wisconsin to Southern California in three days on a motorcycle, but it’s not much fun. The most direct route is 2,200 miles, so you have to cover about 750 miles per day. My wife Barbara and I did it in 1980 on a Suzuki GS1000, going to Elkhart Lake to cover the AMA races. I felt like a spent bullet when I got there.

This trip would be different. No wasted, sacrificial miles, no entire states disposed of in a mind-numbing blur. I set aside six full days.

Well, some wasted miles. It was October when I left, so the plan was to blast as far south as possible on that first day to avoid any potential snow. As it turned out, I need not have worried. The weather was warm and beautiful. I hit the interstate and made Cuba, Missouri, the first night, then rolled south on two-lane roads all the way through the Ozarks, on Highways 19 and 9 to Hot Springs, Arkansas, for the night—hundreds of miles of lightly traveled twisting road through some of the prettiest country on Earth. From there I cruised down through Arkadelphia and Hope (Clinton’s hometown), then took I-30 into Dallas to see my brother, Brian, for a day.

Then it was Highway 67 across most of Texas, another two-lane through beautiful rolling ranch land, across the oil country of the Permian Basin, and up onto the *Llano Estacado* on the I-road and into Van Horn, Texas, for the night. The next day, after lunch in Deming, New Mexico, I took the advice of some local riders who were dining at a great little Mexican cafe called *La Fonda* and rode north on Highway 180 to Alpine, Arizona, where I pulled into town at dusk with sleet freezing to my face shield. Luckily, I was wearing my electric vest, which is to hypothermia what garlic is to vampires. Also had the heated grips on high.

Crossing several 8,000-foot passes the next day in cold, sunny weather, I rode another 300-plus miles of mountain curves to Sedona on Highway 260, braking hard for elk here and there. At Sedona, I spent the night with my friends Richie and Marlene, explored Red Rock Crossing (where scores of Westerns have been filmed), and then rode toward California on Highway 60 through cliff-clinging Jerome and Prescott. Richie rode with me part way on his trusty Guzzi T-3.

The rest was an easy, warm desert cruise on I-10 through Banning Pass and down into Orange County and my sister Barbara’s home in Irvine, California.

We celebrated with margaritas and Mexican food at my all-time favorite restaurant, *El Matador* in Costa Mesa. One mile from the Pacific Ocean.

Total mileage on the trip was 2,600. By adding only three days and 400 miles to that former cross-country blast, I'd been able to do most of the trip on two-lanes, with time to ride the Ozarks, tour the ranch country and small towns of Texas, twist through the Rocky Mountains on virtually empty roads, visit my brother and old friends, and cruise the diamond deserts at near-legal speeds, arriving relaxed. What a difference a little time makes.

Any wasted, thrown-away miles dedicated to just plain getting there?

Yeah. Quite a few, even on this trip. Another week on the road would have been ideal. With every trip I've ever taken, time is the hardest commodity to come by. Good things fly by at the edge of your vision, and there's no time to stop.

In a way, I failed again, hitting the interstate on that last day, when I could have crossed the San Bernardino Mountains on twisting roads through Idyllwild, then cut through the Santa Ana Mountains on the Ortega Highway. Some of the best riding ever, only hours from my destination.

Maybe I'll have to retire to finally get it right. Hurrying through life is a hard habit to break. Especially on that last day, falling toward home.

June 1999

THE DAYTONA FACTOR

"You going to Daytona this year?" I asked my friend Jeff Weaver. Jeff is a fellow member of the Slimey Crud Motorcycle Gang, and we were all at the Come Back In, located in the wintry heart of downtown Madison, Wisconsin, having one of our disorganized, random "meetings," which consist mostly of hoisting a few beers from the dark, ninety-weight end of the viscosity spectrum while waiting for spring.

Jeff grinned from somewhere behind his substantial beard and said, "Daytona? Of course I'm going. I am Muslim and Daytona is Mecca. I have to go. Besides, it's the week that breaks the back of winter. A reason to celebrate."

That pretty much sums up my own motives for going every year. In deepest March, it's the only show in town, and when you get back it seems that winter is almost over. You wait for the snow to melt with the same impatience you feel when an old TV is warming up and you can hear the sound, but there's no picture. Still, you know the picture is coming. It always has before.

This year I drove down with another friend and fellow Crud, Mike Puls, towing my rusting bike trailer with his 1994 Buick Century station wagon. Mike, a Madison cop who just retired after thirty years on the force, had never been to Daytona Bike Week. He decided to take his 1984 Yamaha RZ350 Kenny Roberts Replica, and I my trusty 1979 Moto Guzzi 1000SP.

We left at some ungodly hour of the morning with the Weather Channel threatening snow and rain just to our west, drove straight south through Illinois, "The Endless State," and cruised into Kentucky past the portals of Fort Campbell as usual, this time on the thirtieth anniversary of my induction there. (Yet I feel like exactly the same person now as I did then—still saving for my next motorcycle.)

Stopping for the night in Murfreesboro, Tennessee, in a blinding rainstorm, we made Daytona the next evening, right at dusk, subsisting only on twelve pounds of Georgia pecans and peanut brittle. Plus McDonald's finest.

Actually, we stayed at Flagler Beach, well north of Daytona, in a nice old motel across the road from the ocean, a spot discovered by yet another fellow Crud, Stu Evans, who had trailered his BMW R90S to Florida and had already checked in.

So how was Daytona this time around? A superb year, by my reckoning.

Clear, sunny weather, and the AHRMA vintage races were good, with more people competing than watching, which is just as it should be. We also watched Superbike qualifying. Mike and I sat in the grandstands at the exit of the infield, where riders accelerate hard onto the banking while heeled over—it's a great place to see how the bikes are handling and what the riders are doing about it.

Star of qualifying was Anthony Gobert, who put his Ducati on the pole and set a new lap record. On his hottest lap, he actually appeared to lose the back end of the bike three times in "our" corner and catch it without ever backing off the throttle—an amazing performance. I would have abandoned hope and crashed all three times, in just this one corner. If you multiply that by Daytona's nine distinct turns, that's twenty-seven crashes per lap. Maybe that's why I was in the stands, rather than riding a 996 for Vance & Hines. No decent team will hire a guy who crashes twenty-seven times per lap.

Hero of the week, however, was Miguel Duhamel, who, riding injured, won both the 600 and Superbike races for Honda. He had plenty of horsepower to work with, but still put on a stunning display of riding. Duhamel looks as if his tires are never actually in molecular contact with the track, but just sliding, spinning, and floating around the circuit on a boundary layer of wishful thinking and pure aggression. Masterful riding.

On the Saturday before the big race, Mike and I spent most of the day at the Woods bike auction in nearby De Land. If there was a lesson in this year's auction, it's that you should restore your motorcycle only as a labor of love, rather than hoping for big profits. Buyers are pretty hard-headed these days, and I think the era of giddy speculation has given way to the era of calm calculation. There were bargains to be had. Some year I'll bring money.

Riding back from the auction at night, we stopped at the famous Gene's Steak House and were seated in a room where the entire Yamaha team was celebrating its supercross victory. We had just noticed that Randy Mamola was sitting a few tables away when a waiter opened a side exit door right next to our table, and in came Wayne Rainey and Eddie Lawson to join the Yamaha gang.

Ah, Daytona. You look around sometimes and feel as if you're at Mount Rushmore, brought to life. The Great Ones are all there, roaming the Earth.

Just before we left Daytona, I took a ceremonial swim in the cold ocean—just long enough to give myself an ice-cream headache, and a few other physical problems too lengthy to mention here—and we were off for home on Monday.

Thanks to my careful program of deferred trailer maintenance, we suffered a spun trailer bearing near Paducah and had to have the inner race ground off and new bearings installed at a machine shop just down the road from Possum Trot, Kentucky. I am not making this up.

Driving north through Illinois, "The Land of Standing Water," we cruised into drifting snow and high winds, just at the Wisconsin border.

Doing my best *Dumb and Dumber* imitation, I said to Mike, "Have you noticed that we've been driving on clear, dry roads for two days, and the first place where you can't ride a motorcycle is right about where we live?"

Mike just grinned and said something about spring being on the way.

And so it is. As I write this, a week later, the snow has already melted and two robins have appeared in our yard. We have been to Mecca and the back of winter has been broken. The TV tubes are warming up, the sound is on, and the picture is almost here. A reason to celebrate.

August 1999

MOTORCYCLIST'S CALENDAR

One fine day last April, the wind suddenly quit blowing, the leaden skies slid east, the cold rain lifted, and the sun came out. A week of rain had washed all the salt off the roads and they were clean and dry.

I looked out my window as I shaved in the morning, stared at the sun beaming down on impossibly green grass the color of Easter basket lining, turned to my befoamed visage in the mirror and said, simply, "It's Gassing Day."

And so it was. One by one, I started up my four motorcycles and took them to the gas station to put new fuel in their tanks. I rode over to a Mobil station in the nearby village of Brooklyn, Wisconsin, because it has pumps that take credit cards outdoors, so you don't have to go inside to pay, standing in line behind some whiskey-voiced woman with a spare cigarette behind her ear who's buying an endless succession of scratch-off lottery tickets.

Anyway, I got all the bikes gassed up, but when the job was done I felt somehow incomplete. It seemed a day as significant as the firing up and fueling of motorcycles in spring should be accompanied by some sort of gala festival or solemn ceremony to commemorate the moment.

The Pagans knew how to do this stuff, after all. They'd break into song and dance at the slightest provocation by nature: winter solstice, summer solstice, running of the smelt, the festival of the turnip harvest, the molting of the vipers, etc. A few of them still linger on in Western culture. Until only a few decades ago, people in my hometown still danced around a maypole on May Day. What was that all about? An ancient spring fertility ritual, no doubt, whose symbolism modesty prevents me from even imagining.

What motorcyclists need, it seems to me, are a whole new set of festivals and holidays that have real meaning in our calendar lives, now that television

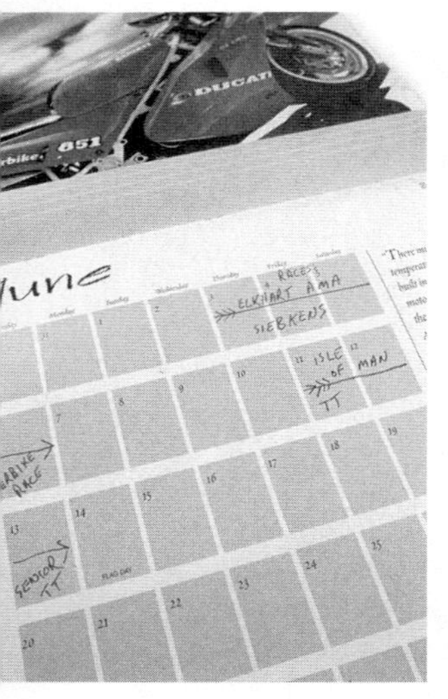

and too much ambient light have made us largely unaware of the movements of planets and stars.

I'm open to suggestions before the calendar actually gets printed, but here are a few possibilities:

Gassing Day: Yes, let's start with the one I've already mentioned. This could be a movable holiday, subject to weather, held on the first Thursday in April in northern climes, earlier elsewhere, and not at all in Florida or Southern California, where every day is Gassing Day. Parties held on Gassing Day should probably feature some high-octane libation, such as aquavit or mescal, which could be ceremonially tossed onto a bonfire, when not being downed, causing a huge flame-up and much applause, while symbolizing the miracle of combustion. Gifts of high-quality neoprene fuel line and see-through filters could be exchanged, as well as exquisitely crafted petcocks.

St. Siebkens Day: Usually celebrated the second weekend in June. This is a day many of us celebrate each year at Siebkens Hotel in Elkhart Lake on the weekend of the Superbike races. People in other parts of the country will have to pick a favorite racetrack, a notable race, and a good hotel. Siebkens has an outdoor bar set up behind the courtyard of the charmingly old-fashioned hotel so that guests can park their bikes along the alleyway across from the tables and bar. On a warm night, with a drink in your hand, old friends gathering and a row of forty or fifty bikes to examine under the festive lights, it's easy to see why the Greeks realized the gods occasionally relent and shower us with divine favor. Thanks should be given. I usually overtip the bartenders, and in the morning drink only strong coffee with aspirin, leaving my breakfast untouched as an offering to St. Siebken.

TT Senior Sunday: Unfortunately very close to St. Siebkens Day, it's the holiest day in all motorcycling, marking the running of the Tourist Trophy Senior on the Isle of Man. Those who cannot attend are encouraged to hoist a pint of something dark and observe a moment of silence for those lost in the last great real road race on Earth. It is also a day of atonement and pardon, in which American fans are admonished to forgive Carl Fogarty for complaining about

Daytona—he did, after all, set a lap record on the Island when most Superbike riders wouldn't even go near the place.

The Feast of St. Taglioni: Observed mainly by *Ducatisti* on the good doctor's birthday, this important feast, second only to TT Senior Sunday, is normally celebrated with fast rides on red bikes and symposia on desmodromics followed by a traditional dinner of pasta putanesca washed down with a good Barolo. Arias from Rossini, Verdi, and Puccini should be sung, or at least listened to.

Wearin' o' the Aerostich: A post-harvest celebration marking the first day of autumn on which you go for a ride and turn around after two miles to put on warmer clothes. Hot chocolate with marshmallows is the customary sacramental drink, after a steaming shower that turns your skin red.

Anointing of the Gas Tank: This marks the end of our ecclesiastical motorcycling year and is a time for reflection and thinking of moving to a warmer climate. While any layman can add Sta-Bil to a gas tank, this ceremony is best performed by someone with big, beefy arms who can shake the whole bike to mix the stabilizer in with the fuel. Any dirge or requiem can be used for background music. A shroud should be pulled over each motorcycle, unless the bike needs a total rebuild. Now's the time.

Ah, I've run out of room, without even getting to the Seven Holy Days of Daytona or the Adoration of the Chromed Accessories in Sturgis. Next time.

September 1999

SLOW SEDUCTION

I was pretty impressed about five years ago when my friend David Knox showed up at Elkhart Lake for the Superbike races, having ridden all the way from Minneapolis on his brand-new 916 Ducati.

"You must have the neck vertebrae and wrists of a twelve-year-old," I told him as we shook hands. David shrugged cheerfully. "It's really not that bad," he said.

Not bad for him maybe. David let me ride his 916 to dinner that evening (my first ride ever on this legendary bike), and I quickly decided it was too uncomfortable for anything but racing, where sheer terror takes your mind off luxury.

When we traded bikes again, I was quite happy to get back on my Ducati 900SS. The 900SS lacked the shrink-wrapped, condensed precision and smoothness of the 916, but it was friendlier. Or maybe just more familiar. Nothing else feels quite like a 916, and a first ride can be more notable for its alien strangeness than for revealing the bike's deeper virtues.

So that's where I left it. Smug and satisfied, I was safe from the allure of the 916, even if I thought it was the most beautiful motorcycle of the decade, and I reveled in its racing successes.

Well, then, I rode through the late 1990s on two successive 900SSs, happy as a clam, until last year, when a small crack appeared in the great wall of certainty.

I was on a Lotus Tour of the Italian Alps, trying out the new, revised 900SS, when I found myself traveling with two dentist riding buddies from San Francisco, Serge Glasunov and Ai (actual name) Streaker, alias "Streak." They were riding a pair of rented Ducatis, an ST2 and another new 900SS.

After a few days on the road, I asked at dinner one night how they liked their rented bikes. They both looked at each other and shrugged. "They're all right," Serge said, "but we both have 916s at home. I wouldn't trade my 916 for either of these bikes." Streak gravely nodded his assent.

"Hmmm," I said. "Interesting. But how far can you ride on your 916s?"

"We take a lot of all-day rides and long weekend tours," Streak said. "No problem."

"The secret," Serge added, "is that you do not leave the Ducati dealership without putting on a Corbin seat and a set of slightly higher clip-ons. If you do that, you have one of the greatest sport bikes ever made, and you can ride it all day."

The frayed wires of belief were starting to sputter and smoke in my hard-wired cerebellum.

It usually takes one last jolt to blow the fuse, however, and that came last winter, when I got to ride a brand-new 996 *CW* test bike over the Angeles Crest Highway. Pretty much the same bike as the 916, but with a little more displacement and power, and refined clutch and brake feel.

The ride was about an hour's worth of sweepers, switchbacks, hairpins, dips, rises, and high-speed free fall down the back side of the San Gabriel Mountains. At some indefinable moment, perhaps twenty minutes into this ride, I knew I was a goner. My simple life had been recomplicated by lust. That's too crude a word. By appreciation.

The 996 is simply a wonderful motorcycle to ride. It's still severe in town or on dull, flat roads, but absolutely inspired in its natural habitat, the corner, and the short distance between corners. Six years of intense Superbike competition have filtered into the soul of the 996 in a way that is hard to explain. The bike is small, quick, beautiful, and compact as a diamond in the arrangement of its functional pieces. It's a sublime machine, even to one who can barely scratch the surface of its profound capabilities. I loved it.

So of course when I got home I started hanging around Bob Barr's Ducati shop in Madison, much the way a teenage boy hangs around the front porch of a girl who reads D. H. Lawrence novels and paints her toenails a lot. Bob, you see, had a 996 on the floor.

After about my fifteenth visit in which I casually sat upon the 996 while chatting about nothing in particular, Bob said, "I believe you ought to buy that bike."

And I said, abruptly, "I believe I will."

Strangely enough, I happened to have a checkbook smoldering in my back pocket, filled with funds from the recent sale of my old 1982 900SS.

Bob and I worked out a loan for the balance, and within a few days the 996 was in my garage.

I've got 1,000 break-in miles on the bike now. For the first 600 I had to keep it below 6,000 rpm, which was not too much of a cross to bear because the engine is immensely torquey, and in top 6,000 is still good for about 110 miles per hour.

Now I'm at the 7,000-rpm break-in level, and that's harder. The engine is ramping up for a power burst toward its 10,700-rpm redline, and it wants to keep going.

Comfort? Perfect on winding roads and at high speeds, where the wind lifts your chest like an air foil, and the bars are right where they should be. In town, it's fair-to-wretched. A little too much neck bend and weight on wrists. After break-in, I may succumb to the Serge and Streak Program of Comfort Enhancement. We'll see.

It's a bike of high limits—and high limitations—but I find myself caring less and less about the latter. It makes everything else I ride feel too large, or puffy and soft as a marshmallow. Its ascetic leanness has grown on me.

When I'm not actually looking at the bike or riding it now, I find myself at night leafing through the pages of Julian Ryder's book, *World Superbikes: The First 10 Years*, gazing at Kel Edge's superb photos of Fogarty, Corser, Kocinski, and the rest, smoking to victory. Or watching Foggy lead yet another championship points chase on Speedvision.

There's a lot of vicariousness built into Ducati's Superbike, I admit, a lot of rub-off magic.

As Wayne and Garth would say, "I am not worthy." But I don't care. The 996 is a thing to behold, and its virtues transcend the owner's limitations.

October 1999

TRACK TIME

"This is the last straw," I said, hopping up and down while exhaling deeply and trying to zip up my racing leathers. "I gotta get in shape and lose some weight."

It was a pretty pathetic sight. There I was at Willow Springs last winter, taking part in a 600cc sport bike comparison test, trying to shoehorn my 6-1, 192-pound frame into a set of leathers once sold to a guy who looked just like me but weighed 172 pounds. It was like trying to jam a cheap plastic rain suit back into its pouch.

Once zipped into the leathers, however, I had a wonderful time on the track—my first such outing in many years—and returned home to the frozen tundra of Wisconsin with my jaw firmly set in new resolve to *(a)* lose weight and *(b)* buy myself a modern sport bike that would allow me to participate in various track days around the Midwest. The joys of the racetrack were back in my blood.

Part A of the Big Plan began that very month, at Daytona Bike Week, when I bought myself some new running shoes and began jogging again. I've been at it ever since, and am up to about forty miles per week now. I've also been riding my bicycle a lot. I'm down to 167 pounds, feel great, and am contemplating entering my first-ever marathon later this fall. More importantly, though, my leathers fit again.

Part B was realized when I sold my old bevel-drive Ducati 900SS and bought a new 996 a few months ago.

Okay. All dressed up in leathers that fit, armed with a new bike. Where to go?

"Why don't you sign up for the Team Hammer Advanced Riding School & Track Ride," my old touring buddy David Knox suggested over the phone.

"It's just before the Superbike races at Road America. A bunch of us from the Twin Cities do it every year, and then stay on for the race weekend. It's a good school, and you get a lot of track time."

Perfect. I called Team Hammer in Wildomar, California, and found myself talking to none other than Trudy Ulrich, wife of my old *CW* colleague John Ulrich. The Ulriches publish *Roadracing World & Motorcycle Technology* and also manage the Team Hammer school. Trudy sent me a registration form, I sent in my $285 for the one-day school (track rides for graduates are $185), and I was set.

Well, almost. I still had to tape my headlight and all plastic lenses on the bike, take off the mirrors, fill a cooler with food and energy drinks, load everything into my van, and show up at Elkhart Lake at 7 a.m. on a Wednesday morning.

I had expected a small tribe of students lost in the vastness of Road America's parklike grounds, but the race weekend was already in full swing when I arrived, the paddock crowded with big Superbike team transporters and lots of privateers, many of them using the Hammer school to warm up or learn the circuit. Thirty students lined up to register for the school, 25 more signed up for the track-ride sessions.

I had also expected an eclectic mix of new and old motorcycles, but the vast majority were the latest open-class track weapons: Yamaha R1s, Suzuki GSX-R750Ss, Honda 900RRSs, Kawasaki ZX-9Rs, Ducati 916s and 996s. Seems most of the people who sign up for these advanced schools like to mix it up with their pals and are not interested in bringing up the distant rear.

My friends from the Twin Cities—David, Tony, Peter, Bob, and Paul—showed up on almost exactly that mix of motorcycles. David had a new yellow 996 with carbon fiber pipes and a computer chip. A fast, serious crowd. My bike, just barely broken-in, was still dead-stock.

David was right about the school; we did get a lot of track time. Five separate half-hour sessions, interspersed with classroom talks on technique and racing setup, taught by many-time WERA National Endurance champ Michael Martin and Team Hammer crew chief Keith Perry.

The track sessions started slow, building quickly to whatever speed we could stand, riding in groups of five, each with its own instructor. By the end of the day, our sessions were essentially chaperoned road races, flat-out—or as close as we could get to flat-out in our own minds. It's quite humbling to think you've got a fast sweeper nailed and then have an instructor cruise by on the outside, looking back over his shoulder and gesturing to follow him.

You would feel worse, I suppose, if he were eating a sandwich.

Nevertheless, we ended the day highly pumped up, and glowing with that sense of satisfaction that comes from pushing harder than you thought you could. And not crashing. I collected my diploma, loaded my Ducati (tires nicely cooked to the edge of the tread), said goodbye to my Minnesota friends, and motored home in my van with the A/C on high. It had been a very hot day—the kind where it takes two hapless bystanders to help peel off your soaked leathers. Even when they fit.

So, was it worth all the months of running and riding and the $285?

Yes.

You learn many things at a track session, but I've always thought the most valuable gift of the racetrack is faith in your tires. Every year that I don't ride on the track, my cornering lean angle gets about two degrees more upright and I start to forget just how hard you can lean on a good set of modern motorcycle tires.

The track brings it all back into focus. This renewed insight doesn't necessarily make you ride faster on the street, but it lets you ride more safely because you have a better sense of how much traction is left in reserve. And there's usually a lot more than you think.

Most of the crashes I've seen over the years (or almost had myself) have stemmed from a simple lack of belief. Halfway through a botched corner the rider says, "I can't get out of this," and subsequently gives up and crashes, as if surrendering to fate.

Track time makes you believe in your tires again. Especially the unused, shiny parts, with those little rubber bristles on them.

February 2000

BRITAIN VERSUS JAPAN, 1973

This is how motorcycles die, I thought to myself as I rode away from the repair shop. Someone looks at the complexity, the cost, and the relative payoff and decides the bike just is not worth fixing. The end of the line. Why does it happen so much more often to Japanese than European or American bikes?

The sudden impetus for this reflection came last week, when I took my recently reacquired 1975 Honda CB550 in for a carb synch and float-level check at Motorcycle Performance, a shop run by my friend Bill Whisenant.

As mentioned in a recent column, I'd made the mechanical refurbishment of this bike my little autumn garage project, installing a new battery, brake hydraulics, carb O-rings, plugs, points, tires, etc. In only a few weeks, my $600 jewel had become a $1,200 jewel, but that was all right. It was a nice bike to ride and it ran well.

Okay, fairly well. There was a flat spot off-idle and the two left spark plugs were showing a dark, fluffy richness. Which was why I decided to turn it over to Bill's considerable expertise. Mechanic Chris Neff reset the float levels slightly, synched the carbs accurately and even ran the bike on their dyno. Thirty-six peak brake horsepower at 9,000 rpm!

After all this fettling, the bike ran beautifully, but Bill told me the two left plugs were still a bit dark. "Probably due to the left-side mufflers, which you haven't replaced yet," he said. "They look good externally, but are probably starting to 'implode' from rust and carbon, so they don't flow as well."

"So I need new mufflers on the left side?"

Bill raised one eyebrow. "If you want to put that much more money into this bike . . ." he said, leaving the question open to logic and common sense. "As you know, they cost about $300 a set."

Interesting comment. Without saying it in so many words, Bill was respectfully suggesting that there are rational limits to how much money you might want to sink into a 1975 Honda CB550. If I spent $300 on mufflers, I'd have a $1,700 jewel, including Bill's modest charge for his tuning work.

Was this too much for a nice, useable old semi-classic Honda with 12,000 miles on the clock? Maybe so. The bike was right on that cusp of value and repairability, where a really serious engine problem might send it to the boneyard. No one would ever fix it. Maybe not even me.

Meanwhile, I had a nice, smooth and uneventful 200-mile Saturday afternoon ride in the country, then pulled back into my garage, where I parked the Honda next to my 1968 500 Triumph Trophy T100C.

They made an interesting contrast, sitting side by side.

Almost contemporaries, really. Triumph quit making the Trophy 500 in 1973, and that was the year Honda introduced the CB550, which was really only a mild update on the 1971 CB500. So if you were looking for a 500cc streetbike in that era, you might have bought either of these bikes.

My Triumph is older than the Honda but has fewer miles on it—only 6,000. This is probably a testament to its limited charm as a highway cruiser. It becomes very busy above fifty-five miles per hour and gives the impression that sustained speed will soon result in some grave mechanical disappointment. Also, things fall off, partly from engine vibration and partly because the antiquated suspension is brutally stiff.

The Honda, on the other hand, cruises with serene, electrical smoothness at seventy miles per hour and intimates it would be happy to do this forever, while soaking up road bumps with steady aplomb and grace.

It turns-in about as nicely as the Triumph, handles well (as Bill says, it doesn't have enough power to do otherwise), and corners better than the T100 over bumpy surfaces. The Honda has brakes; the Triumph doesn't.

What other differences? The original Honda instruments still work perfectly, while the Triumph speedometer recently broke—for the second time. The Triumph clutch and primary chain have also been replaced twice, but I don't think the Honda clutch cover has ever been off the bike. A good thing, too, because those typical cheesy Japanese Phillips-head screws might never come loose.

Nevertheless, I would happily ride the Honda from Wisconsin to California right now (except for the snow), and wouldn't even consider it with the Triumph, except on some kind of dare or far-fetched journalistic experiment.

It's hard to imagine that anyone who test-rode both bikes new in 1973 would have decided to buy the Triumph, unless for its superior off-road capabilities, by which time it was already eclipsed in that function by much lighter Japanese and European two-strokes.

So, the Triumph belongs in the dustbin of history and the Honda is perfect, right? Not quite so. The Trophy has a few things going for it.

While its internals are weaker, the Triumph has a hardier exterior. The original pipes have a nice patina, but are not rusting out. Its 32-year-old stainless-steel fenders look like new, while the Honda's cheap spray-on chrome is spider-webbed with hairline rust.

But the Triumph's biggest virtue is probably its simplicity. No need to "synch" that one carb. A Triumph carburetor gasket kit costs about two dollars, while the Honda needed four of them, at fourteen dollars each.

The Triumph will probably need three or four engine rebuilds before the Honda is worn out, but someone will do it because the twin is simple and the parts are few and available.

Essentially, Honda's 550 embodies the triumph of engineering brilliance over average materials, and the Triumph is just the opposite. The Honda has quality where it needs it, and is cheap where it doesn't. The Triumph is randomly elegant.

I like them both, but have to confess I've been riding the Honda more. And will probably continue to do so.

Right up until that sweet-running, complex four starts making ominous noises from deep within.

March 2000

BACK IN THE DIRT

"No, I don't need to borrow any off-road riding equipment," I told my friend Gary Elmer over the phone. "I haven't ridden a dirt bike since I did the Barstow-Vegas dual-sport ride eleven years ago, but I still have all the gear from my desert riding days in California."

Gary had just invited me to go riding on his family's 600-acre farm nearby. Gary rides a much-modified Honda CR250, but he also has a Kawasaki KDX200, available for guests. "Got a helmet?" he asked.

"Yeah, I've still got the original Bell Moto III I bought the first week I worked for *Cycle World* in 1980."

There was a respectful silence on the other end, and then Gary said, "Better check the helmet lining. It's probably dust."

After I hung up, I dug into the back closet and found the old canvas Duluth pack where my off-road riding gear has languished, clean and carefully folded, these many years. I unbuckled the leather straps and dumped everything out on the bed.

One red-and-yellow *CW* jersey, name on back, no moth holes; one pair all-leather Malcolm Smith motocross boots with strap-and-peg buckles; deer hunter–orange high socks; motocross pants with *Cycle World* emblazoned down both legs; three pairs of variously armored gloves; two pairs of goggles with limp headbands and foam disintegrating; and one white Bell Moto III helmet.

I tried the helmet on, and when I took it off, most of the inner liner was stuck to my head in small tufts and streamers of black foam with the consistency of sphagnum moss from an Irish peat bog. I looked like a Rastafarian from County Cork.

So much for the helmet. Ten summers in a hot storage closet had not been kind to it. I carried it by the strap out to the trash can in the garage and threw it away, along with the two pairs of decayed goggles. Everything else was useable, if dated, but I'd have to wear my black open-face street helmet and the Smith ski goggles I bought last winter.

So dressed, I jumped on my 1968 Triumph 500 and rode off toward Gary's farm.

A couple of cars whizzed by (as they will, when you ride a Triumph 500), and I must have made a strange sight on the highway: "Look, Dad, a guy going to a 1970s costume party!" For in truth, all my riding gear, bought in January of 1980, was twenty years old, at least. Unbelievable.

Quite frankly, my sense of nostalgia has been fading as of late. I'm sick of the old century and glad to see a new one arriving. I vowed to get some new stuff. And maybe another dirt bike—a *new*-generation dirt bike. If I enjoyed riding in the dirt again, that is. We'd see.

Gary's farm turned out to be something of a dirt bike fantasyland, an ideal mixture of wooded trails along a creek, open hayfields, sweeping hills, gullies, and—best of all—a series of long-abandoned limestone quarries that left behind a kind of unreal landscape of ponds, small cliffs, ravines, and steep climbs and descents, mostly overgrown with a carpet of grass. Into these natural features Gary had engineered a spectacular series of jumps and ramps, using a Bobcat to build up the terrain.

He showed me one of his favorite jumps, a dirt ramp higher than my head, built at the edge of a deep thirty-foot ravine.

"I won't soon be jumping over this," I told Gary as I peered uneasily over the edge. Gary laughed and made a run at it with his CR250, blasting over the ravine in a high arc (feet off the pegs for show) and landing easily on the other side.

There is an athleticism among good dirt riders now that I don't think was even imagined when I started fooling around in the dirt in high school. Watching Gary leap and fly around the farm, I realized I am never going to learn to ride like this, just as I am never going to play the guitar like Eric Clapton.

But that doesn't keep me from enjoying my guitar, and it didn't keep me from having a great afternoon on the Elmer farm. The KDX200 is a delightful bike (at least at my level), light and easy to turn and steer, with a surprising amount of low-end grunt for digging up steep hills. It's also about 275 percent better than the last dirt bike I rode.

Gary also let me ride his CR250, which even I could recognize as yet another noble step upward in suspension control and steering precision—with explosive, trigger-pull power. There's something about a real motocrosser . . . I am not worthy, but I could get addicted.

At the end of the afternoon, we each took my Triumph Trophy 500 on a lap of the farm, just for fun. And Gary pronounced it, "surprisingly, not that bad." I knew what he meant. The Triumph, which feels arthritically stiff and undergeared on the highway, actually feels more at home—more fluid, if you will—in the dirt. The suspension handles dips and ruts at moderate speed pretty well, and the engine always seems to have just the right kind of torque on tap to pull it through anything.

Nice to discover that an early dirt bike (and seven-time national enduro champion), in its element, still has some genuine magic to dispense.

But my next off-road purchase won't be a vintage bike.

When you've been away from these things for a while, the latest generation of dirt bikes makes you feel as though Time itself has reached out to hand you an unexpected gift. As if to say, "Here's what we were doing while you were away."

It's not as easy to ride off-road here in southern Wisconsin as it was in the deserts of California. You have to have a friend like Gary with private land, or else travel a fair distance to the public fire roads and trails up north. But, whatever you have to do, it's worth the effort.

I think I'm due for another dirt bike.

And, while I'm at it, some new riding gear (maybe I could sell my old stuff to Mike Myers for his next *Austin Powers* episode). If I upgrade every twenty years, I won't need any new equipment until I'm seventy-two.

April 2000

THE PENDULUM

About a month ago, I walked into a southern Wisconsin motorcycle shop, Mischler's BMW/Harley, just to look around, and immediately noticed a beautifully restored Norton 850 Commando parked among the usual lineup of used Harleys and BMWs.

"Where did this come from?" I asked a young man behind the parts counter.

"A guy named Bob Lee traded it in on a BMW R1100RS," he informed me. "It used to belong to some motorcycle journalist."

"Well, I'll be . . ." I muttered.

It was my old bike, of course. The black-and-gold 1974 Commando I sold to Bob five or six years ago.

This particular Norton was becoming well traveled. A friend of mine had found it north of San Francisco in Santa Rosa, California, in the late 1980s and hauled it down to Southern California, where we were living at the time. I bought the Norton from him and, when Barb and I moved back to Wisconsin in 1990, the bike came with us in the moving van.

I rode the Commando for about six years, then, in one of my periodic "life-simplification" garage-cleaning purges, sold it to Bob. He continued the rolling restoration I had begun, repainting the tank, polishing the metalwork to a high luster, and so on. It looked good. And now it was sitting in a dealership in Beaver Dam, Wisconsin.

"Did Bob say why he decided to trade it in?" I asked Art Mischler, the shop owner.

Art grinned. "His riding buddies finally convinced him he had to get a modern bike so he could *go* places with them, instead of just working on his Norton."

I laughed and said, "I think that's why *I* sold it."

"Want to buy it back?"

"Not this week," I said. "I recently sold two of my less practical bikes and bought an R1100RS myself. So I can *go* places," I added, "instead of just working on my Norton, so to speak."

Now, I hope you readers noticed that when Art offered me a deal on the Norton, I said, "Not this week."

I did not say, "Never."

I have learned in thirty-seven years of motorcycling not to burn my bridges. I have a genetic weakness for certain types of motorcycles, and no matter how many times I clear them out of my life, they seem to reappear in one form or another.

I've often thought of this tendency as "the pendulum," an analogy much beloved of historians, who have long noted the swings back and forth between left and right, largesse and conservatism, etc., in American government.

In motorcycling, however, the swings are not those of political doctrine, but of mood, engineering philosophy, and a relative willingness to endure either embarrassing material excess or grim asceticism in the name of experimentation and the never-ending search for truth. Of course, a lot of it also depends on whether your last bike was a joy to own or something akin to the Curse of the Pharaohs.

In any case, there's a pattern to these swings, and there may even be more than one pendulum. There are probably half a dozen, in fact, and they all have different things written on them.

One is the Masochistic Sport bike/Tolerable Road bike pendulum. I've been bouncing back and forth between these extremes all my adult life—or at least for the past twenty years. I pick that number, because twenty years ago was when I bought my first bevel-drive Ducati 900SS. After several years of that experience, I sold it and bought an all-purpose streetbike, a Kawasaki KZ1000 MK. II, which I then rode for most of a decade as my main bike.

But then the focused, unadorned purity of Ducatis began to appeal to me again and I bought another Ducati. Since then, the pendulum has swung through this cycle any number of times, mostly alternating between comfortable, useful VFR750s or various BMWs and ridiculously uncomfortable but infinitesimally lighter and more agile sport bikes. The beat goes on.

Then there's the Tragically Flawed Charisma/Predictable Utility pendulum. This might also be called the Olde British Bike/Rest of the World polarity. Essentially, you ride a British bike for a while, then get sick to death of fixing it, so you sell it for something well engineered, then start missing the unapproachable beauty and mechanical charm of some old vertical-twin or single and find yourself with another lovely leaker. A bad memory helps here.

Another is the Harley/Other Bikes pendulum. This is where you buy a Harley and enjoy riding it until you finally overdose on the tough-guy "lifestyle" posing that surrounds this marque and move on to something else, mostly out of protest.

But then you begin to miss the unique mechanical presence, real-world functionality (i.e., Road King windshield and seat), and the relaxing, torquey gait of a big twin on a cross-country trip and find yourself hanging around the Harley dealership again.

There's a Japanese/European pendulum as well, one that pits thorough, trouble-free engineering, 16,000-mile tune-up intervals, and a favorable performance-dollar ratio against the handcrafted, heart-warming eccentricities of bikes apparently designed by individuals rather than committees. Or at least by smaller committees. Who drink too much espresso.

There are no doubt other extremes of action and reaction, and I've been hit by most of them. Over and over again.

But these days, for reasons that are unclear (age?), the pendulum seems to be swinging more often toward the utilitarian, sound-value end of the arc. Maybe it's just a temporary attack of common sense—or transcendental new-millennium wisdom—but lately I've become less tolerant of pointless discomfort, mechanical unreliability, and overpriced exclusivity. I'm becoming more fond of bikes that simply work, while carrying as little sociological baggage as possible. As time goes by, I just want to ride.

But that doesn't mean I've quit thinking about my old Norton, sitting there on the showroom floor. Still beautiful, and all alone. And for sale.

December 2000

ORTHOPEDIC BIKE

It was not a great beginning for a 6,000-mile motorcycle trip, but by midmorning I was tired of waiting for the weather to clear, so I put on my clammy rain suit and hit the road. As I left our Wisconsin home and headed for Oregon, the rain hammered down in sheets while bolts of lightning actually struck trees on both sides of the road ahead of me and wind whipped the leaves into a white froth. Not a nice day.

I knew within twenty-five miles of home I'd made a mistake. Not by leaving in the rain, but by changing the handlebars on my Harley-Davidson Road King, just two days before the trip.

The stock bar made me lean forward from the waist a little too much (I thought), so I'd foolishly installed some "Big Sky" touring bars—the kind that come back to meet *you*.

Should have tried them out on a short, experimental trip. Now I was pinned, bolt upright, against the back rise of my seat with no way to change position. My lower back—always a lurking source of trouble—was starting to ache. Should I return home and put the stock handlebars back on the bike?

Nah. There's nothing I hate more than turning around at the beginning of a long trip. If the bars still bothered me after a day or two, I'd stop at a Harley shop on the road and change them. Maybe in South Dakota.

As I crossed the Wisconsin River at Spring Green, the sun came out, so I pulled into a McDonald's parking lot in Richland Center to take off my rain gear.

Naturally, I sat on a curb to peel my rain suit over my boots and immediately threw my back out. Big time.

Nothing to do but lie on the grass and pop a couple of the muscle-relaxant pills and aspirin I always carry with me (since Daytona three years ago). Then I staggered into the restaurant, got a Coke, and waited for the pills to kick in.

After about an hour—and probably just before they were about to throw me out for vagrancy—I shuffled back to the bike, put on my Malcolm Smith Gold Belt, turned around, and rode home. Carefully.

Pain pills, sleep.

The next morning, I lurched out to the garage and stared forlornly at the Harley. A long-planned vacation in ruins. My wife Barbara already had plane tickets to fly out to Sunriver, Oregon, to meet me. We had a cabin rented, and a bunch of our California riding buddies were meeting us there for a week in the Cascades. Then we were supposed to ride down the coast to Orange County for my niece's wedding. Barb would fly home and I would ride back to Wisconsin. What to do now?

I couldn't get back on the Harley because sitting bolt upright made my vertebrae feel like a stack of dominos about to topple over. Changing the bars back involved disassembling the headlight, which was too much work in my stove-in condition. Yet I had to ride.

I walked over to my old 1984 Silver Smoke BMW R100RS with 91,000 miles on the odometer and stared at it. The RS was a bike I'd sold four years ago and then just bought back from my old friend Mike Puls this summer, in a fit of nostalgia. Barb and I had ridden it to British Columbia and all through the West in the summer of 1991. A good old friend, and still running fine. Mike had just put new Metzelers on it, changed the oil, and installed a new battery.

I carefully climbed onto the saddle of the old Beemer, stretched my arms forward to the short, back-angled bars, put my feet on the roomy but moderately set-back pegs, and felt my back muscles relax as my spine stretched into a wonderful underslung concave slouch.

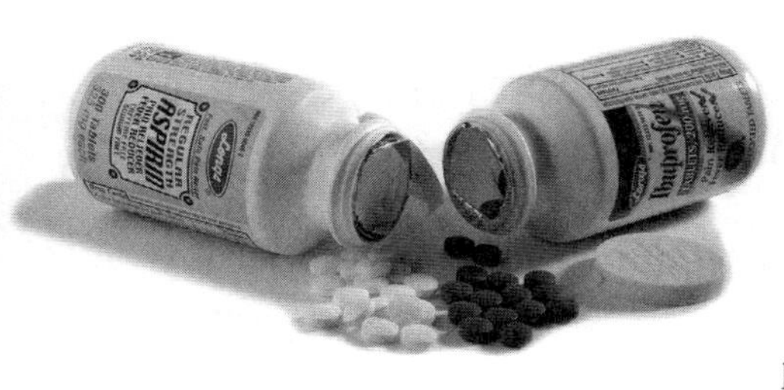

It felt . . . good.

Better than sitting in a chair or standing. Better than lying in bed and looking at the ceiling. Better than anything I'd tried.

"Maybe I should just sit here and have my meals delivered," I mumbled to myself. "Or maybe I should ride to the West Coast and let my back heal as I ride."

So I transferred my luggage—slowly—from the Harley to the BMW, put on my helmet and jacket and left.

I did four 500-mile days getting to Oregon, via Pipestone, Minnesota; Gillette, Wyoming; and Idaho Falls. Everything was fine—as long as I stayed on the bike. At gas stops and motels I had a little trouble straightening up, walking around like an early hominid from one of those "Ascent of Man" charts you see, somewhere between Neanderthal and the first amphibians. I'm surprised anybody rented me a room. No restaurant meals during the day; I snacked my way west at gas stations, to avoid being off the bike. The classic Butterfinger lunch.

The hot tub at our Oregon cabin (real rustic) helped, and I was able to take several day rides through the Cascades. Barb and I then rode down the coast to Southern California for the wedding. I changed the oil and adjusted the valves and spent four days riding home, through Sedona, Arizona; Colorado Springs; and Grand Island, Nebraska.

When I got home, my back was vastly improved. Almost normal.

A week later, I'm fine, back up to running four miles a day, riding my bicycle, and able to hoist a twenty-ounce beer can with either hand while eating nachos.

I changed the bars on the Harley, and it feels much better now. But still not quite as good as the old Beemer. After thirty-five years of riding all kinds of bikes, the RS remains my personal long-distance comfort champ. It has a wide, flat seat; a little weight on your outstretched arms and wrists; a little on the arches of your boots; with footpegs you can stand up on when you want to stretch or soak up road bumps.

It's some other kind of champ, too. With 97,000 miles on the odometer now, it used just half a quart of oil in 6,000 very hot miles of western road and ran flawlessly the entire trip. It was fast on the plains and fun in the mountains. At least a dozen times during the trip I found myself saying, "This is a great motorcycle."

Good to have the old girl back. And just in time to save the trip. If I didn't like the bike so well, I'd open a back-pain clinic and rent it out.

January 2001

RIDE HARD, RIDE SHORT

It was one of those midwestern autumn weekends you'd like to frame and put up on the wall so you could look at it all winter. Balmy and clear, with the maples nearing full color and the wind "counting its money and throwing it away," as Carl Sandburg put it so nicely, scattering golden leaves across country roads. The wind smelled like dry leaves and grain dust from corn harvesting.

Which is a good thing, because I did not. I reeked of wood smoke from sleeping in a tepee all night, next to a campfire.

Yes, we recently acquired an actual plains-style Indian tepee and have erected it on the lower pasture overlooking our creek.

We camped in it this past weekend with a bunch of our friends, roasting hot dogs and marshmallows on sticks, much as Lakota warriors might have done if they'd had a grocery store nearby, instead of ten million buffalo.

Good times, but when I got up in the morning and walked out the east-facing door into the first rays of sunlight, it was time to shift back into the present century and ride. A big day around here: The seventh-annual autumn Slimey Crud Motorcycle Gang Cafe Racer Run.

As I've noted in previous years, this—and the spring run—are essentially semi-disorganized affairs in which interesting bikes in the cafe-racer tradition are encouraged to show up at a country bar in Pine Bluff, Wisconsin, and then randomly ride about sixty miles to another country bar called Sprecher Tap in the village of Leland, for an afternoon of bike appreciation. Not a real long ride, but then the Slimey Crud motto is, "Ride Hard, Ride Short."

This year, I looked over my meager four-bike "collection" and decided to ride my black 1977 Harley XLCR. What could be more appropriate, after all, than a motorcycle that actually has the words "Cafe Racer" in its official factory designation? It's as easy as picking out clean underwear with "Wednesday" stamped on it.

A nice assemblage of bikes showed up again this year, approximately 500 of them. My favorite was a cafe-racerized "Black Bomber" Honda CB450, looking very Dunstall-period correct, with upswept pipes, a long, low tank, and a bum-stop seat. None of this prepackaged stuff, like mine.

Motorcycle Performance of Madison brought a Kawasaki drag racer they started up for the crowd. It revved with an unearthly, eardrum-shredding bark and filled the air with exotic fumes that made everyone's eyes water. It was wonderful.

Late in the afternoon, our Slimey Crud President for Life, Dr. Kenneth Clark, mounted the front steps of the Sprecher Tap to thank all the riders for being there and not crashing their brains out on the way. He said people had been calling all week to ask if the unpublicized run was being held as usual, and he said, "Of course it is! This event has taken on a life of its own. We couldn't stop it if we tried!" Much cheering.

Then, on a more somber note, he reminded the crowd that one of the founders of the Cafe Racer Run, Bruce Finlayson, had died of cancer this past summer.

"We Cruds all took up a collection and dedicated a park bench to him," Ken explained. "It's at Brigham Park, up in the hills near Blue Mounds where we all used to ride together. It overlooks the valley, at the place where we scattered his ashes. If you ride past there, you should stop and rest awhile. The bench has a plaque with his name on it."

It suddenly occurred to me, while looking out at the crowd, that you could see the faces of nearly all the people who took care of Bruce when he was sick.

Like so many families, his was widely scattered around the United States, so it was friends who looked after him when he became ill. An old friend from Michigan named Kathy did most of the hardest work, but the Cruds helped, too. We all drove Bruce around, ran errands, and put on rides and gatherings to try to condense the pungency of life as best we could. Another old friend, Phil Schilling, the former editor of *Cycle*, flew all the way out from California to visit and help out, then returned a few weeks later for the funeral.

Bruce knew everyone in the motorcycle world. He raced at Daytona in the 1960s; restored Ducatis, BMWs, and old Hondas; and wrote articles for motorcycle magazines. He was a fast guy of almost magical smoothness, who could ride like the wind.

And in the end, it was mostly just other riders who looked after him. People in leather jackets; the other family.

Odd how that happens, I thought. All but a small handful of my own good friends, after fifty-two years of life, are motorcyclists. The effect, no doubt, of some unspoken agreement on how life should be lived.

I rode home alone that afternoon and took a little detour, the XLCR hammering up the winding valley roads out of the Wisconsin River Valley, climbing County Highway F to Brigham Park, which stands on Military Ridge in a natural grove of sugar maples.

It didn't take me long to find the new redwood park bench. The bronze plaque on the backrest reads:

BRUCE M. FINLAYSON
1945–2000
SLIMEY CRUD MOTORCYCLE GANG
RIDE HARD, RIDE SHORT

I sat there for a long time, taking in the view. You can see all the way back down to the Wisconsin River Valley, and beyond, to the bluffs at Devil's Lake. It is, to my mind, one of the finest views on Earth.

Late in the afternoon, a wind came up and began to blow steadily, rustling the trees. There's something about a warm autumn wind in this part of the country that's a little unsettling. It sounds like the audible passing of time, the hidden clockwork behind the scenery, moving way too fast and sweeping another season away.

I rode home on the back roads, taking the long way around, listening to the beatific sound of those siamesed pipes until it was almost dark.

March 2001

STOCKING UP

When you live in Wisconsin, you can never be sure exactly when your last ride of the season will take place. Some years, it snows at Halloween and goes downhill from there. Other years, a strange, soft Indian autumn lingers or reappears well into December and you find yourself riding down roads flanked by stark, leafless trees through balmy air that seems to have been wafted up from New Orleans.

This past fall, riding ended for me in mid-November. We had one last gloriously warm weekend when I packed in a bunch of riding in a sort of frenzy of last-minute activity, like a Yukon gold miner loading up on provisions at the Dawson general store before winter hits.

On Saturday morning, I put on my ancient enduro gear, mounted my trusty BMW R100RS, and rode fifty miles through the hills to the cabin-in-the-woods home of my friend Toby Kirk, who had invited me to go dirt-bike riding near a place called Yellowstone Lake. Toby jumped on his XR500, lent me his XR200, and we spent the afternoon trail riding forty or fifty miles through deep woods and open fields.

When I rode back home in late afternoon, Toby went with me partway on his Triumph Sprint. We stopped in the historic Swiss town of New Glarus for a mandatory visit at Puempel's Olde Tavern for a beer and one of their famous Limburger and onion sandwiches. This cheese is so deadly, it's kept in a foil wrapper inside a Ziploc bag inside a big glass jar in the refrigerator. Like many of my favorite foods and drinks, it's an acquired taste, shunned by millions.

We dined on the front deck, under umbrellas in the sunshine, with recorded Swiss music oomping from a distant speaker somewhere up on Main Street. Guys on Harleys thundered by wearing do-rags; a Gold Wing simmered through town, husband and wife communicating by helmet hookup, like deep-sea divers out of water. A perfect day.

The next morning I woke up and, lo, it was still sunny. Much colder, but still sunny. The weather forecast warned of freezing rain by late afternoon, the map showing those nasty slanting lines moving across Iowa and Minnesota in a broad front, like the Third Armored Division. Time to ride again.

This time I mounted up on my old Triumph 500 Trophy, the green 1968 T100C I've had for years. For some reason, whenever I sense that a ride is to be my last of the year, I always head toward the Triumph. It has some benedictory significance to me, like a final blessing on the season.

As usual, the Trophy started first kick, even though it had been sitting for two weeks. I notched into first gear, headed down our driveway, and turned to cross the old iron overhead-trestle bridge that crosses our creek. The bridge has been closed for ten years, condemned as unsafe. To keep people from driving across it, county road workers dumped big piles of dirt at either end. These make wonderful jumps, of course, and I never miss an opportunity to do my *Great Escape* routine, sans barbwire, with the Triumph.

Significantly, the Trophy is the only streetbike I own that *can* jump over these mounds without high-centering or crashing in a pile of fiberglass. This is one of the reasons people used to buy Triumphs.

Over the leaps, but where to go?

I gravitated eastward about twelve miles, past the little town of Albion, and found myself drawn once more on "The Quest," a strange little private search for a lost farmhouse.

It's a charming old sandstone house with walls as thick as a castle's. My old friend Ward Paxton was renting the place the winter after I came home from Vietnam in 1970. A bunch of us went out there for a party one night and ended up taking a moonlit walk over the nearby fields. There was a small frozen lake just behind the farm and a dry-docked sailboat covered with snow on the shore. We walked on the lake under the stars and the extreme cold was making the ice harden and contract, sending thunderous cracks across the ice like jagged earthquake faults and breaking glass.

That's it. Just a small, pleasant memory filled with cosmic wonder, and I've always wanted to see the place again. I was going with Barb then, and we were all so young, nobody married yet or settled into any career, the future stretching out mysteriously like that black sky full of cold stars.

I know about where the place should be—it's only about fifteen miles from where we live now—but in 1970 we arrived in a Chevy cargo van full of people (Moroccan carpets, Boone's Farm Apple Wine, etc.) and I don't remember exactly how we got there. Or how we got home. I could call and ask Ward exactly where it was, but that wouldn't be any fun. I'd like to find it by accident while riding the Triumph around.

I narrowed the farmhouse location to one of three small lakes on the map and circled on a series of back roads, but didn't find anything that looked right. Late on Sunday afternoon, the long shadows disappeared into chilled gloom as the first clouds of that storm front moved in, so I gave up the search, headed home, and pulled the bike into my workshop just as pellets of sleet began to rustle on the roof. I didn't realize until I stopped how cold I was. Frozen through without noticing.

Unless we get some freakish warm weather, that was it; the Triumph is parked for the winter.

On Monday morning, my old pal Pat Donnelly called and asked what I did all weekend.

"Rode a couple of motorcycles," I said. "I went dirt riding with Toby Kirk, then exploring on the Triumph."

Pat told me he went riding all Saturday afternoon on his Ducati 900SS. "Beautiful day," he said. "Perfect."

The shorthand of pleasure.

You have to admire any activity whose texture and essence are impossible to explain in any quick and facile way. The best things always seem to be that way: riding, flying a light plane cross-country, canoeing a river, fishing a stream, mountain climbing, or racing just about anything.

A thousand impressions are noted and kept, to be contemplated later. And sometimes we run all winter on the voltage stored away.

April 2001

RAMBLING ROADBLOCKS

One fine summer afternoon a couple of years ago, I was batting around the hills of southwestern Wisconsin on my old Harley FLHS when I suddenly realized the hour was growing late.

Turning up the wick a bit to get home in time for dinner, I came around a corner on a small country road to find myself at the back end of a long parade of very slow-moving cars and pickup trucks. Little old ladies with gray hairdos in vanilla-plain sedans, farmers hauling milk cans, the usual rural mix.

"Okay," I grumbled to myself, "who's causing this logjam in the middle of nowhere? Manure spreader? Corn picker? Elderly farmer?"

Alas, I came around the corner and crested a hill to find the slowdown was caused by a long line of thirty-five or forty motorcycles, all chuffing along at about forty-nine miles per hour. A riding club of some kind, no doubt. The bikes were staggered down the road in perfect symmetry for at least half a mile.

The cars ahead of me, of course, were afraid to pass. They always are. First, it appears there's no room to pass because it's unclear whether any of the bikes have left a large enough gap to fit a car into the procession.

Second, people are afraid. They move out and take a look down that long column of motorcycles and can almost see the headline in the paper the next day: "Local man blunders into motorcycle gang; is badly beaten." Or worse yet: "Grandmother accidentally kills four bikers out for peaceful Sunday ride."

Both bad scenarios, and most people don't want to cause trouble. So they drive forty-nine miles per hour and wait for deliverance.

I, however, am an impatient person, so I simply put on my turn signal, twisted the throttle to its stop, and moved out to pass on a long, downhill stretch of straight road. Rather than hopscotch a few bikes at a time and risk disturbing the formation, I simply held it open and passed the group in one long swoop, waving to people as I cruised by.

On the following Monday morning, I stopped into a local bike dealership to buy an oil filter and overheard an interesting conversation.

"Yeah, it was a nice ride," a customer was telling the clerk, "but on the way home, some *jerk* (this wasn't the actual word he used) pulled out and passed the entire group." He shook his head sadly, "No lane discipline."

Could he have been talking about me? Maybe. On the other hand, he didn't mention that his group was holding up a long line of cars and trucks, so maybe it was some other club.

As I stood at the counter, I said, "I passed a long line of bikes myself yesterday, but they were holding up traffic, and I had to get home."

This news was met with silent stares. After a short, uneasy silence, commerce resumed. If we had been in the Long Branch Saloon, the piano player would have gone back to hammering out "Buffalo Gals." No harm done.

There is probably a divergence of vision here as to what riding fun is all about. I have to admit that I have never been tempted to join one of these large group rides, except as part of some charity event or an officially organized parade—a mass ride to the track at Daytona or Elkhart Lake, with cops blocking the intersections and spectators waving from the roadside. And even then, I would rather watch than participate, because you get to see more bikes and watch the people go by.

Generally speaking, I don't enjoy riding with more than four or five other bikes. I've found that beyond that number, you spend more time waiting at gas stations or watching your mirrors than you do riding. Two or three bikes is even better, and solo, many times, is best of all.

In truth, one of the things that attracts me to motorcycling is the very absence of "lane discipline," or any other vaguely militaristic concept. I observe the usual rules when riding in groups—staggering bikes, making room for others who are passing, etc.—but it's a long way from my favorite moral exercise. (Actually, I can't think of a favorite moral exercise, but never mind that for now.)

The point here is not to portray myself as some free-spirited renegade, but only to say that riding seems more fun to me when it's a little looser and you are free to make your own decisions.

A riding buddy of mine, who occasionally goes on these big Sunday rides, has pointed out that the reason these groups are often so slow is because it's the road captain's job to make sure no one is left behind. The group, therefore, travels at the speed of the slowest rider, and that rider is often a beginner.

A nice communal concept, and kindhearted at its core, but my own feeling is that a new rider who cannot maintain the speed limit should go off by himself or herself and practice awhile. No need to speed, but you shouldn't be holding up a pickup truck full of hay bales, either. Or the local Model A club.

I don't know what to suggest to these large riding clubs that would enable them to enjoy the scenery, have a laid-back ride, and still let faster traffic through. Perhaps there is already some protocol in place, such as the periodic roadside stop, or a set of predetermined gaps in the flow of bikes, and I haven't heard about it.

But something should be arranged. Blocking the flow of traffic gives motorcycling a bad name. The sport is popular now, but we are still in the minority and don't need to be earning the enmity of ordinary motorists. Or even their sympathy.

One of my favorite Gary Larson cartoons is called "Charlie Parker in Hell." It shows the famous alto sax jazz genius seated on a stool in an underground recording studio, surrounded by speakers. Nearby, the devil is seated at the control panel, grinning to himself and putting a record on the PA system. "Let's listen to a little more Guy Lombardo," he says.

We all have our own personal versions of hell, I guess, and one of mine would be an afterlife in which I am trapped in a perfectly staggered line of motorcycles, going forty-nine miles per hour through eternity. With cars backed up behind me.

To paraphrase my old riding buddy Gil Nickel, if I ever find myself on a winding road, holding up a line of cars with a motorcycle, I will carry the shame to my grave.

And maybe beyond.

May 2001

FREE BIKES AND OTHER CURSES

So there I was on Sunday night, working quietly in my garage and wondering if I would, at any moment, go up in a big orange ball of flame.

The problem was, I'd just dumped a full gallon of gasoline into the tank of a newly acquired green 1973 Honda CB350G and I'd forgotten these things have underslung cross-over hoses to equalize the fuel level in both sides of the tank. This one was disconnected, so fuel was spewing all over the place.

And I, like that famous Dutch boy, was trying to reach under the tank and plug the dike with two fingers on the spigots. Meanwhile, gasoline gushed over the bike and down the insides of my coverall sleeves, flowing into a huge puddle that spread ominously in all directions, like the dark borders of Fascism in one of those old World War II documentaries.

As I knelt in the fuel, looking in all directions for something to plug the tank, my overhead workshop furnace kicked in, igniting the propane with the usual loud WHOMP!

This was not good.

What would my friends at the funeral say? Probably, "What was he thinking?"

To which the terrible answer would be, "Apparently, nothing."

Acting decisively, I lifted the unlocked motorcycle seat with my chin and wrenched the entire tank off the bike, tilting the fuel away from the outlets. I ran outside with the tank and opened the garage doors to lean out the fumes in my workshop, which was running a little rich, you might say.

Fifteen minutes later, I had the floor cleaned and everything back in order. No fire. Saved again.

By now you may be wondering what a person of my advanced age is doing messing around with a nonrunning version of a small-bore motorcycle I last owned and rode twenty-eight years ago.

That's easy. Someone gave it to me. And I cannot turn down a free motorcycle. Especially a model of the exact year and color of the bike that was given to me brand-new as a birthday present by my wife, Barbara, when I got out of the army and finished college on the G. I. Bill and was basically broker than I have ever been.

Here's how I got it: The phone rang last week and the caller was a young motorcyclist/engineering student named Neel Vasavada. Neel and I have chatted at several motorcycle functions, and last year he showed up at one of the biennial Slimey Crud Cafe Racer Runs with his college roommate, who was astride none other than a thrashed-looking green 1973 CB350G—the last year for this model and the only one with a front disc brake.

"Gee," I said, "just like my old one. They sold millions of these bikes, but I haven't seen one on the road in years. I'd love to find one myself."

"We paid seventy-five dollars for this one," Neel said. "Found it on a farm in Iowa."

"Well, if you ever decide to sell it, lemme know," I said. (Note how this phrase just slips off my tongue, from years of practice.)

So last week, Neel called up. He'd graduated and was taking a job in California. His roommate had abandoned the old 350 in a snowdrift in the backyard of a student apartment, so Neel had pushed the bike to nearby Foreign Car Specialists, a shop where I used to work as a mechanic, and where Neel had been wrenching part-time.

"How much do you want for it?" I asked.

"Nothing," he said. "I just want to find it a home. There's no title . . ."

So naturally, I threw my aluminum loading ramp right into the back of my Ford van and headed into Madison, Wisconsin, to collect my free bike. Which was, as advertised, a little rough—slightly bent front wheel, multiple dings in the faded tank, drooping turn-signal stalks, rusted chain, etc.

Into the van it went, and I drove home glowing from that strange euphoria produced only by a new old bike that needs a serious cleanup and may actually run someday. Who knows?

At this point, before you discover the bad crank or the spent cam chain, the sun shines, bluebirds tie your shoelaces, and the world is filled with latent joy.

I spent Sunday cleaning the bike and discerned that it needed, cosmetically speaking, a new tank, seat, and mufflers, as well as a straight front wheel. Honda doesn't stock most of this stuff any more, so I called a friend named Don Omen. Don has a garage and a metal shed filled with more old Hondas than I have blues CDs. He also has a random collection of parts.

"I don't have many parts for the CB350s," Don said, "but I have a complete green 1973 CB350G that's pretty nice, cosmetically. I just bought it from a schoolteacher. It has a nice tank, good chrome, decent wheels, and tires and perfect mufflers. The seat is fair. I also have the title for it."

Every part I needed, in one neat package. "How much do you want for the whole bike?" I asked.

"Oh, three hundred and fifty dollars?"

So, for the second time in one weekend, I found myself driving home with a CB350 strapped in my van. This one looked so good, I tilted the rearview mirror so I could keep an eye on it.

Don also sold me a new factory seat for the bike, right out of the box, for $175. So I now have an immaculate $525 CB350 "parts bike" to support my thrashed free bike. Or vice versa. Or maybe two parts bikes, at $262.50 each. Hard to tell what I've got.

Of course, the costs have not ended. I also ran out and bought one new battery. And some carb cleaner. And a new clutch lever. And tune-up and disc-brake rebuild kits.

With a battery installed, the free bike started right up and ran fine. The expensive one also started and idles okay but won't rev (this is the one that spilled all the gas). Probably has the usual clogged jets from sitting and needs a carb rebuild. A couple of surprisingly costly rebuild kits should fix that.

Ah, well, I saw it coming. When you acquire a piece of your own past, you have to be prepared to pay a little something for winding back the clock. And when you've sold a keepsake you shouldn't have, penance may be due.

December 2001

CANADIAN DUCKS

"It's all set," my friend Mike Cecchini said over the phone, long distance from Bethesda, Maryland. "I've entered you in the Ducati Owners Club of Canada annual rally at Grattan, Michigan. I've rented a garage at the track, which you can share with me, and I got you a room at the Candlestone Motel near the track."

"Okay," I said, chuckling at the irresistible streamlined efficiency of it all, "you finally pinned me down. I'll be there."

Mike has been trying to get me to go to this rally for about ten years, like an evangelist attempting to lure his wayward brother to church on Christmas Eve, certain that the inspirational atmosphere will effect a permanent life change.

Normally, of course, it doesn't take a lot of prodding to make me hang around a racetrack full of Ducatis and other European bikes for a weekend, but this particular event has been cursed. I've planned to go half a dozen times, but every year, like celestial clockwork, there's been a wedding, a funeral, a family illness, or some other train wreck that's forced me to miss it. Nearly all my *Ducatisti* buddies have attended by now, but not me. No. While my friends have been dragging their knee pucks through Grattan's famous Soupbowl turn, I've been standing in front of an industrial church fan in a tux and a ruffled shirt the color of mint sherbet.

Not that I don't approve of marriage—heck, what would I be without it? Illegitimate!—but it makes a poor substitute for a track day.

This year, however, I defended the sanctity of that weekend like a pit bull with a pork chop and allowed nothing to interfere, even if I had to stretch the truth at times. ("Sorry, I'd love to attend your anniversary dinner, but I'm beginning a long prison sentence that weekend at Alcatraz. Alcatraz is closed? Damn! Well, maybe it's Devil's Island they're sending me to.")

I not only cleared the weekend for myself, but found that my pal Pat Donnelly was free and would be able to come along with his Ducati 900SS SP. We decided we would load our bikes in my van and take the Manitowoc-Ludington ferry across Lake Michigan from Wisconsin, avoiding Chicago traffic.

I had initially planned to bring my own 900SS, which is virtually the spittin' image of Pat's, but just three weeks before the Grattan rally I learned that a gentleman named Jim Blundell, who bought my old Ducati 996 two years ago, was thinking of selling it. After the usual obligatory thrashing nights of sleepless fiscal indecision, I decided to buy it back.

Jim had put only 500 miles on the 996 and had kept it in immaculate condition. How could I resist? This is a bike I bought new, broke-in myself, and ran on track days at Elkhart Lake. I sold it in a fit of practicality and have regretted the decision ever since.

"Why do you need *two* red Ducati sport bikes?" my wife Barbara asked, stunned.

"The 900SS is a better all-around streetbike," I explained, "but the 996 is a magnificent track bike." She wandered off in a trance, apparently dazzled by logic. (Note to self: Take wife to Tahiti, if you can ever afford it.)

I didn't explain to her Jack London's theory that *"I like"* are the two most powerful words in the human vocabulary, and they tend to blow away all our philosophical constructions like a house of cards. Also our retirement savings.

Anyway, I got the bike, taped the lights, removed the sidestand, changed the potentially slippery antifreeze over to water, and applied my new DOCC numbers to the fairing and sides in crisp white numerals, slightly misaligned by me for that accidental Toys-R-Us effect. Pat and I loaded our bikes and leathers, drove to Manitowoc, boarded the USS *Badger* car ferry (an oddly un-nautical name; can badgers swim?), and chugged to Michigan on white-capped seas. We drove south through Michigan's apple and cherry orchard country and got to the track just before dark. Mike's garage was the one with the Bimota flags flying, and his SB3 poised within.

We unloaded bikes, dined, slept, and the next morning we rode.

The Grattan rally has grown from a casual gathering of a few hard-core members to a big event with 194 riders and 250 bikes registered for the track sessions in five groups, based on speed and experience. Pat, who had never ridden a bike on a racetrack before, was in the orientation group. As a relatively late entry, I was placed in the theoretically tame fast touring group, which was okay with me. I hadn't been around Grattan since my very first motorcycle race in 1979, a cold, rain-drenched affair on my Box Stock Honda 400F, and I needed some orientation myself.

As it turned out, there were way too many entries in the "hot shoe" class, so every group had its share of fast riders and there was always someone to chase or—more often—blow your metaphorical doors off. And there was plenty of track time, at least four twenty-minute sessions a day—and lots of volunteer track marshals and instructors in orange vests (Mike among them) to show you the way around. As the weekend progressed, Pat and I both got progressively faster and smoother, happily without crashing.

So, did we have a good time?

Does the Pope live in the same country where Ducatis are made?

I hesitate to expound, fearing to drive up registration, but the track is fun (even run backwards, which is how we did it on Sunday), the outdoor evening track dinners (Thai and Italian) are wonderful, there are plenty of cold beers opened at the end of the day, and the Canadians who run the event have a relaxed, low-key sense of contagious good cheer that seems to permeate the weekend. It's a great bunch to hang out with.

Pat, who normally races formula cars, had such a good time on two wheels he's thinking of getting a bike strictly for track weekends (an Aprilia RS250?), and I felt that the sacrifices I made to get my 996 back were vindicated by this one weekend alone. But there are many more ahead. Mosport, perhaps, and the DOCC rally at Grattan again next year. Gotta go. Pat says he's coming back, too. The Jack London syndrome really works.

I think Mike knew that when he made our reservations.

February 2002

CAFE RACERS OF THE DISCO DECADE

Yesterday was a day of big motorcycle plans. It was projected to be one of the last warm, balmy days of late autumn by our "Storm Team" TV weather forecasters, who, I've noticed, seem to issue a forecast every day whether there's a storm coming or not. But I suppose they can't call themselves the "Dead Calm Team" or the "Gloomy Overcast Team" or just the "Usual Crappy Weather Team." It wouldn't sound dramatic. Still, I can remember when it was just "The Weather." But I guess that was too obvious.

But back to bikes. I decided to take advantage of this warm windfall of nonstormy weather by running my small collection of bikes (one at a time) to the nearest gas station for a fill-up augmented with a few ounces of Sta-Bil in the gas tank. Winter preparation for impending storage, in other words.

First, however, I had to drink my usual five cups of coffee on the front porch and jitter my way through the motorcycle classifieds in the morning paper.

"Uh, oh," I said aloud, setting down my coffee cup.

"What is it?" my wife Barbara asked, concerned.

"A 1975 400F Honda for only $900."

"Uh, oh," she said.

Low miles and excellent condition, it said, with an aftermarket 4-into-1 header and the original exhaust system. I walked to the phone and called the owner, who lived in the nearby big city of Madison, Wisconsin. We agreed to meet at his rented storage garage in a back alley, so I drove into town, first sticking a checkbook into my back pocket and throwing my ramp into the van, just in case.

When the garage door opened and I finally saw the Honda, I breathed a huge sigh of relief. The bike was rough. Repainted gas tank, dented headlight, badly restitched seat, acid corrosion on the swingarm, etc. Not for me. I used to take on projects like this when I was slightly stupider (yes, such things are possible), but I have finally come to realize that restoring Japanese bikes in bad condition will always cost you about $2,000 more than just going out and paying top dollar for the nicest one in existence.

I say I breathed a huge sigh of relief because I need another motorcycle in my garage like a hole in the head, and by *not* buying the 400F I immediately saved myself the purchase price, restoration costs, insurance premiums, and a long wait in line for plates and registration at the DMV.

Still, I am almost helpless not to go look at a Honda 400F when one appears in the paper. Why? Because it's a sublimely beautiful bike from an era of motorcycling of which I am inordinately fond, the age of the mid-1970s cafe racer.

The 1970s, of course, have gotten a bad rap on nearly all fronts: The Vietnam war fizzled to a pathetic rout; Nixon resigned in disgrace; the Iranians held our hostages forever while we did almost nothing about it; most fashions were dreadful; cars got uglier, harder to work on, and less powerful; and rock 'n' roll (with a few bright exceptions) got so bad, thousands turned to disco, just so they could dance to something.

(Egan's Universal Cultural Rule No. 8: Humans will dance. If you stop them one place, they'll go somewhere else. We are a butt-shaking species that likes to get down, get down tonight.)

But amid all this squalor and degeneration, motorcycles actually got better in those years. This is a strange thing to say, coming from a Brit-bike guy steeped in 1960s Triumphs, Nortons, Velocettes, etc., because this is when most of those companies died off. I hated to see them go, but they had their best work behind them (still available for restoration and riding, even now), and there were new and exciting things in showrooms to take our minds off the British debacle. Specifically, a fine generation of factory-built cafe racers.

Let's look at the period from 1974 to 1978, for example. In those few years you could have bought one of the following, brand new: a BMW R90S in moody Silver Smoke or shimmering

Daytona Orange; a silver-and-blue bevel-drive Ducati 900SS SP with "race-kit" Conti mufflers and big Dell'Orto carburetors; the brutally lovely black Harley XLCR Cafe Racer; that stunning classic, the Moto Guzzi V-7 Sport, or its 750S3 and 850 Le Mans progeny; the formidable Laverda 750 SFC or Jota; the muscular Kawasaki Z-1R and, of course, the jewel-like Honda 400F I mentioned, plus the 550 Supersport as well. Even England—home of the cafe-racer concept—managed to crank out the John Player Norton racer replica at the last minute.

This is an extraordinarily nice group of bikes to choose from. Unlike some of my 1960s favorites, most of these motorcycles were fast and reliable, with good brakes and handling that was either adequate or downright superb. They also had an intense mechanical presence and spare, classical styling that reflected an honest relationship with function. You didn't get the feeling the designers had run out of ideas and were just adding curves and plastic for the hell of it. Also, there wasn't much plastic.

Years ago, I wrote a piece for *Road & Track* about all the cars that were available the year I graduated from high school, 1966. I noted that it would cause no hardship for me, esthetically or functionally, if some strange law required that I buy no car built after my graduation. Just drop off my Cobra, Sting Ray, GT350, 911S, and E-Type, please. I'll get by somehow.

I'm not sure I'd want to be stuck in the 1960s, motorcycle-wise, but I could certainly get by on that batch of mid-1970s bikes. And if I were in the mood to collect motorcycles with some theme in mind, that is where the thematic center of my collection would lie, pivoting on a fulcrum placed somewhere around 1975.

I love my few modern bikes, of course, but to turn on your garage lights and find an R90S, 900SS, V7 Sport, and XLCR sitting there would not be too hard to take. With, say, a nice clean little 400F for flavor.

Almost makes up for disco. And Iran and Watergate . . . and those chocolate-brown bell-bottomed leathers with big collars flapping in the wind.

No matter how bad things are, the gods always leave us something to live for. Humans will dance.

April 2002

THE MOUSE THAT ROARED

"I've decided to get a motorcycle again," my old buddy Jim Wargula told me over the phone one Saturday morning last month. "I was wondering if I could come over and take a ride on your Ducati 900SS. It's one of the bikes I'm considering, but I've never ridden one."

"Sure," I said, "come on over. It's a nice day for a ride."

I hung up the phone and smiled reflectively (or so I imagined, having no mirror handy).

So Jim was getting another bike. At last.

Jim and I go way back. We met in college when we both showed up for freshman orientation week in 1966, lugging electric guitar cases and Fender amplifiers down the hallway and into our respective dorm rooms. Immediately thereafter, we plastered our walls with motorcycle pictures. Instant friends.

We later bought Honda 350s the same year (a CB and SL) and bought new Norton Commandos the same week, doing a lot of riding together.

Jim got out of motorcycling, though, about twenty years ago during the Soccer Dad Years, and has not ridden since, except to bum an occasional ride on one of my bikes.

Still, he never stopped looking at motorcycles. Riding was on the back burner, but always at a slow boil. All he had to do was turn the heat up a notch. Which he had apparently decided to do.

So Jim showed up at my house that Saturday morning with his old helmet and leather jacket. I fired up my 1995 900SS SP for him, rolled out the old BMW R100RS for myself, and we mounted up and headed into the hill country of southwestern Wisconsin for a two-hour ride.

When we got back, Jim slowly turned off the ignition, sat on the bike for a few minutes, and then took off his helmet.

"Well, what do you think?" I asked.

He turned and looked at me quizzically. "If you owned one of these," he asked, almost accusingly, "why would you want any other motorcycle?"

"I don't know," I admitted, glancing self-consciously at my other five bikes.

"Gotta get one," he said. "A full-fairing SP, just like this. Your assignment, Egan," he said with mock *Mission Impossible* gravity, "is to help me find one."

So that afternoon I called my pal Mike Mosiman in Fort Collins, Colorado. Mike is a motorcycle addict who spends more time on the Internet searching for motorcycle bargains than most people spend breathing. "We need an SP," I told him.

Mike called back fifteen minutes later and said, "Okay, I got on the Net and found you a nice one in Cleveland. A '96 SP with only 4,000 miles; rejetted, sprocket, high Ferracci pipes. Owner sounds like a nice guy, says it's immaculate and wants around $6,000 for it."

I passed along this information to Jim, and the next day he called me back. "Want to go to Cleveland with me this weekend and pick up a red Ducati?" he asked.

"Sure," I said, "sounds like fun."

"Oh, by the way, can we take your van?"

"Sure," I said. "Do you need anything else? Shoes or anything?"

"No, just your van, and some help loading the bike. I have shoes."

So we drove to Cleveland, picked up the bike (immaculate, as represented), and stayed overnight near Toledo on the way home. Jim bought me dinner at a Mexican restaurant and we toasted his rebirth as a motorcyclist with a couple of margaritas.

Right after we got home, winter arrived, so Jim now has the SP enshrined in his basement workshop until spring. In the meantime, he's been reading Ducati books, collecting old 900SS road tests, logging on to Ducati websites, visiting Ducati shops, and looking at carbon fiber accessories that cost more, per ounce, than good caviar.

Jim is a computer engineer for a power utility company, so I gave him one of those "I have a Ducati on my mind" posters that depict a computer desk with a bright red photo of a 900SS taped up on the wall of an office cubicle.

When I call Jim up at his office these days and say, "What are you doing?" he always replies, "I'm working on a computer program and looking at my Ducati poster."

He's got it bad.

Which I am happy to see.

Ten years ago, I wrote a column called "All My Rowdy Friends," in which I lamented that many of my old riding buddies—including Jim—had given up riding, playing guitars, or just plain going out of doors, for the tightly focused pleasures of the computer screen.

When I would call Jim at home on a weekend to talk about bikes or guitars, I could always hear his keyboard clacking in the background, even as he talked. His conversation seemed distracted by whatever was on the screen.

I work on a word processor all day myself, but trading a Sunday-morning ride in the country for a few more hours on the computer in a dark office seemed like a bad deal to me. Almost creepy, in fact, like a science fiction plot from *Invasion of the Body Snatchers*, or some story in which our brains are slowly taken over by a race of passionless aliens. It seemed to me that all forms of real physical activity—riding, hiking, flying, running, bicycling, sailing, etc.—were being supplanted by small, furtive movements of the aptly named mouse on its little foam pad.

Now, happily, this relationship seems to have been reversed, with computer technology put in its proper role as servant rather than master.

Through the dual miracles of the Net and e-mail, our friend Mike was able to find Jim a bike in fifteen minutes, and Jim was able to negotiate a deal that night. This little exchange in cyberspace set in motion the wheels of a half-ton Ford van, two days of road travel, a Mexican dinner, the whirring of a margarita blender, the acquisition of a beautiful red Ducati, and the promise of a coming summer filled with sound and motion.

When I'd call Jim ten years ago, he was talking about motorcycles but thinking about computers. Now he is still on the computer, but thinking about his motorcycle. Which sits, even now, poised for spring in his workshop. I believe this is called technological progress.

May 2002

A TRIP TO THE BARBER

Twenty-two years ago, when I was hired at *Cycle World*, my wife Barbara and I sold our house in Wisconsin and moved to California. Determined to avoid the dreaded L.A. freeway commute, we rented a little house in Newport Beach, about six blocks from the *CW* office.

As we settled in, I soon realized that Newport and its next door neighbor, Costa Mesa, were filled with small pockets of industrial magic. Hidden in the back alleys and side streets amid the palm trees were virtual rabbit warrens of garages and shops that specialized in the most arcane and exquisite crafts.

There were builders of sailboats and restoration shops that concentrated on nothing but Jaguars, prewar Alfas, old Moto Guzzis, or vintage sprint cars. Ron Wood, famed builder of flat-track Nortons, had a shop just a few blocks away. The sheer concentration of technical skill and artisanship within walking distance of our house was enough to boggle the mind. Mine, anyway.

Of all these shops, however, my favorite was a place called British Marketing, owned by a genial expatriate Brit named Brian Slark. Brian's specialty was Nortons. He had worked for Norton's off-road competition department in England before moving to the United States in 1964. He also wrote a technical column for the *Norton Owners Club Newsletter*, which I avidly read. He was a skilled rider, a desert racer who had ridden for the Greeves ISDT team at the Isle of Man in 1965.

Being on my second Norton Commando at that point, I naturally dropped by now and then for parts and advice, or just to talk about bikes. Brian and I were pretty much on the same philosophical wavelength regarding the good, the bad, and the ugly of motorcycle design, and we soon became friends.

Eventually, Brian sold British Marketing and moved to St. Louis. There, he set up a business with Dave Mungenast, searching out, restoring, and selling old

British bikes that had been neglected or forgotten in the barns and garages of the Midwest.

During all these years, Brian and I have stayed in touch. We call each other about once a month to talk about bikes, though Brian sometimes calls just to taunt me about the weather in Wisconsin.

"Took a two hundred–mile ride Sunday on my KLR650. Lovely day, seventy degrees. What'd you do this weekend?"

"Ran the snowblower for two hours," I typically reply. "Then I fed some whale meat to the sled dogs."

To make things worse, Brian and his wife Dian moved even farther south seven years ago, to Birmingham, Alabama.

"I've taken a job with George Barber as an in-house consultant at the Barber Vintage Motorsports Museum," he told me. "You've got to come down and see this collection. It's wonderful, and we're adding bikes all the time. Nice riding around here, too. Warm weather, great roads."

Since then, Brian has invited me to come down several times, but I've never managed to break free and make the trip. Until last week.

My Ducati-riding buddy Pat Donnelly called on a cold winter afternoon and said he was selling his vintage Lotus 31 race car to the Barber museum. "They're adding a few cars to the motorcycle collection," he said. "Would you like to help me tow it down there?"

On my way at last. Pat and I towed the Lotus down to Nashville, stayed overnight, and got to Birmingham at noon the next day. Slark met us at the museum, a rather nondescript industrial building in the heart of town, and introduced us to George Barber.

Barber, who made his fortune in the dairy business, immediately struck me as a modest and thoughtful man, with a real love—and knowledge—of cars and bikes. The Barber Museum may not look like the Guggenheim from the outside, but to walk in through the front door is to enter another world; you feel like a treasure hunter opening an old chest to find it filled with the Crown Jewels.

Inside, well-lighted and immaculate, are bikes beyond belief, about 750 of them. The old and the new, the great and the humble. Streetbikes, race bikes, dirt bikes. Gileras, MVs, and Hondas ridden by Surtees, Agostini, and Hailwood. Ducatis, Triumphs, Nortons, and BSAs of every era. Bultacos and Montesas. All the great Italian and British singles; Harley flat-trackers and roadracers . . .

I won't belabor the point any further (we already did a full story about the museum on these pages), but this is certainly the biggest and most comprehensive motorcycle collection in the world. If you haven't been there, go. Give yourself at least a day to look around. Two would be better.

We would like to have spent a lot more time ourselves, but Pat had to get home, and Barber wanted to show us the *new* motorcycle museum and racetrack he's building twelve miles east of Birmingham.

I had heard about the new track, but I guess I expected some kind of a small, glorified go-kart course built around a roadside museum. This is not the case. The place is huge, both in vision and scale.

It's a wide, 2.4-mile circuit set in 740 acres of rugged Alabama forest. The track swoops uphill and downhill in a natural amphitheater that is being landscaped with flowers and shrubs and grassy hillsides for spectators. It's a massive project, grander than anything I'd imagined, all in a jewel-like setting.

Barber drove us around the track in his van, unreeling a billiard-table-smooth surface full of great dips, rises, and sweepers, with lots of runoff area and enough width to permit easy passing and line changes. Especially for motorcycles. The track is being built to meet the safety requirements of all current sanctioning bodies, and it is supposed to open in the spring of 2003.

I think it may just turn out to be the nicest racetrack in North America. With the world's best motorcycle museum sitting on the front straight. In a warm southern climate.

Brian is talking about building a log home in the woods near the track and museum. On a large piece of property with a dirt bike trail. If he does, I may just stop answering the phone.

June 2002

A STEAM SHOVEL AND A PIECE OF EARTH

One of our enduring Egan family anecdotes alleges that when I was three years old I sat on the lap of a department store Santa in St. Paul, Minnesota, and told him I wanted "a steam shovel and a piece of earth" for Christmas.

He laughed (presumably like a bowl full of jelly) and asked "Why a piece of earth?"

"Because the ground is frozen," I explained, "and I need something to dig."

Nothing ever changes.

We had a blizzard here in Wisconsin last weekend. The ground is frozen and I still need something to dig.

Why? Because I acquired a marvelous new piece of earthmoving equipment recently, in the form of a dual-sport bike.

Yes, after a shameful dozen years without a dirt bike of any kind, I have finally purchased another motorcycle that doesn't automatically fall down and stick its legs in the air at the sight of gravel.

When we lived back in California, I regularly rode the desert on either *Cycle World* test bikes or my own well-worn Honda XL500. But when Barb and I moved from California to rural Wisconsin in 1990, I sold the old red desert sled, thinking to get something newer and lighter.

Alas, it didn't happen. I've occasionally ridden borrowed enduro bikes on friends' farms, but haven't bought another dirt bike myself. Seems the better off-road trails are a distant tow—or street ride—from our home, so my dirt longings have been confined to the usual tire-kicking and brochure gazing, until this past December.

Okay, the premonitory rumblings are older than that. They started two years ago, when I took a Harley sidecar rig down to Baja for a *CW* feature story. The Harley and side-hack were fun in their own way, of course, but hardly as liberating as a dirt bike in Baja. Of which there were many passing through the villages where we stopped, ridden mostly by small groups of friends off-roading it through this lovely and wild 1,000-mile peninsula, which is one of my favorite places on Earth.

This trip naturally gave me a renewed dose of Baja Fever, for which there is no cure but to ride there. I've been looking at my old maps and guidebooks ever since. So has my Ducati-riding buddy Pat Donnelly, who Jeeped the full length of the old Baja 1000 route with me fifteen years ago. We're cooking up a similar bike trip now, for this coming autumn.

Call this Dirt Bike Incentive No. 1. No. 2 came in the person of one Paul Roberts, the drummer in our garage band, which we call The Defenders Blues Band, or just The Defenders for short. Some call us tone-deaf.

Anyway, Paul's family owns a weekend cottage and 300 acres of wooded land in northern Wisconsin, and they have a dirt bike/snowmobile trail running through it. The place is also near a big recreational loop through a national forest. Paul has invited Donnelly and me to go riding there this summer.

He also says the cottage has a refrigerator capable of cooling beer or making ice cubes for margaritas, both of which are food for thought. Or what passes for thought among the Defenders.

Dirt Bike Incentive No. 3, you might say, is anecdotal. In the past year I've had at least four acquaintances tell me their dual-sport bikes, originally purchased for trail riding, have gradually become their favorite *streetbikes*, by virtue of their light weight, simplicity, and nimbleness.

So, fully spring-loaded to acquire a dual-sport bike, I walked into our local Suzuki/Honda/Yamaha shop just before Christmas (always a good, selfless place to look for gifts for the whole family) and what to my wondering eyes should appear but a leftover blue 2001 Suzuki DR650, marked down $700 in an end-of-season blowout sale. One of a handful of finalists I'd been considering.

Alas, the dealership also had a leftover DR-Z400S—another of my favorites—on sale at almost exactly the same price. So here was a real quandary.

On one hand, the DR-Z would be a much lighter (by thirty-three pounds) and nimbler dirt bike, but the DR650, with its big torquey motor, slightly wider seat—and lower seat height—might make a better blaster for the wide-open sections of Baja and the back roads of Wisconsin.

In the end, I came down on the side of the slightly better roadability of the 650. So, with Mrs. Claus' approval, I handed a bank check to my salesman friend Tym Williams just before closing time on Christmas Eve and trailered the bike home smack dab in the middle of the first real snowstorm of the season.

But a week later the snow melted, and our strange, on-again/off-again winter of 2002 continued. Since then, I've sneaked in three weekend rides on the DR. No dirt time yet (the turf is still frozen solid, and I want to get some DOT knobbies on the bike), but lots of miles on narrow, winding pavement strewn with loose sand and gravel. Lots of dead-end farm roads full of potholes and dirt. Places I would never explore on most streetbikes.

The DR works beautifully on these rough old rural roads, but what's more enlightening is how much I'm enjoying it on clean, normal pavement. Smooth, torquey, and fast, it cruises easily between seventy and eighty miles per hour and flicks through corners effortlessly. Amazing what light weight, narrowness, and wide handlebars will do for you.

Meanwhile, only time and some exposure to real dirt will tell if I should have bought a lighter, smaller dirt bike like the DR-Z. But for right now, I'm having so much fun on the street with the DR, it almost doesn't matter.

In any case, I'll soon have a chance to sample a DR-Z 400S and do a little home-brewed comparison test. My buddy Donnelly found one last week, slightly used, at a local dealership. And he actually rode it home, suffering only minor frostbite.

Meanwhile, the Baja maps are out and the guidebooks are open. Our own little vigil light flickering here in the dark church of winter.

We have our steam shovels, at long last, and we're looking for a nice piece of earth.

July 2002

GREAT MYSTERIES OF MOTORCYCLING

As a motorcycle magazine guy, I am occasionally singled out as a lightning rod for complaints—generally couched in the form of questions—about the state of the bike industry, motorcycle design, new technology and so on.

Usually, of course, I have no good answers to these questions because I'm wondering about them myself.

Just the other day, for instance, my old buddy Jim called and said, "How come all the bike magazines keep saying the Ducati 998 has a 'dated' trellis frame and 'dated' styling when it's the best-looking sport bike on Earth, easily the best-looking bike in the whole Ducati lineup, and it keeps winning the World Superbike Championship every year?"

"Beats me," I said. "I like my 996 just fine, and wouldn't change a thing on the 998."

Then I walked into a local bicycle shop owned by my friend Phil, who is an avid sport bike rider, and he asked, "Why have so many manufacturers quit providing centerstands on new streetbikes? Don't those engineers ever have to lube a chain or remove a wheel?"

"Beats me," I said. "I like centerstands, too. I can't imagine why you would leave one off anything but a pure race bike."

You see the problem. These people wonder about the same things as I do, but I don't have any answers for them. All I can do is shrug. I call these the Unanswered Questions of Motorcycling.

And there are many. Some have been asked of me by others, and some have sprung from my own incomprehension. Here's a brief sampling:

- Why would anyone make an "adventure-tourer" so tall and top-heavy that a grown man can't pick it up when it falls down?

Which it will, in the worst possible circumstances, because it's so tall and top-heavy.

• When Harley-Davidson deleted the standard tach and luggage rack from the FLHS and slightly restyled it as the Road King, why did the price go up $1,700?

• Why do television motorsports directors think really awful Thrash Metal makes a good musical soundtrack for roadracing and motocross?

• Why does a 400cc dirt bike with a thirty-seven-inch seat height and DOT knobbies go so much faster down a tight, winding road than a low, sleek 147-brake horsepower sport bike with fat, sticky race tires?

• How come there are so few Hell's Angels named Jeff or Timmy?

• Why are two-strokes so often described as sounding "cheap" or "tinny" to the human ear when, in many applications, they are clearly superior?

• Why is tin so cheap, anyway?

• Why were the fatal mechanical flaws in old British bikes so quickly evident to their owners, but not to the factory engineers and test riders?

• Why does the feet-forward cruiser riding position feel so bad when you ride fast? Why does it feel safer to lead with your head?

• How can Nicky Hayden high-side and tumble without apparent injury, while I throw my back out raking leaves?

• Why do squared-off and triangular mufflers always remind one of Buck Rogers and cheap plastic ray guns?

• Why are Montesa T-shirts still cool after all these years?

• Why can't Kenny Roberts Jr. grin once in awhile, like Dave Aldana did? And still does.

• Why do Italians style both the world's most beautiful bikes and the most comically awful?

• As a motorcycle traditionalist, why do I not miss adjusting ignition points? At all. Ever.

• Why do polyester dirt bike jerseys that are made to "wick away moisture" always smell so much worse than cotton jerseys? Why can't they wick away stink?

• Why was Kevin Cameron born with so many more brain cells than I was?

• How did I survive on the OEM streetbike tires of the 1960s? Am I charmed, or are there really guardian angels? Is this Heaven?

• Why are so few motocross champions involved in acts of terrorism?

• Why would anyone, including me, want to assume a roadracing riding position, so effective at 180 miles per hour on the straights of Road America, on a trip to the bookstore?

• Why doesn't somebody make a quiet helmet so I can ride my R100RS without going deaf or wearing earplugs that get stuck in my ears outside the restaurant window?

• How did the reborn Triumph company get all its traditional names turned around, so a Tiger is now an off-roader and a Trophy is a big heavy touring bike?

• Why does the Richard Thompson song "1952 Vincent Black Lightning" always fill a person with a wistful and expensive sense of longing, especially when he's drinking Guinness in his workshop late at night?

• Why was Mike Hailwood the last Isle of Man TT winner whose English I could decipher?

• Why would anyone try to sell a used 1998 Harley for $2,000 more than a readily available new one?

• Why do so many motorcyclists play guitar, and vice versa?

• Why don't the French make more motorcycles, when they are surrounded by the bike-mad Germans, Spanish, Italians, and Brits?

• Why do so few of our dinner guests want to watch *On Any Sunday* or *V-Four Victory* as often I do?

• If loud pipes save lives, how come so many people who have them crash?

• Why do rain-proof plastic overmitts make you feel like a Doberman trying to open a wall safe?

• Why doesn't that stinky guy in the BMW ads take a shower?

• If Kenny Roberts Sr. won his many championships, as he admits, on a diet of cheeseburgers, why does he train young racers on health food? Scientifically speaking, shouldn't he order more cheeseburgers?

• Why can we never have a president who *rides?* Are BS and motorcycling mutually exclusive?

These and many other matters remain mysteries that may never be solved.

August 2002

BACK IN THE DEZ

A few weeks ago, I called my old friend and former *Cycle World* editor, Allan Girdler, to tell him I would soon be flying in from Wisconsin for a California visit. "Want to go riding dirt bikes in the desert?" I asked. "Maybe up in our old stomping grounds around Stoddard Wells?"

"Lord," Allan said, "I haven't been up in the high desert in years. Is it still there?"

"I think so," I replied, "unless it's all been closed for riding, or developed into tract housing."

"Still got your riding gear?"

"You bet, as we say in Wisconsin. I just bought all-new stuff to replace the 1980 gear I got the year you hired me. New helmet, pants, jersey, knee protectors . . . all I need is new boots."

"What's wrong with your old boots?"

"They're the old style," I explained, "with leather straps and pegs. My back is so bad I can't spend that much time bent over, pulling on those straps. I need the new kind, with overcenter latches."

"Too bad," Allan said. "My back is okay, but my hearing isn't so good anymore."

"I tell you what," I said, "if you'll buckle my boots, I'll listen. Maybe if we get six or seven of us old guys together, we could form up as one fully functional human being."

I flew into California the next week to visit my sister, Barbara, and gave Allan a call. We had arranged to go riding on Sunday morning, with Allan meeting me with his pickup truck at the Arco station near Corona. "There's just one small problem," I told Allan. "*Cycle World* doesn't have a dirt bike I can borrow at the moment. I'll have to see if I can rent something."

"Easy solution," he said. "You can ride my XR250 and I'll ride my XR100."

"Jeez, Allan," I said, after a moment of thought, "that's a pretty small bike for the desert. Why don't you let me ride the 100, and you take your 250?"

"It'll be fine," he said. "Besides, you're bigger than I am."

Tactfully spoken. Nice of him not to use the words "big galoot" or "oafishly large" in that sentence.

So meet we did at the Arco station, driving the pickup toward Victorville and climbing into the warm, crystalline desert air. It would be great to ride in the Mojave again, a place for which there is really no substitute.

I had my first ride in the "dez," as it was called around the office, when I came to work for *Cycle World* in 1980. It was an initiation ritual in those days to take the New Guy out to the desert, set him on a dirt bike, and beat him to death with his own incompetence. If he survived, he got to keep his job.

Managing editor Steve Kimball and art director Paul Zeke took me on that first ride. They set me up with a Yamaha XT350 and said, "Follow us!" Then they took off cross-country in a cloud of dust, leading me through sand washes, over berms into sudden road cuts, up incredibly steep mountainsides, and down breathtakingly vertical trails littered with boulders and loose gravel. Needless to say, I crashed my brains out.

In one incident, I endoed the XT on a steep downhill and the engine landed on my right ankle. Which I then needed to kick start the flooded bike. I had a little trouble getting my boot off that night, and I still walk funny on that foot.

But I learned a lot, in a hurry. Dirt riding, like roadracing or flying, is the art of the possible. You have to learn what can be done and what should never be done, where to go fast, and where to go slow. That first ride was a crash course—literally—in all those skills. I survived and went back many times. As a 32-year-old desert novice, I was no threat to Brad Lackey or Bob Hannah, but at least I quit crashing my brains out. And I had fun.

Allan hit his turn signal as we came up to our traditional Bell Mountain Road exit north of Victorville and saw a sign that had once said Off-Road Vehicle Area, but now had a NO stenciled in front of those words. We pressed on toward Lucerne Valley, nevertheless, and soon saw a sign that said "Off-Road Vehicle Area 6 Miles." That was more like it.

When we got there, we pulled off and parked in exactly the same spot my first ride had begun twenty-two years ago. There were two or three other pick-ups in the area, a mixture of families putt-putting around the nearby trails, and a few serious fast guys blazing off into the distance. We changed into our gear, started the bikes, and took off in the general direction of the famous Slash X Bar, that dirt biker oasis of lunch and fluid replacement in the high desert.

I needn't have worried about Allan getting along on the little XR100. He rides the thing a lot, practicing for his favorite hobby, vintage flat-track racing, and gets around on it just fine. Allan is one of the few people I know who actually seems to be getting faster as he gets older.

The desert was especially dry this year from lack of winter rain, and the trails seemed a bit looser and sandier than usual. At least once during the morning I repeated those two mantras of low-level dirt bikers everywhere: "I hate sand," and that other classic, "I hate rocks."

Despite these two intermittent geological plagues, most of the trails were fine and we had a nice ride over to the Slash X, stopping for cheeseburgers and Cokes to replace the calories we'd squandered getting all heated up in the whoops.

By the time we rode back to Allan's truck, it was late afternoon and all the other trucks and families had packed up and left. We loaded our bikes, changed into street clothes, and Allan broke out a couple of cans of iced tea from his cooler.

I stood there drinking, looking out at the Mojave and feeling the friendly rays of the sun against my face, radiating warmth into my only slightly sore muscles. The visibility was perfect. You could see a hundred miles. The sky had the deep blueness of outer space.

I thought of Kurt Vonnegut's famous question, "What could be nicer than this?"

At the moment, I couldn't think of anything. We climbed into the truck and drove south into the growing stream of weekend traffic heading home into the L.A. basin.

"I guess the desert is still there," I said later as we hummed along the interstate.

"I guess it is," Allan said.

September 2002

RED BIKES OF THE NORTH

"Funny how we call them Canada geese," I told my buddy Pat Donnelly, "as if this were where they *really* live, even though they spend half the year down south. Why don't we call them Florida geese, or Louisiana geese?"

"I don't know," Pat said patiently. This is the kind of brilliant question he has learned to endure without flinching in our many years of friendship.

We were standing on the cold, windswept shores of Lake Huron's Georgian Bay in the little town of Blind River, Ontario, watching the geese fly north into an unseasonably chilly spring.

We'd stopped for the night at a local motel, partly because we were tired from driving all the way from Madison, Wisconsin, and partly because Blind River appears in a Neil Young song called "Long May You Run," which Young says was written about his first car, so it seemed like an appropriately mechanical, gearhead kind of place to stop.

In front of the motel sat my Ford van, loaded with leathers, helmets, lawn chairs, donut crumbs, and two Ducatis—my 996 and Pat's 900SS SP. We were headed to Mosport, Ontario, just east of Toronto, for a track weekend with the Ducati Owners Club of Canada (DOCC).

Last summer, Pat and I went to the DOCC weekend at Grattan, Michigan, where everyone had praised Mosport as "a real Ducati track," meaning fast, smooth, and full of big, sweeping turns. "You'll love it on your 996," track marshal Claus Flieschman had told me. "You can really open it up."

When you are in your mid-fifties, of course, this sometimes sounds like a mixed blessing. I have reached that unfortunate age where, at around 140 miles per hour, I begin to visualize the big circlip that holds my rear axle nut in place and wonder casually whether I put it on right. Still, I love fast tracks for sheer speed euphoria, and because hitting sixth gear on a sport bike with

the throttle pegged is a form of private revenge for the two big speeding tickets I got this year. ("You say seventy-one miles per hour is dangerously fast? In what gear? First?")

When I ran at Grattan last year, the 996 was dead stock, but over the winter I spiffed things up with a new set of Remus carbon fiber canisters, performance chip, a carbon fiber front fender (big speed increase here), a bigger rear sprocket, and a set of Dunlop D208 GPs to replace the flogged OEM rubber.

In the morning, we left Blind River headed toward Sudbury, stopping briefly at a small campground where Pat and I camped on our first motorcycle trip in the fall of 1968. A cold, rain-soaked odyssey to Montreal that would have cured any sane person of motorcycle touring forever, but had no apparent effect on us. Except for my buying a van with a heater, of course. From Sudbury, we turned south on Highway 69 through Parry Sound toward Mosport. This was not the fast way from Wisconsin to Mosport, but we'd decided to take an extra day for a great arc through the scenic north woods of Upper Michigan and Ontario on two-lane roads. Well worth it, even if we missed seeing Gary, Indiana.

Arriving at Mosport late on Friday afternoon, we ran our bikes through tech and met old friends from the DOCC. This club is the very fulfillment of my private theory that the short riding season here in the North Country simultaneously intensifies our passion for motorcycling and makes us crazy as bedbugs, much as extended prison time or six years of high school might do. It also causes us to drink beer in the evening, by way of compensation. The DOCC is a fun, lively bunch.

After tech, Pat and I checked into a Howard Johnson's in nearby Bowmanville, found a good Italian restaurant in Oshawa called Fazio's, ate enough to unravel my Valentino Rossi Look-Alike Weight Reduction Plan, and then got up early the next morning to make the orientation session for riders who'd never seen the track before. An hour later, we were lapping.

Claus was right. Mosport is a great Ducati track. It's also just a great track, period. A high-speed rollercoaster nestled in real hills, with blind brows, hero dips, and steep climbs. Big fun. My new pipes sounded much faster than the old ones, the chip and gearing were perfect, and the new tires were the best I've ever ridden on.

When I went out for my first open session, I was reminded why Ducatis win so many races: *(a)* They put power down in big, broad, useable gobs of friendly torque at any rpm; and *(b)* they don't want you to fall down. The chassis is your friend—it absorbs your own imperfections like a blotter. Always a good thing, in my case.

I ran a little hot over the hill into Turn Four on one lap and suddenly remembered the immortal words of my friend (and fellow DOCC member) Mike Cecchini, who once said, "When you get in trouble, just lean over farther." Simple advice, but on the 996 it always works. So far.

And it seemed to work for a lot of people. Speeds were high, but there were only three minor crashes all weekend, among 200 entrants.

Most of the bikes were from the 916 family, with 900SSs next in popularity, mixed with Monsters, 851s, 888s, a few Guzzis, Aprilias, Cagivas, and a good selection of vintage bikes—bevel-drive twins, singles, and a few Harley-Aermacchis. The event is for all European and American bikes, but Ducatis are the glue that holds the thing together.

After our last track session on Sunday, Claus invited a bunch of us back to his house, twenty minutes from the circuit, to have pizza and beer while we watched World Superbike at Silverstone. There, Troy Bayliss put on the most amazing display of rain riding—or riding of any kind—I've ever seen. On his red 998.

On the drive home the next morning, I said to Pat, "What would all of us have been doing this weekend if Ducati had gone broke, which it almost did, back in the 1980s?"

Pat thought about that for a minute, and then he said, "I don't know."

I didn't know, either. It was another of those pointless questions, like the one about Canada geese. Sometimes the world unfolds just as it should.

October 2002

A TALE OF TWO SUZUKIS

Never has the ownership of a well-liked motorcycle been so tragically brief.

As mentioned in this column a few months ago, I bought myself a leftover 2001 Suzuki dual-sport DR650 last winter, as a critical part of my grand scheme to take a long off-road Baja trek next fall. That, and do some trail riding in northern Wisconsin with my friend (and ace drummer in our garage band) Paul Roberts. Paul's family owns a 300-acre farm there, with lots of woods and a cabin on a lake, right next to the Chequamegon National Forest trail system.

After riding the bike for a couple of weeks, I decided that it was *(a)* one of the most fun, most carefree, go-almost-anywhere road bikes I'd ever owned, and that *(b)* it was a little large and heavy for the dirt riding I had in mind.

So I went creeping back to Tym Williams, my salesman friend at the local Suzuki shop and said, "Just for the sake of conjecture, how much would it cost me to trade the DR650 in on one of your leftover DR-Z400S models?" He took this proposition to the unseen sales manager in the glass booth and came out with a trade-in deal that was only about $300 above the "No way, no how" maximum I'd contrived on my way to the dealership.

I stared blankly into space for a moment and then said, "Oh, what the hell. Sure, let's make the trade." Then I added, "Life is short."

This is a phrase people my age use to talk themselves into almost anything. It's probably sold more Harleys, among other things, than all the advertising on Earth. No one above the age of fifty wants to waste a summer (especially a short Wisconsin summer) riding almost the right bike. We have to make lightning decisions here.

Anyway, I made the trade, signed the papers on the 400, and five minutes later my friend Doug Haltine, who is a complete singles nut, walked into the dealership and bought my "old" DR650 before the engine had a chance to cool. It's a crazy world.

So away I rode on my new blue DR-Z, heading home in a misting rain. The 400, I quickly verified, is nowhere near as pleasant on the highway as the DR650—it's more wound-up and edgy, higher-strung and lower-geared, with a bit more vibration and less roll-on torque. It likes to hum down the road at sixty or sixty-five miles per hour, while the 650 wanted to cruise at eighty. The 400 is also about three inches taller, and more awkward at stop signs.

But a quick run down some pathetically short trails I'd cleaned up around the edge of our property (two days with a rented Brush Hog) revealed I'd made the right decision for serious woods riding. The DR-Z is simply lighter (thirty-three pounds), narrower, and more agile, with better gearing for the dirt. As a friend of mine said, "The 650 is really a streetbike for people who like to ride trails once in a while, and the 400 is a dirt bike that can legally cross the highway."

Except for the dual-sport tires, of course, which are no great shakes in the dirt. I got out my fine collection of long-neglected tire irons and installed a set of Pirelli MT-21 DOT knobbies—without pinching the tubes, for once. Then, with Baja in mind, I ordered and installed an IMS four-gallon plastic gas tank (which almost fits, after much grunting, shoving, and filing of mounting holes, befitting the imprecise nature of plastic) and put on a set of Moose brush cutter–type handguards. Ready to roll.

And roll we did. Paul invited me and three of his longtime dirt-riding buddies—Dean Ellison, Larry Wiechman, and Brian Barker—up to the cabin for a weekend of trail riding. Not to mention watching the sun go down over the lake, listening to the loons, and standing around a bonfire at night while drinking the random beer and/or margarita and watching Monty Python's *Holy Grail* on the rustic VCR in the cabin.

Despite this riotous northwoods nightlife, we managed to rise and ride early both mornings. On Saturday we hauled our bikes to a trailhead, suited up, and hit the trails. A sixty-five-mile loop of them, with a stop for lunch at a lakeside bar-and-grill. Paul rode (should say, "rode the wheels off") his Polaris four-wheeler; Brian, the Honda CR250 he motocrosses regularly; Dean, an elegantly simple, fast, and hard-starting 1982 Husky 430 two-stroke; and Larry, his trusty 1983 XR500 Honda. These guys have been riding dirt bikes all their young lives and they ride like bats out of Hell, while I'm just getting back into it, so I had to ride my butt off to stay within dust-eating range. But pushing yourself is how you learn, and I picked up some speed and had a great time, on two fronts.

First, I was unprepared for the general wonderfulness of the trails. Wide, sweeping corridors through the forest with tight turns, fast turns, S-bends, dips, hills, hard-packed dirt, loam, rocks, sand, water crossings, and mud wallows. Mile after mile of uncrowded trails hard enough to be challenging, but not brutal enough to ruin the day for a novice.

The other nice surprise was the DR-Z. The motor, which packs only moderate wallop on the street, works superbly in the dirt. It pulls with almost electrical smoothness from no revs to its considerable redline, and buzz-saws up steep climbs and through heavy mud (except when you high-side while cleverly switching ruts in the middle of a bog) with a kind of intrepid, unstoppable tenacity.

Handling? Accurate, easy-turning in the rocks, stable in fast turns, with a plush ride that seems to soak up anything. At the end of the day, I couldn't think of a single complaint, and the bike had already come to feel like a good friend.

Now that I'm home, I must admit that I miss the smooth, torquey DR650 a bit as a back road exploring bike. If I were a richer guy, I would have kept it for just that, as I am not tempted to ride the knobby-shod DR-Z much on the street.

But for the woods of the north, the switch was a good one. And probably for Baja as well. When you are truly off-road, lighter weight is always the vortex with the irresistible draw. The DR-Z400S is no featherweight motocrosser or pure, stripped-down enduro bike, but it's very good indeed for a bike that can legally cross the highway.

November 2002

A MORNING IN ITALY

My brother Brian—whose job has him traveling even more than mine—and I are solidly agreed on at least one thing: When you arrive in a strange city, the best way to find out where you are—physically and culturally—is to get up early in the morning, leave your hotel, and go running and/or walking.

Which is what I did recently in Borgo Panigale, Italy.

Borgo Panigale is the suburb of Bologna where the Ducati factory is situated, and I was there for World Ducati Week, staying at the conveniently close Amadeus Hotel.

While I am not normally an early riser, the usual jet lag tricked me into thinking it was morning at about midnight, so after a largely sleepless night of watching incomprehensible soccer matches and an old John Wayne Western dubbed into Italian, I finally threw myself out of bed just before dawn and put on my running shoes.

Hitting the street in front of the hotel, I headed down the *Ave. Marco Emelio Lepido* toward the Ducati factory, which was only about five blocks away. The streets were almost empty—Italy is not a country where people feel duty-bound to rise in the dark and rush to work so people will think of them as "team players." The random Fiat, a few scooters, and bicycles went by. A bakery and coffee shop opened its doors and unrolled the awning over its outdoor tables, the aroma of hot-baked bread tumbling out in a thick cloud of seduction. Yet I did not tarry.

Onward I ran, turning onto a narrow sidestreet called *Via A. Cavalieri Ducati*, past a bus-stop shelter with a big poster of Valentino Rossi holding up a bottle of *Nastro Azzuro* (Blue Ribbon) beer. Presumably not from Pabst. Will the day ever come in the United States when a roadracing hero is a poster boy for a major brand of beer? You've got to love Italy.

Inside the guarded gates of the Ducati factory, WDW2002 pennants were flying. Rows of 998s, Monsters, and STs were poised for our upcoming press ride to the racetrack at Misano on the Adriatic coast, and the walls of the factory were painted with huge murals of the World Superbike team in action.

I trotted as far as I could around the factory grounds without running onto the nearby *autostrada*, then doubled back and found myself passing *Santa Maria Assunta*, an old church of faded brick, where bells in the tower began ringing and mostly elderly people converged from different parts of the neighborhood for morning mass.

On the corner, a flower shop was selling bunches of flowers to dozens of old women dressed in black, who then made their way by foot or bicycle down a long tree-lined lane to the gates of a walled cemetery. The lane had bronze plaques with flowers on them placed every three feet for its entire length, bearing the names of Borgo Panigale's war dead from World War I. A lot of casualties for what must have been a very small village in 1918. All the young and fit, the romantic, and the energetic. What would it do to a little town like this? Tear the heart out of it, probably. Yet there was quite a bit left. Borgo Panigale, Ducati's hometown, is to motorcyclists, at least, a very large part of the heart of Italy.

A man in blue coveralls unlocked the cemetery gates, and the gathered crowd of visitors streamed in. I walked discreetly into the edge of the cemetery and looked around. A huge place, extending behind the church. Some of the tombstones looked very old and weather-beaten, while others followed the twentieth-century Italian practice of embedding a photograph of the deceased in the headstone. Not such a bad idea. Seeing the portrait of a son killed in World War II or a mother who has passed away adds a dimension beyond the chiseled name. Faces tell us everything, and contain their own stories.

Strange, but on previous brief visits I'd always thought of Borgo Panigale as a sort of modern, created-from-nothing industrial park, appended to Bologna in the last fifty years or so. But on closer inspection it was an entirely real town with a long history. As a friend of mine once said, "Every acre of Europe has been owned by hundreds and hundreds of generations, going all the way back to Neolithic times, and they've all added a little something, or taken something away."

You could feel that bone-deep age even in the neighborhood around the Ducati factory. In the backyards of nearby homes you saw old wells, fragments of ancient stone walls, gnarled olive trees over tiled patios, roof timbers in barns too large to have come from a modern forest. And in those same backyards were Fiats and Alfa Romeos. And Ducatis. Shiny new things that, nevertheless, managed to look as though they belonged.

As I jogged back to the hotel, traffic was picking up. In the flow were a surprising number of Ducati Monsters. These quick, agile bikes seem to be the new national urban motorcycle of Italy, a high-performance Vespa alternative.

When I got back to the hotel, I showered and went down for breakfast, to get ready for our mass ride from Bologna to Misano. I drank dark roast coffee, ate a typical Italian breakfast of buttery cheese, dark bread, and sliced sausage (they don't call this place Bologna for nothing), and found myself wondering how much of my enthusiasm for Italian bikes was derived from the culture that produced them.

Just as every British bike had a certain appealing Druidic content built into its engine and frame, suggesting narrow lanes, greenwood forests, and thatched roofs, Ducatis seemed to have evolved naturally from the roads and villages and hills that surround the factory. When you park a red Ducati against a stone wall on the *Via Emelia*, it looks perfect, just as a Norton does when it's parked in front of a half-timbered pub. Not a trace of historical discontinuity.

In the end I decided that, while I like riding motorcycles, I may also be using them to pay homage to foreign places where I feel inexplicably at home. The purchase price is partly tribute, like coins in the collection box when we light a candle in an old cathedral.

December 2002

THE THOUSAND-MILE RIDE

For many years, our little local motorcycle club of like-minded sport bike misfits, the Slimey Crud Motorcycle Gang, has staged an annual Thousand-Mile Ride—of widely varying length.

This event has proved useful as an adjunct to club solidarity and an acid test of saintly tolerance toward those who have a mystical sense of passing time, or can't program alarm clocks. The foul-ups and misunderstandings have been legendary—mostly thanks to the use of high-quality earplugs—but somehow the Gang has always sallied forth and returned home more or less as a unit, having had good fun.

Most of these rides have been planned around the concept of free housing, the route chosen to include one or two stops at cottages or homes owned either by members themselves or by distant friends and relatives whose memories often need prompting vis-à-vis their relationship to some nearly forgotten Crud. ("Hi, Uncle Bob! Remember me? Little Jimmy? I'm all grown up now, and these are my motorcycle friends!")

Unfortunately, I have never managed to go on the annual Thousand-Mile Ride before, thanks to scheduling errors where I foolishly let work or family responsibilities interfere with the main business of riding. Which, of course, is what we were put on Earth to do, good works notwithstanding.

So this year I kept my calendar clear and was pleased to see that the proposed route would take us from Madison, Wisconsin, all over Michigan's Upper Peninsula (UP) with a dip into the LP to join forces with our Detroit chapter at the weekend getaway farm of Greg Rammel. A nice long ride (1,600 miles, actually) on beautiful roads.

But what bike to take?

My 1995 Ducati 900SS SP would be fun, except for the slightly stiff springing and the lack of hard luggage. The Harley Electra Glide Standard I acquired last spring (my fourth in a long series of baggers; I can't seem to stay away from these things) would be pleasant to ride, except for the usual Harley Quandary—the stately, mellow Electra Glide can keep up only with itself or other Harleys. And the Cruds are a hard-ridin' bunch, mounted mostly on Ducatis, BMWs, Cagiva Gran Canyons, 1200 Bandits, etc. Fast bikes that like winding roads.

In the end it came down to, as it always does, my silver 1984 BMW R100RS, which had just turned over 100,000 miles and now had an odometer full of zeros. Reborn, as it were. The old Beemer still had everything I needed: hard luggage, good wind protection, 240 miles of fuel range, decent handling, and 135 miles per hour of available speed. As an added bonus, fellow Cruds Randy Abendroth and Tom Pirie would also be taking their own R100RSs, so we could ride in close formation and do our own impression of the Berlin Police Department.

In preparation for the trip, I cleaned and detailed the aging Beemer, bead-blasted and repainted the stone-chipped black valve covers, changed the oil, and adjusted the valves.

And, bright and early one Wednesday afternoon, we were off. Keeping true to our club motto, "Ride Hard, Ride Short," we stopped almost immediately for the night in Appleton, Wisconsin, to pick up Tom and eat the requisite huge dinner at a roadside supper club.

Daylight took us through Green Bay, Escanaba, and Manistique, across the high and windy Mackinaw Bridge down to the crossroads village of Levering, Michigan, near Greg's farm. Some of us stayed at the farm, while the overflow took over a nice little motel in Levering, where we sat at picnic tables on a warm summer night and drank a few beers and some excellent cheap wine from a liquor store across the street whose neon signs winked at us seductively all evening, nearly driving us mad with desire.

In the morning, my roommate Tom took a couple of Excedrin and said, "I will never drink that much again as long as I live. Maybe less or maybe more, but never that exact amount."

On Friday, we explored the Grand Traverse Bay area, then went out to Greg's farm, where we rode dirt bikes through the hills and had a fine party, with much food. It was already shaping up into what I would later call "The 2002 Health and Fitness Tour." Ride, eat, drink, sleep, ride. For six days all our exercise came from walking to restaurants.

Saturday, twelve of us rode 320 miles up to Copper Harbor, stopping for lunch at Seney, where Ernest Hemingway famously got off the train to go trout fishing when he returned, wounded, from World War I. We spent a day exploring the great winding roads along the south shore of Lake Superior, then rode across to the Lake of the Clouds, and down through the Porcupine Mountains to Mike Puls' cabin in northwoods Wisconsin.

Most of the guys stayed at Mike's the next day for fishing and boating, but I had to ride home because we had guests arriving that night. I said my goodbyes and rode the last 250 miles solo in a light, misting rain, after five days of perfect weather.

When I got home late in the afternoon, Barb was off at work, and it was cool and silent in the house. I sat in a chair in the living room, my ears still ringing from wind and highway sounds. Looking across the room into my office, I could see a large stack of mail cascading down onto a sprawl of previously unanswered mail. Next to the phone in the living room Barb had left a list of 14 phone messages. And the light on the answer phone was blinking with five new messages. Just outside, the lawn needed mowing.

Back to the world of faxes and phone calls, meetings, e-mails, doctor's appointments, home repair, and work. For a whole week, I'd almost forgotten about all of it, living purely in the present, like one of the Lost Boys in *Peter Pan*, or a sailor on an old whaling ship, cut off from land and all its communications.

I sat there and made a private vow not to miss any more Thousand-Mile Rides with my friends. They are what all the other stuff is for, and the only way most of us have left to run away to sea.

January 2003

A PURE RACE BIKE

It was just like being thirteen again. That was the age at which I illegally rode my homemade Briggs & Stratton–powered minibike all over the back roads of Wisconsin one summer. No driver's license, plates, headlight, or brake lights. Just me and the minibike, chugging along at fifteen miles per hour and keeping a sharp eye out for the Juneau County Sheriff. And hoping, if caught, to throw myself on the "earnest, resourceful youth who could be doing worse things, like sniffing glue, after all," defense.

And here I was again last weekend, at the somewhat overripe age of fifty-four, riding a totally illegal motorcycle down the back roads of Wisconsin, keeping my eyes peeled for cops, and hoping to avoid arrest. No headlight, plates, or brake lights.

Only this time I wasn't exactly chugging. "Crackling" would be a better word, though still at modest speed, thanks to a draconian break-in procedure.

The bike in question was a brand-new Aprilia RS250. I had, just the day before, purchased it from my salesman friend Scott Siem at a Ducati/Aprilia/MV Agusta shop called Corse Superbikes in the little town of Saukville, Wisconsin, near Milwaukee. The RS250, for those who are not familiar with it, is a race-track-only GP-replica with an Aprilia-modified Suzuki RGV liquid-cooled, 249cc, two-stroke, ninety-degree V-twin engine, said to put out sixty-eight brake horsepower and to propel the 295-pound bike (dry) to 137 miles per hour.

This bike was at the heart of the now-defunct Aprilia Cup Challenge, a one-make race series introduced in 1999. In the United States, the RS is now used mostly in club racing and for track days. Europeans have a street version of this bike with lights and turn signals, of course, but in this country only the stripped-down race version can be imported and sold.

For the past three years, I've been doing track weekends on my Ducati 996, leaving the headlights taped and numbers on the bike. No road use at all—for that I prefer my good old 900SS. The 996 is a wonderful track bike, but heavier than it has to be for its current purpose. So I had planned, over this coming winter, to throw some money and time at the 996, to lighten it up with a monoposto race seat, headlight-free upper fairing, carbon fiber instrument pod, genuine magnesium race wheels, etc.

We're talking $3,000 to $4,000 here, added to a motorcycle that was already the most expensive new bike I ever bought. Not to mention the $2K worth of canisters, chip, sprockets, etc. already added. I was getting into serious money here, for a bike that could easily be thrown down the track at any moment by a clumsy oaf such as myself.

Anyway, last month I took the 996 to a Ducati Owners Club of Canada track weekend at Grattan, Michigan, with my old buddy Pat Donnelly and his 900SS. The day before we left, Pat called and said, "My next door neighbor, Jeff Schiffman, would like to come with us. He just bought a slightly used Aprilia RS250 yesterday."

"Great!" I said. "Maybe I can bum a test ride and find out if I really want one of those things."

I told Pat I'd been looking at the Aprilias ever since they were introduced at Daytona three years ago and was wondering if I could live with a two-stroke and its legendary peaky powerband, oil-injection, ring-ding exhaust note, lack of engine braking, and all the rest. I do, after all, think of myself as "a four-stroke guy."

But bum a ride I did. Jeff kindly let me take the RS out for a full twenty-minute session on a hot Saturday afternoon at Grattan. A jab of the kick starter had it running, and I was off.

Impressions?

Instantly light, agile, quick-turning, and fun. The engine pulls surprisingly well from 6,000 rpm up, with broad, useable torque up to about 9,000, when a nice "Holy smoke!" rush to its 12,000-rpm redline kicks in. Easy to ride, and the least amount of work I've ever done in fast transitions. When I came in from the session, I was elated. Also about half as overheated and sweaty as I'd been on the 996. A few people warned me I wouldn't like the lack of compression braking, but I hardly noticed. I tend to brake hard and reassuringly early (not to say panic) rather than coast into fast corners, without much transition time.

The RS250 had nowhere near the wonderful, soul-satisfying torque of the 996 exiting corners, nor the big-bore muscle while blasting down the straight. It also had cheaper hardware and cobbier paint. But it was very quick and lots of fun. And I think I was getting through the snaky back section of Grattan faster and more easily. Compared with everything else I've ridden on a track, it felt almost weightless.

So, when I got home, I debated whether I should put more money into lightening and de-streetifying the 996, or buy a pure race bike that started out 140 pounds lighter from the factory. After a few weeks, I reluctantly decided to sell the fast and lovely 996 and try something completely different, variety being the spice of life and all.

Back when I raced Box Stock Kawasaki 550s and 750s in the early 1980s, I always imagined my next track bike would be a Yamaha TZ250, a pure racing motorcycle without one ounce of fat.

But then my friend and colleague Jeff Karr actually bought a TZ250 and raced it for a season. He said it was a blast, but very maintenance-intensive. Lots of pistons, barrels, bearings, gaskets, etc. Working on the bike, he said, was a full-time hobby. The polar opposite of cheap, worry-free Box Stock racing.

So I gradually let the 250 GP dream drift away, like so much Castrol premix smoke. Never did ride a race bike that hadn't been on the street first.

And now, twenty-one years later, here I am, running up and down the little country road near our rural home on the nearly weightless RS250, laying down a light haze of two-stroke smoke, and putting on the required break-in miles. And watching for cops.

Just as I was at the age of thirteen.

If I get arrested, I don't know if they'll go for the "earnest, resourceful youth" defense again.

Maybe I can tell them I'm senile.

February 2003

THEM ICE-COLD BLUES

It rained all night the day I left
The weather it was dry.

And cold, apologies to "Oh Suzanna" songwriter Stephen Foster. Unseasonably cold, and windy. One of those late-October days when the dark mood of the sky tells you the party's over, chum. A distinctly winter wind was raking across our yard with icy fingers, rustling the leaves. I looked at the thermometer outside. Thirty-one degrees. Fahrenheit.

And standing nearby in our garage was my Harley Electra Glide Standard, packed and ready for travel. It was poised for a 640-mile trip from Wisconsin to Nashville, where I would visit my brother and his fiancée, then borrow a new Triumph Bonneville, and ride it down to the Mississippi Delta.

I'd been asked to do a Blues Country story for our annual *Adventures* magazine, and had been looking forward to the trip all summer.

Except summer, it seemed, was gone.

The overnight low had suddenly dropped twenty-five degrees, and the Weather Channel showed the Canadian jet stream looping deeply south like a deadly blue snake. So I put on my long johns, wool sweater, insulated touring boots, street leathers, and Belstaff jacket. I briefly considered wearing my two-piece Aerostich suit, the warmest thing I own, but decided it was too unrustic for a descent into the hardscrabble Delta. Can't have a hellhound on your trail when you're wearing Gore-Tex. Besides, it might suddenly warm up again down there, and I'd want to wear just my blue jeans and leather jacket.

I walked out of the house like the Man in Black, sweating profusely, but instantly feeling the heat leach out of my being like a horseshoe quenched in cold water.

I went out to the garage and fiddled around my luggage for a while, cleaned my face shield a second time, and then came back into the house.

I got another cup of coffee and looked out the window at our 1988 Buick Park Avenue, the luxurious "winter salt car" I'd bought three years ago for a mere $1,800. At 146,000 miles, it still ran perfectly. Leather upholstery, superb sound system . . . heater . . . cupholders . . .

Barb, who was reading the paper, looked up at me. "I thought you were leaving early, so you could be in Nashville before dark," she said. "It's almost 8:30 now."

"Yeah, I know," I said, "but frankly I'm thinking of taking the car down to Nashville. It's really cold out there."

"Oh no!" she said. "You've been planning this trip all summer. It's half the reason you bought the Harley, for those long highway trips."

I looked at Barbara and wondered if I should accept spine-stiffening advice from a person wearing a bathrobe and fluffy slippers with bunnies on them. But she was right. I had planned this ride for a long time. And it might be the last ride of the year.

So I rode off into the frosty morn.

All day I rolled south, down through Illinois, across the Ohio and Tennessee rivers, and into Nashville twelve hours later, just after dark. The big Harley's bat-wing fairing protected my upper body well, but my feet and shins quickly went numb. At Bloomington, I experimented with some vinyl lowers I'd borrowed from a friend, snapping them over the crash bars. These protected my feet, but forced more cold air up into my chest and face. A bad trade. I took them off.

By the time I reached my brother's house, my lower legs were like two blocks of wood. Nothing three hours in a scalding hot shower couldn't fix, however, and I soon recovered.

I traded the Harley for the Bonneville at a shop called Castle Motorsports, rode the twisting Highway 100 to Memphis in a cold rain, then spent four slightly warmer days touring the Delta. Then it was back to Nashville, and home on the Harley.

Riding north, I passed the gates of Fort Campbell, Kentucky, where I shivered my way through winter basic training in 1969, and the air was *still* frigid. I stopped in Mount Vernon, Illinois, and bought some thicker wool socks from a sporting-goods store.

Just after dark, I stopped for gas in Rochelle, Illinois, bought a newspaper, and stuffed it in my jacket for more insulation. The sales clerk said,

"I can't believe you're riding a motorcycle on a night like this."

I rolled into our driveway at 9 p.m. with a fairly advanced case of them low-down shakin' chills, after eight days and 2,300 miles of riding.

Nothing three hours in a scalding hot shower couldn't cure.

The next day, I went out to the garage to unpack and stopped for a moment to ponder the old Buick. Ah yes, the Buick. Quite a device. Heater, cupholders, windshield wipers, windows . . . roof. When the weather got bad, you couldn't beat it. Yet, I suddenly realized I hadn't wished for one moment of the trip that I'd taken my car instead of the Electra Glide.

I have found that cars, unless they are old and funky (MG TC) or very high performance (Ferrari), or both (Cobra, E-Type Jag), tend to dull our memories of travel, while motorcycles amplify them and etch them clearly in our minds.

Some years ago, I wrote a column about overnight lodgings and noted that I had never forgotten a campsite nor clearly remembered a motel room. Exposure to weather nearly always sharpens our perceptions. Likewise, I can still remember the two years I spent in the army, almost minute by minute, because much of it was hard and challenging—and mostly outdoors. But the earlier years I spent in school have been largely reduced in my memory to a handful of highlights and low points.

Road travel is like that, too. What we call luxury is sometimes nothing more than the absence of sensation. Too much ease becomes a sort of opiate. Feels good, but you forget where you are. And where you've been.

Which is all a long-winded way of saying I'm glad Barb talked me out of taking the Buick.

Next year, however, I might take the Aerostich suit and wire up my electric vest. In humans, unlike computers, there is such a thing as too much memory.

March 2003

FAMOUS HARLEY MYTHS

Rode my large Electra Glide to the doctor's office a few weeks ago, right before the Moon of the Frozen Garage Door Hinges arrived and forced me to store my bikes for the winter.

I strode into the examination room carrying my leather jacket and helmet, and the nurse—the one who takes your blood pressure and makes you put on that backless gown that makes you feel like a cast member from *Night of the Living Dead*—said cheerfully, "Looks like you rode your bike in today. What kind of motorcycle do you have?"

"A Harley-Davidson," I admitted. (I always hate to say this because it's such a common answer these days. How much more interesting to say, "I rode in on my Velocette Venom Clubman" or "my trusty Tohatsu Run-Pet." Anything to break the monotony.)

"Oh," she said, her eyes lighting up somewhat, "my husband would *love* to buy a big Harley, but we don't have $25,000 to spend on a motorcycle right now."

I frowned as she pumped up the boa-constrictor cuff that slowly squeezed the life from my rippling bicep and said, " Well, I don't either, but my Electra Glide Standard was only $13,700."

She smiled and looked at me as if I'd said she could get a new Mercedes for about the cost of a dozen eggs, and then handed me a striped, backless gown. "Put this on," she said. "The doctor will see you in a few minutes."

So I shed my motorcycling identity and soon sat shivering in that humiliating gown, thinking about this misconception of Harley prices.

Ah, yes, the $25,000 big twin. I'd heard this a thousand times. Okay, maybe only a few dozen times, but it's surprising how often you tell someone you have a Harley and that person says, "Must be nice to have $25,000 to blow

on a motorcycle." Somehow, in the public's mind, any big, glittering Harley has become fixed at that price. Where did this idea come from? Boasting owners with a taste for exaggeration?

Okay, in truth, I suppose it is possible to spend that much. If you buy a bike from one of those rip-off, "Bikes in stock now!" dealers and then glom on a big-bore kit and a couple hundred pounds of chrome eagles, you could probably stagger out of a Harley shop having been shorn of $25,000. But then you can do the same thing by getting drunk and ordering too much Chateau Lafite at a French restaurant. An act which is uplifting, but not required.

In any case, the $25,000 Harley is not the only odd myth in circulation; another favorite of mine is the odd notion that, "Harley riders trailer their bikes everywhere."

For some reason, many nontouring riders I know have the impression that most Harley riders haul their bikes to within 300 yards of, say, Sturgis and unload them in a Wal-Mart parking lot before putting on their riding duds and parading grandly down Main Street.

People who believe this probably are not getting out of the house often enough. Or out on the open road. I rode to Sturgis on my Ducati a few years ago and found myself in a virtual lemming-fest of long-distance Harley riders converging from all points of the globe. A few bikes were trailered, but those were mostly overbuilt or overtuned custom showbikes.

On my many cross-country trips, I have to say that most of the bikes I see being ridden through the middle of nowhere, bearing dusty license plates from distant states, are Harleys. Followed closely thereafter by BMWs and Gold Wings. Most of the trailered bikes I see are Daytona-bound in winter.

Another interesting urban legend I often hear or read is, "Harleys are all owned by stockbrokers who wear Rolexes."

Now, Harley-Davidson sold 263,000 motorcycles last year, and is hoping to sell 289,000 of its 2003 models. That's a lot of stockbrokers, especially in this economy. Personally, I know only one stockbroker, and he doesn't ride a motorcycle or wear a Rolex, but what if he did? Are stockbrokers less worthy to ride bikes than, say, truck drivers or skilled machinists? Of course they are—especially those who have turned my retirement funds into a distant echo floating through cyberspace—but that's neither here nor there.

In any case, I feel the notion of big shots on Harleys is greatly exaggerated. Surely these guys buy their share, but they are not the people who keep the production lines rolling.

I recently took my bike into our local H-D shop for its post-break-in inspection and decided to wait for it. So I spent the whole Saturday morning drinking coffee and reading magazines in the hospitality area. For three hours I watched customers come and go, and never for one minute felt I was hanging out on Wall Street. Coming through the door were guys buying oil and parts, young couples and their kids arriving by Saturn wagon to look and dream or order a bike, middle-American retired couples traveling across the country. A few apparent rich dudes, but mostly ordinary working people.

So those who worry that Harley is losing its constituency among mechanically minded folks who actually know how to produce real goods of measurable worth can rest easy—unless, of course, we send all our remaining industrial jobs to Mexico and China. Then Harley, and the rest of us, will find out exactly how many stockbrokers there really are.

The last myth I was going to mention is the old notion that Harleys break down more often than other bikes.

Well, I've had one Shovelhead from the supposedly dreaded AMF era and five modern Harleys in the past twelve years—three Evos and two Twin-Cams, and I've never had a problem with any of them. Not one thing has gone wrong. Until last week, of course, when the shift lever fell off my Electra Glide on the interstate.

Maybe I should have sold some of my priceless blue-chip stocks and bought the $25,000 version—and a trailer to go with it.

April 2003

TWO-STROKE LANDFILL

In that great division of household labor that defines every marriage, one of my regular jobs is to load the Econoline van with trash every other Saturday and haul it to the dump. Living out here in the sticks, you see, we have no curbside pick-up. In fact we don't even have a curb.

I know what you're thinking: What fun it must be to go to the dump and fling all that old stuff over an embankment and watch it crash and tumble into the junk below!

Well, it isn't like that anymore. The dumps of my youth, where you could heave a busted stove, an old car battery, and half a dozen paint cans into a swamp and then shoot them with your .22 Winchester, are gone. We aren't allowed to poison the ground water for eternity anymore. Instead, everything is separated into dumpsters. More ecologically sound, but not quite as physically satisfying. Nevertheless, there are compensations.

I made my regular dump run a few weeks ago and was sorting our cat food cans into the recycle bin when Dick, the guy who oversees the dump, walked up.

"Say," he said, glancing at the Harley, Ducati, BMW, Aprilia, and Triumph stickers in the back window of my van, "you like old motorbikes, don't you?"

"Why, yes," I testified truthfully.

"Well, somebody brought a little Honda scooter out here and they were just about to heave it into the scrap-metal dumpster when I stopped them and told them to set it to one side. It looked too nice to throw away."

I walked over and looked at the scooter, which turned out to be a black 50cc Honda Spree. It was pretty clean and almost complete, missing only a set of body panels around the engine and the top half of the air cleaner housing.

Also, there was no ignition key. I noticed the white plastic oil-injection tank was empty.

"Somebody probably ran it out of oil and fried the engine," I said doubtfully. I pondered the neat little scooter for a minute, and then said, "I probably shouldn't take it home. Every time I pick up a machine like this, it ends up costing me about $500 and a month of spare time . . ."

"Okay," Dick said with a good-natured shrug. "Just thought I'd ask."

So I drove out of the dump with an empty van, proud of my self-control, watching the Spree disappear in the rearview mirror. It sat there quite elegantly on its tiny centerstand, with snow flurries sifting down upon it out of the dark sky and settling upon the seat. Rather a bleak sight.

Halfway home, of course, I pulled off the road and stared into space for a while.

My friend Pat Donnelly had a Spree he used as a pit bike for vintage race weekends. Maybe he could use some spare parts. Or maybe I could make the thing run and use it as a pit bike for myself. Seemed a shame to throw it away.

So I did a U-turn and went back for the scooter.

"All right!" Dick said happily, as he helped me lift it into the van. "I knew somebody would rescue this thing!"

"Yes," I mumbled to myself as I drove away, "and that somebody is always me."

When I got the Spree home, I took the body panels off and cleaned everything up, tried to charge the questionable battery, added two-stroke oil to the injection tank, added gas, and attempted to hot-wire the ignition.

Nothing. No life from the starter motor or ignition lights. I didn't find out until later that you have to pull one of the two brake levers in to make the ignition work. Also, this Spree was a 1985 model, with no kick starter, so I had no way to turn the engine over, what with the enclosed variable belt drive. Was the piston stuck? Did it need a key to work at all?

Caving in to my total ignorance (and lack of shop manual), I decided to take it to an expert. I'd heard of a repair shop in nearby Madison called Scooter Therapy, known among university students (and older pit-bike aficionados) for doing good repair work at a fair price, so I hauled the Spree into town.

Talking to the shop owner, I was amazed to learn that Honda hadn't produced the Spree since 1987. They'd sold so many zillion of them—at roughly $300 apiece—and there were still half a zillion running around campus, fourteen years later. Good old Honda; every few decades they put the whole Youth Culture back on wheels.

A few days later, the shop called and said the Spree was fixed. Bad vacuum petcock, they said, and a bad oil tank valve, which allowed the crankcase to fill with oil. Also, the drive belt was badly worn. They replaced all this stuff, found some matching used bodywork, put in a new air cleaner and battery, and did a tune-up, all for $232.

Or a little less than the luggage rack I just bought for my Harley.

I took the Spree for a short test ride and was reminded again how liberating it is to have something really light and agile—and effortless to park. The thing goes only about thirty miles per hour (by law), but gets there quickly.

When I rode back to the shop (my hair blown straight back like a Katzenjammer Kid), the owner laughed and said, "I wish I had a picture of the grin on your face."

So now I've got a two-stroke pit bike for those track weekends with my two-stroke Aprilia RS250 next summer, after not owning any two-stroke machine—other than a Homelite chain saw and a weedwacker—for the past twenty-five years. Ring-Dings-R-Us.

I'm glad I went back for the Spree. Old, broken motorbikes, no matter how humble, are not the same as other junk. They aren't in the same class as discarded microwave ovens, empty paint cans, or old refrigerators. Their capacity to provide happiness, once they are brought back to life, is all out of proportion to their cost or physical mass.

And no one ever sat up late in a workshop, drinking a beer and gazing contentedly at a recently resurrected, freshly waxed kitchen appliance.

May 2003

BATTERY LIFE

Not too long ago, a reader sent me some photos of his sizeable motorcycle collection, all arranged row-upon-row in a beautiful new garage. He had a lot of nice bikes, including quite a few of my all-time favorites, such as a black-and-gold Ducati 900SS SP, circa 1980, and a perfectly restored '67 Triumph TR6C.

My favorite photo, however, was not of the bikes.

Emblematic of bike collections everywhere was a snapshot of a tall metal storage shelf filled with motorcycle batteries. Tall ones, short ones, long ones. Mixed in with this stunning industrial display of lead and acid were half a dozen Battery Tenders with their various lights glowing green or red, all draped with more wires and hoses and alligator clips than an Intensive Care Unit in a cardiac ward. You could almost smell the sulfuric acid fumes and hear the soft, gurgling percolation of gas bubbles.

I stared at that picture for a few minutes and wondered if I should have it silk-screened onto a T-shirt with the subtitle, "Winter Riding in Wisconsin." Those batteries, more than any other image I could think of, represented the glowing embers of enthusiasm, waiting to flare up again in spring. Passion on the trickle charger, as it were.

This photo also reminded me that my own bikes had been sitting for a while, so I retired to my posh, heated workshop to do the annual Battery Thing where I take them all out, clean off the white powdery stuff, sand the terminals, burn acid holes in my favorite pair of blue jeans, and trickle charge everything on my battery bench.

Yes, I too have a dedicated spot for the handling of batteries. It's a Sears metal workbench with plywood bolted to the top. It's way over in the Toxic Corner of my garage, next to the parts cleaner, as far as possible from any painted surface.

I am a great respecter of the corrosive properties of sulfuric acid. When I was a car mechanic in the 1970s, a guy walking through our shop accidentally tripped on some battery-charger wires, throwing a spark that blew the top off the battery in a BMW 2002 that was parked in the bay next to mine. *Blammo!* I saw it happening and turned away just in time to miss a face-full of acid.

We doused everything with water immediately, but the car was ruined. So was my shirt. Nasty stuff, acid.

Anyway, I was overdue for a little winter battery maintenance, and in preparation for my long-postponed, much-ballyhooed, but virtually imminent, dual-sport ride in Baja, I went out to the garage the other night to change the oil in my Suzuki DR-Z400S. But first a little warmup.

It being winter, I cracked open the garage door, aimed the exhaust pipe into the great frozen outdoors, set the choke, turned the key, and hit the starter button.

Nothing.

As in nil. Not a whimper from the starter motor, nor even a sign of life in the LED instrument cluster. Weird. Only a month earlier, I'd taken a short ride during a break in the weather and the engine had cranked like a house afire, but now the battery was dead.

So I pulled off the left side panel and removed the long, narrow "maintenance-free" battery, which lives on a little shelf under the seat. I hooked up my one-amp Battery Tender for an overnight slow-drip power transfusion. But no lights came on in the charger. Odd. Perhaps the battery needed a bigger jolt to get going. But I hooked up my two-amp and six-amp units, successively (yes, to paraphrase the New Testament, my house has many chargers), and nothing happened with those either. No bounce of the needle, no hum of the charger. Nothing. I might as well have hooked the battery clips to a chunk of 2x4. This little beauty was dead, and not about to be revived. Have to get a new one.

Next I turned my attention to my nearly new but dormant Aprilia RS250 track bike. I turned the key and there was not a hint of life in the LED instrument pod. So I took its tiny battery out (same as the nearby Honda Spree's) and tried to charge it, with identical results. Another nonconductive block of wood. Have to get a new one.

Moving down the row, my Ducati 900SS and old BMW R100RS both had enough juice to light their headlights, but not quite enough to turn their engines over more than once. Those batteries came out and took their places on the charging bench, soon gurgling happily back to health.

The Harley cranked and started right up (but should probably get a trickle charge), and I didn't even try the old 1968 Triumph Trophy 500. That bike's little gel-cell has been dead for two years, but the bike always starts first-kick in the spring and the lights work fine.

Odd that the only bike I have that starts and runs predictably is equipped with a kick starter, a dead twelve-dollar battery, and thirty-five-year-old Lucas electrics. So much for our brave new technology.

But then I have felt for many years that the motorcycle battery—even in its most modern form—is an odd throwback to some earlier era, the one piece of equipment that has really improved not at all since I bought my first bike in 1963. And I continue to be amazed that any manufacturer would bury a battery deep in the bodywork of a bike where it cannot be immediately reached.

Battery failure is the third certainty in the world, right after death and taxes.

It can be just as expensive as taxes, too. That little black short-lived maintenance-free unit on the DR-Z cost me $126 at the dealer. After ordering one yesterday, I am still bleeding from the ear. The Aprilia battery, on the other hand, was only eighteen dollars, so maybe that evens things out.

My little bike collection right now, at seven motorcycles, is slightly beyond my normal, self-imposed limit of five, and I've been thinking of selling a couple of them to simplify my life and make a little more room in the garage. When I explain this plan to people, I tell them I have too many bikes.

But, in my own mind, I never really have too many bikes. There is no such thing. I just have too many batteries.

June 2003

SECRETS OF TRAVELING LIGHT

On our official Slimey Crud Motorcycle Gang 1,000-mile road trip last summer (which was 1,600 miles long, thanks to a slight miscalculation), one of our most revered members from the Detroit contingent, Wil Laneski, revealed a scientific breakthrough in lightweight packing technology that virtually stunned all of us at breakfast one morning.

Over our bacon and eggs, some of us straining to focus on our coffee cups through the dim haze of headaches from a small amount of extremely cheap wine drunk happily the night before, Wil revealed that his riding buddy Dennis Lappin always throws his underwear away after every day of riding.

Yes.

Wil woke up one morning on a bike trip to find his morning coffee boiling away over a roaring campfire of split oak and Jockey shorts.

Seems Dennis saves his threadbare underwear throughout the year—the kind most of us throw away in case we are ever in a car accident so the hospital won't think we don't have health insurance, or in case the nurse looks like Renee Zellweger—and uses it strictly for motorcycle trips. Each day, he throws it away, so his luggage gets lighter and lighter as the trip goes on.

Needless to say, this is nothing short of brilliant.

And it's a concept that's right up my alley. Like most of us, I have not just underwear, but all kinds of apparel—socks, T-shirts, etc.—that wear out every year and are simply deep-sixed. Why not save them for a motorcycle trip? In fact, a perceptive fashion critic might suggest that my entire wardrobe could be discarded, one piece at a time, on a motorcycle tour, with no great loss to the world.

In any case, it was an interesting revelation to one who has spent years trying to pack light, not just for motorcycling, but also for backpacking, canoeing, bicycling, piloting light aircraft, etc. Seems I've spent half my life weighing things in my hands like a human balance beam and wondering if I can take them along on a trip.

The most extreme example came along in 1987, when Barb and I circumnavigated the United States in an underpowered 1945 Piper Cub. The Cub, for reasons of weight and balance (not to mention its ability to stagger off the ground), is rated for only twenty pounds of baggage, which is not much for two people who have to travel for six weeks. And, in an airplane, this weight limit is not a mere suggestion—too much weight in the wrong place can kill you. So we learned to travel very, very light.

We could not throw any clothing away on our airplane trip—we had only two of everything and had to wash and dry things in the motel room each night—but we did devise a few other strategies worth remembering, and I used them again in packing for a two-week off-road trip in Baja. Here are a few conclusions reached, before and after the Baja trip:

• It is never necessary to carry shampoo or soap. Even the kind of cheap, godforsaken motels I patronize usually have a small bar of soap that works for everything.

• If you are a guy, get a really short Marine boot-camp haircut just before the trip, as I did for Baja and the Cub trip. Then you are not tempted to carry a comb, hairbrush, fancy styling mousse, or a tin of Dapper Dan Pomade, which caused George Clooney so much trouble in *O Brother, Where Art Thou?*

• Paper is heavy. Mail unneeded maps, brochures, etc., home as you travel. We had about fifteen pounds of unneeded sectional charts waiting for us when we finished the Cub trip. If you must take a book along (and I must), take a thin, ageless classic that you can read over and over again, such as Walt Whitman's *Leaves of Grass* or *Cheerleaders in Heat*.

• As much as possible, take riding gear that doubles as rain wear. I now wear waterproof riding boots (no more of those torn Totes in the tank bag) and a Gore-Tex jacket, saving the leather stuff for shorter trips and sunny days. When it rains, only some light rain pants are needed. In cooler weather, I take a two-piece Aerostich suit, though the pants are rather bulky to store if the weather gets hot. I also have some Gore-Tex touring gloves now that work for nearly all weather.

• Always carry all your cash in $100 bills. Or 500 peso notes, in Mexico. No one will accept them, and you'll be forced to use a credit card, saving weight and space on bulky change. At most gas stations, gift shops, and roadside motels a $100 bill is as unspendable as a 1934 stock certificate from the Trans-Manchurian Railway Company. Having only $100 bills will also prevent you from buying trashy souvenirs and bulking up on snacks.

• Put all your high-powered emergency back-pain pills—Codeine, Vicodin, etc.—into a single white plastic Bufferin bottle, rather in than many bottles. Try to remember the shape and markings on each one, so you can find the right pill by touch in the utter darkness of a cheap, godforsaken Mexican motel room when they've turned the generator off at bedtime.

This is just the tip of the weight-saving iceberg, of course. I'm sure there are many more things we could all think of, such as the old cut-the-handle-off-your-toothbrush hint we used to see in backpacking guides. Forget that. Brushing with a short stub of a toothbrush makes you feel like a fool. And look like one, according to bystanders.

Also, as one last suggestion, I would advise you not to register with your correct home address at any motel in which you intend to abandon your old underwear.

July 2003

ACCESSORY FATIGUE

Spring rains had not yet washed all the salt off our Wisconsin roads, but I had to go for a ride anyway.

"I can go over the mufflers and wheels with some Windex and a rag later," I reasoned aloud. "I'm sure that will get all the salt off. In the meantime, I must take this new motorcycle for a ride!" My voice rose in a crescendo of near-madness from cabin fever.

The bike in question was a new/leftover 2001 dark-blue Ducati ST2 that I had just acquired in the most convoluted set of swaps and trades since the creation of the former Yugoslavia.

Essentially, I had decided in some midwinter mood shift that I had way too many old bikes that Needed Something and decided to roll about three of them into one modern, useable motorcycle whose owner's manual was unstained by blood and drain-oil fingertips.

Salvation appeared during a winter visit to Corse Superbikes in Saukville, Wisconsin, where my salesman friend and sometime riding buddy Scott Siem pointed out that they had this very nice, heavily discounted ST2 sitting right there on the showroom floor. Trades accepted.

Truth be told, I had an ST4S in mind, so I did not act immediately. I hadn't spent more than about fifteen minutes on either model of ST, so I made a quick telephone survey of friends who owned them.

There was strong loyalty on both sides. ST2 owners (including *CW*'s Brian Catterson) told me to buy an ST2. "Broader torque band, less shifting, less maintenance, cheaper to buy, sweet-running 944cc water-cooled, two-valve engine—a secret weapon and emerging classic for the motorcyclist of refined judgment," they said. "Responds beautifully to pipes, air cleaner, and chip."

"Get the ST4S!" said three ST4S owners I know. "How can you argue with an extra thirty-four brake horsepower, Öhlins shock, lighter wheels, stickier tires, and a fully adjustable front fork?"

Actually, my own instinct was to buy an ST4S. When I used to take my 996 track bike on one of its rare Sunday morning street rides, I'd inevitably say to myself, "If I could have this engine in a slightly more comfortable bike, I'd never stop riding." Well, the ST4S was Ducati's answer, with luggage.

Nevertheless, I chose the ST2. Why?

Well, because it was there; because the price was too good to resist; because Ducati's dark blue is such a nice color even Barb urged me to get the bike; and because I wanted to find out why three or four really good riders I know had found it to be such a satisfying motorcycle.

So the other day I finally took off on the first of several early spring break-in rides, salt be damned. I've done just 250 miles so far, still keeping it at the prescribed rpm, so I haven't really sampled its true potential. Nice bike, though. Light, compact, well-finished, good luggage, instinctive steering and turn-in, taut yet compliant suspension. Very civilized.

Of course, I'll have to make the usual Ducati changes.

The seat is hard as a rock, so I'll order a different one right away. The exhaust note isn't too Lawn-Boyish, but I'll probably get some slip-ons for better flow and lighter weight. The stock mufflers feel like barbells from the local fitness center.

Then the mandatory performance chip. And, like all Ducatis, this one is geared to the moon. A few more teeth on the rear sprocket would make it nicer everywhere. And the handlebars would benefit from about a one-inch rise.

But I've made none of these changes yet. I like to leave things stock during break-in, as a performance baseline for any future changes. Also, this tactic makes the bike sound cheaper when you tell your wife what you paid for the thing. Costly accessories made of titanium, carbon fiber, emeralds, and gold can be sneaked in later, when things have calmed down.

However, I must say this: I am dragging my feet just a bit on making all these changes. Why?

Perhaps because I have made them too many times in the past twenty years, on too many different bikes. Never mind Ducatis; I could write a chapter on Harleys alone. Accessory Fatigue is setting in.

Sitting on the wide shelf above my garage door at any given time, I generally have at least two sets of perfectly good OEM mufflers, a couple of stock but uncomfortable streetbike seats, and a dirt bike tank that's too small for a decent afternoon loop through the woods.

In a nearby cabinet drawer, you will normally find a couple sets of brand-new, beautifully anodized final-drive sprockets; a few unused drive chains (too short), still with clean, gleaming gold side plates; a minor collection of carburetor jets, computer chips, and air cleaner elements; and rejected alternative clip-on handlebars.

Never mind the money that all this stuff cost to replace; think of the waste of human time and perfectly good material. If you melted down the world's supply of cast-off stock Harley mufflers alone, you could build a fleet of aircraft carriers. With aircraft.

Okay, the pipes I can understand. Manufacturers are stuck with ironclad regulation here. But what about seats, tanks, and bars, and all the rest?

Perhaps with our new, slower economy, the makers of bikes will eventually try a whole new marketing strategy to draw us into showrooms. Their brochures will proclaim, "Seats you can sit on! Comfortable handlebars! Gearing that makes sense! Tanks that hold enough gas!"

And, if the Feds would back off on the laws just slightly, they could advertise, "Mellow yet inoffensive pipes you can actually hear, jetted just right!"

I don't expect this to happen soon, so my personal battle to fight waste will consist mostly of buying accessories that could easily be transferred from an ST2 to, say, an ST4S, in case I suddenly find myself unable to live without that extra 34 horsepower. Or the Öhlins shock.

We all do what we can.

August 2003

RIDING THE CHEYENNE BREAKS

It is one of the parables of Chaos Theory that the mere whisper of a butterfly's wing in the rain forests of Brazil can set off an unpredictable chain of wind currents that may eventually cause a typhoon in the South China Sea.

If that's true, the early spring wind that was raking through my friend Rob Himmelmann's place last week was probably caused by a butterfly the size of a B-52 living in Nome, Alaska. It was bitterly cold and windy. And there we were, six of us loading our dirt bikes on Rob's big flatbed trailer in the frigid darkness near Portage, Wisconsin, mechanically tossing our riding gear in the two trucks that would take us Out West.

"I guess we'd better get used to the cold," Rob said. "The Weather Channel says it's supposed to snow tomorrow where we're going in South Dakota."

I said nothing, but had my doubts about this whole enterprise. It is entirely possible in the upper Midwest to misjudge the end of winter and spend a blizzard-wracked weekend holed up in some depressing motel along the interstate instead of riding your motorcycle.

Would this be one of those trips?

Probably. But if we made it to South Dakota before we got snowed in, there would be at least one redemptive pleasure: I would finally get to see the famous "motorcycle ranch."

Rob had been telling me about this place for years. It was a 7,000-acre cattle ranch just north of the Badlands, belonging to Rob's old friend, Randy Babcock.

Randy, Rob explained, was a third-generation rancher on the original family homestead, a great guy, fine rider, and motorcycle buff with a barn full of old Huskys, CZs, BSAs, Triumphs, and Nortons, a cowboy who did all his ranching from the saddle of a Honda XR600.

"You've got to come out and go riding with us," Rob said. "Two or three times a year, Randy invites about a dozen riding friends for a long weekend of trail riding. We ride all day, party at night, and sleep in the old ranch house. Everybody brings food and drink."

"Sounds pretty nice," I said.

"The ranch is beautiful," Rob said. "You have to see it to believe it."

If that glowing invitation were not enough, I had yet another motive for making the trip. Sitting in my garage was a new KTM 450 E/XC I'd bought during the winter, still unridden.

I sometimes suspected the bike was actually looking out the window at the frozen tundra with its headlight, wondering what kind of world it had been born into. But the KTM was going somewhere at last, jammed onto the trailer with Rob's ATK 605, a couple of big XRs, a Suzuki DR-Z400S, a DR250—even an ancient Honda CL160—and we were on our way to the ranch.

We drove all night, and in the morning turned north at the famous Wall Drug. A few miles after the pavement turned to gravel, we were at Randy's place, Cedar Breaks Ranch. The yard was full of trailers and bikes and pickup trucks. I shook hands with Randy, an easy-going, friendly, and down-to-earth guy, and we all went into the ranch house for a breakfast of bacon and eggs.

The ranch was everything Rob said it was, and more. Fourteen of Randy's friends showed up to ride, coming in from Montana, Colorado, Minnesota, and nearby Rapid City. The winter storm we'd feared passed miraculously just to the south, and we rode for three days in cool, partly cloudy weather over beautiful terrain with wide-open fields, sweeping hills, and steep descents along cattle trails into a rugged canyon land called the Cheyenne River Breaks.

Most of us were dressed to the teeth in modern motocross gear, but Randy and his brother-in-law, Butch, led the way in canvas ranch coveralls and red wool hunting caps with earflaps. Worse yet, Butch smoked a pipe while he was riding, and only a few in our group could keep up with these guys. Turns out dressing exactly like Dick Burleson in the new Moose catalog has no effect on your riding talent.

Nor does the modernness of your bike, apparently. A guy named Jeff Ecker, who alternately rode an explosively loud CZ 400 and an old Rickman-Triumph 500, outclimbed and outrode everyone.

And the new KTM? Light, quick, and powerful, with the same feathery tautness I admire in Ducati streetbikes. I loved riding it every minute of those three days.

Between the days of riding, we had three nights of parties in which a certain amount of beer and Old Overholt was consumed, and a few people accidentally rode their bikes through the ranch house, while others watched classic John Wayne Westerns on the VCR or sat drinking around the dining room table, next to a big jukebox with no bad songs on it. We also had three great "guy dinners" with main courses like chili, ranch beans, and barbequed pork. Pure, uncut explosives. No salads or fluffy desserts.

On Sunday we loaded the bikes and headed home, chased by the leading edge of another spring snowstorm. The weather had opened and closed for us like a ticket window with strict hours.

When I got home from Rob's late last night, I was too tired to unload the KTM from my own trailer, so I left it out all night, still festooned with frozen South Dakota cow dung and bits of straw. By this morning the storm had hit big time, and the bike was rapidly turning from orange to white in the drifting snow.

I made some coffee and looked out the kitchen window at this bleak scene, thinking it seemed early for what was possibly the best ride of 2003 to have taken place already. So much for the Weather Channel. Good times are a part of Chaos Theory, too, unpredictable as the motion of clouds.

I guess the breeze of the butterfly's wing, in this case, was the day my late friend Bruce Finlayson introduced me to Rob Himmelmann. And now I've met Randy and his pals and ridden with them through a landscape I could hardly have imagined.

In motorcycling, the repercussions of friendship never stop, even after we're gone.

September 2003

BSAs AND OTHER BIKES UNOWNED

As our pickup truck bored through the dark Minnesota night on I-90, returning from the dirt bike ride in South Dakota I wrote about last month, my friend Rob Himmelmann and I had lots of time to kill, so we naturally talked about motorcycles.

Rob flies through life on a slow drip feed of caffeinated Diet Coke, and I drink enough coffee when I'm on the road to keep Juan Valdez and his whole family up nights, picking more beans. In other words, we were both wide awake, even though it was about two in the morning.

The subject was BSAs.

Rob was, at that moment, wearing a BSA T-shirt, and I knew from visiting his rural home in southern Wisconsin that he had a fair number of these bikes lurking in the wonderfully eclectic motorcycle collection that fills his garage and random storage sheds.

His property, in fact, has a kind of black-hole gravitational field that pulls old bikes in from all over the Midwest, because his buddies know him as a Friend of the Orphaned Motorcycle. When they don't know what to do with that old Zundapp two-stroke or Montesa trials bike, they give Rob a call.

Rob likes all kinds of motorcycles—a BMW R1100GS is his regular long-distance ride—but he especially likes British bikes, and has a soft spot for BSAs in particular. Somewhere on his property—if memory serves—there are five or six Victor 441s, ranging in condition from beautiful to "I think the crankshaft is in those boxes over there."

So, of course, I was picking Rob's brain as we drove along, on the feasibility of actually owning and riding a Victor 441, which I've always regarded as one of the handsomest of British singles—and one of the best-looking bikes on Earth, for that matter.

The lovely tank of polished aluminum and yellow paint; the neat curve of the exhaust pipe as it heads toward the small, tucked-in chrome muffler; the elegantly simple seat; the fundamental rightness of the bike's architecture—all these hit me right where I live. Which is in a seamy world of unbridled motorcycle lust and oil-stained depravity, if you really want to know.

In any case, I've always seen the BSA 441 as one of those bikes you'd almost be willing to restore and hang on the wall, even if it didn't run.

Which I guess they sometimes don't.

The general rep on 441 Victors (a.k.a. "Victims") over the years, as I have received it through a second-hand mixture of innuendo, legend, and probably a little distant envy, is that they are not very reliable.

Wretchedly perfidious, even.

Rob concurred that they had their problems and he wouldn't be inclined to *travel* on a 441, but said they are lots of fun for running up and down the country roads near his home. "I don't push any old bike hard," he said, "or ride it in some way that was never intended when it was new."

It was the basic old bike creed: You have to be sympathetic, keeping your expectations grounded in whatever decade the bike was produced, with an added allowance for age. And always carry tools or a cell phone.

So as we crossed the Mississippi River bridge at La Crosse in the early dawn, I was still mulling over the possibilities of someday buying or restoring a Victor.

Curiously, I've never owned a BSA of any kind. When I was in high school, those of us who liked British bikes seemed to be drawn toward either BSAs or Triumphs, but not both. And I found myself in the latter camp, mostly on the grounds of Triumph's impressive desert and enduro racing credentials and their more understated styling. Less chrome and flash.

I had one friend in college who owned a BSA 650 Lightning, but it blew up on I-94 as he rode to a job interview in Milwaukee, dousing his pants and shiny "job interview" shoes in oil. A connecting rod narrowly missed his foot. We Triumph guys looked at each other sagely and nodded.

A lot of BSAs were blowing up right then; aged machine tools at the factory were causing cylinder bores to diverge (we later learned), producing, in effect, a nonparallel twin and putting a lot of strain on the rods. This reputation made me leery of the Birmingham Small Arms company's twins.

But I loved the looks of BSA singles, and still do.

Maybe it's time to do something about that. I'm not getting any younger, and there are still five or six old bikes on my Short List whose vintage charms I've yet to experience.

As a serial owner of older bikes, I am something of a marque recidivist—I keep going back over and over again to the same brands (in some cases, without learning my lesson). In forty years of riding, I've had multiple Nortons, Triumphs, and old Hondas, but only a few other brands. In restoration projects, I keep falling victim to minor variations on the Commando, Bonneville, Trophy, and Honda. Four themes, going back to them like a stuck record. But no BSAs.

The discerning reader will also notice a couple of other alarming gaps in this largely predictable parade of popular and obvious targets.

Also missing from the lineup is the Velocette Thruxton or Venom one should probably have in this short lifetime, the Bultaco Metralla I've admired since adolescence, the Honda 305 Scrambler I somehow missed on my glacial ascent through the Honda ranks, and the inevitable Harley Panhead, whose engine I can look at for hours, as though through a glass darkly into the past.

That's about it. Not so many bikes, really. And if a person could somehow avoid getting distracted by yet another Norton Commando (never easy), he could probably track down at least a few of these remaining sirens.

Starting, perhaps, with a 441 Victor.

As we motored south toward home into the gray dawn of Wisconsin, Rob suddenly turned to me and said, "Have you ever owned a Zundapp?"

"No," I said, noncommittally.

October 2003

REVENGE OF THE SOCCER DADS

My old buddy Steve Kimball came over from Michigan last week with his son Ben—who just graduated from college—and stayed at our place for a weekend visit in Wisconsin.

It was good to see them again, but they hadn't come merely to visit us, heartwarming as that motive might be. Seems Steve's daughter, Kathy, is a student at the University of Wisconsin, in nearby Madison, and he and Ben were here to help her move from the dorm into a student apartment for the summer.

Some of you who are more than 100 years old may still recognize Steve's name. He was the managing editor of this magazine in the early 1980s, back when I joined the staff as technical editor. Steve and I soon developed a lively friendship based on a tendency to get matching pairs of speeding tickets any time we rode together, as well as a shared sense of humor that relies on damning with faint praise as its core mechanism.

I refer to Steve (who has a navy background in nuclear engineering) as "the Einstein of people who aren't especially bright," and he calls here asking for "the Herman Melville of drive-chain maintenance."

We have a lot of fun, yet seldom resort to actual violence.

Anyway, Steve came over a few weeks ago, and I couldn't help but notice that his motorcycle helmet and jacket were in the back of his family wagon. I also noticed that he was eyeing my new/leftover blue Ducati ST2 with more than casual interest. If the bike had been a daughter, I would have locked her in the attic until he was gone.

"Want to take that bike for a ride?" I offered.

"Sure," Steve said with a muffled voice as he pulled on his helmet and I took a quick step backward to get out of his way.

I looked at him through the fogged visor and shouted, "A good local test ride is to take Old Stage Road over to Highway 14 and then come back on Highway 59. It's a nice little ten-mile loop with some good corners."

Steve nodded, shot down the driveway, and disappeared for about a week.

Actually, it only seemed that long; he was probably gone for less than two hours. As Ben and I awaited his return, I said, "Gee, I hope Steve is okay. There's loose gravel on some of the corners . . ."

Ben grinned. "Oh, he'll be all right. He's just lost. But he'll find his way back eventually."

And he did. Steve came riding up the driveway just in time for dinner. "Nice bike," he said, thoughtfully examining the mechanical details of the ST2. "I'm thinking of getting a newer motorcycle myself."

Like a lot of people who are now in their late forties and early fifties, Steve has had to sublimate his desire for new and fancy motorcycles for a decade or more as he and his wife Denise have ushered their two children through the Expensive Years, that time of life when they needed soccer uniforms, music lessons, straight teeth, the occasional square meal, and—the big one—college tuition.

Unlike a lot of people, however, Steve didn't quit riding; he simply scaled down a bit. During those years, he put his 883 Sportster on the block, and turned that bike into some ready cash and a pair of used Honda FT500 singles, which he bought for $500 each. He also had a Yamaha 550 Vision for a while and an XL250 Honda to run around on in the dirt. Then, a couple of years ago, he really splurged and spent $1,700 on a pristine 1992 Yamaha Seca II. He's been riding that right up to the present.

But with No. 1 Son out of college, No. 1 Daughter nearly through and wife Denise having recently earned her teaching credentials and employed in the local school system, Steve is clearly picking up financial steam and getting that slightly manic "Somebody stop me!" Jim Carrey–look in his eye.

It's kind of fun to see. My riding buddy Jim Wargula is going through exactly the same phase with his kids right now (son Matt just graduated from college), and in the past year he's bought a Ducati 900SS and a BMW R100RS. I get the feeling he's not done yet. We keep stopping to look at new BMWs wherever we pass a dealership. Not to mention Harleys.

But back to Steve: A few days after he and Ben returned home to Michigan, Steve phoned to say he'd sold his Seca II and bought a really clean, low-mileage silver 1998 Ducati ST2. He found it at a local Ducati shop for only $5,500. With luggage, no less. (Only Steve can find deals like this.)

And every time I talk to him on the phone now, he's just been out for an evening ride. Says he loves the bike.

I am naturally quite happy for him and pleased at his impeccable taste in motorcycles (or high suggestibility, whichever you prefer), but there are a couple of observations I'm tempted to make about this gradually unfolding chain of events.

First, I notice that, despite the personal sacrifices Steve made by not blowing money on all kinds of new, trendy, and exotic bikes for the past fifteen years or so, he really didn't suffer very much in terms of riding quality. All of his bikes were fun, quick, agile, comfortable, and essentially *free*. Steve told me he actually made money on his last six bikes. Which is more than I can say.

Also, while it's nice to see Steve and Jim upgrading to faster and more comfortable road bikes that might work better on a long trip, the best part (from my perspective) is that they might have more time in the next few years to take some of those trips. Like we used to. It's never the bikes that hold us back; it's finding the time to use them.

And, as a final thought, I should point out that both Jim and Steve's kids have turned out to be polite, thoughtful, well-spoken, lively, and fun to be around.

I hate to tell these guys, but they could have had a bike with carbon fiber mufflers instead of all those expensive, well-educated children.

And now, of course, they have both.

Here's to graduates everywhere.

November 2003

BOOGIE MUSIC & THEM MEAN OLD BIKER BLUES

Got a package in the mail last week, containing a paperback book with a letter enclosed.

The letter was from a man named Fito de la Parra, who explained that he'd enjoyed a touring story I did recently for our sister publication, *Adventures*, about looking for the roots of the blues in the Mississippi Delta on a Triumph Bonneville.

De la Parra wrote: "Hell, I should have done that ride. Maybe I still will."

He then went on to explain that he was a drummer for a 1960s blues band that's still going strong, and said, "From the gray in your beard in the photos, you look old enough to remember my band, Canned Heat."

The book he'd included was his autobiography, *Living the Blues: Canned Heat's Story of Music, Drugs, Death, Sex and Survival*, co-written with T. W. and Marlane McGarry (available from Whitehorse Press, www.whitehorse-press.com).

Well, Mr. de la Parra got it right. Not only am I old enough to remember Canned Heat, but I've been a huge fan of the band ever since I heard their first hits, "Going up the Country," "Let's Work Together," and "On the Road Again" in the late 1960s.

Our own garage blues band, The Defenders, does several Canned Heat songs (imitating them as best we can manage) and we still listen to the originals over our PA system for inspiration. I love their sound, and de la Parra's superb drumming.

So, of course, I've been reading his book all week, and have been pleased to find that motorcycles figure heavily into de la Parra's life.

He grew up in a well-to-do family in Mexico City, falling in love with motorcycles and American rock 'n' roll at an early age. An outstanding drummer right from the beginning, he worked with a series of nationally famous and well-paid Mexican rock bands, and immediately went out and bought himself a new Triumph Bonneville after seeing Marlon Brando in *The Wild One.*

He writes, " . . . Just as rock music had become an instant passion for me, I realized that motorcycling was going to be a part of my life forever. I was so jazzed, I actually slept next to the bike for the first few nights."

Old Triumphs, however, did not remain a part of his life forever. The Bonneville—his only transportation—broke down so often he frequently missed gigs, and it also affected his love life: "My dates often ended with angry, oil-splattered girls snarling at me by the roadside."

So he sold the Triumph and bought a BMW R60, which gave him no trouble and started a lifelong affair with BMW Boxers. In fact, there's a picture of his entire Mexican band, Los Sinners, sitting on a row of Beemers.

After that, the book is filled with photos of de la Parra and other members of Canned Heat posing with their bikes. Their late, great singer, Bob "The Bear" Hite, was a Harley nut, always working on old Panheads, while de la Parra appears with ever-newer BMWs.

The band's hard-driving boogie music and wild ways earned them a big following among bikers, and it seems to have been biker bars and parties that sustained them during the dark Disco Years, when work was hard to come by.

As one who shares de la Parra's dual passions for motorcycles and blues music, it has always been interesting to me to observe how often these two interests coalesce. Riding bikes and a taste for the purer, less adulterated strains of American music—blues, rock, and traditional country—just seem to go together.

Buddy Holly and Elvis went right out and bought new motorcycles with their first big earnings, as professional musicians have ever since. Most of the Allman Brothers Band were riders (two were killed on Sportsters in accidents that were one year—and one block—apart), and then you have Bob Dylan, John Hammond, J. Geils, Lyle Lovett, and so on. You could probably fill this column with nothing but a list of famous musicians who ride.

Even in our own little six-man blues band, no fewer than four of us are lifelong riders and current Ducati owners. In fact, we threatened to throw both our harmonica and bass player out of the group if they didn't buy red Ducatis and learn to ride, but we then remembered they are two of the best musicians in the band and backed off on this possibly extravagant demand.

Sadly, our own drummer, Paul Roberts, crashed his Ducati 900SS two months ago, breaking many bones, and has been in the hospital ever since. He spent the night unconscious in a ditch and only survived because a jogger heard his labored breathing while running along the highway early the next morning. Paul and his bike were both invisible from the road, hidden in the tall grass. He's in rehab now, doing very well, and we hope to be playing together again soon.

I'm not quite sure what the link is between riding bikes and a passion for good traditional music, but at times it seems almost like two halves of the same gene. Our motorcycle club, the Slimey Crud Motorcycle Gang, is filled with guys who have (by my exacting and weird standards) perfect taste in music. Not a Lite Music fan in the bunch, and there are no bad tunes played at our parties, ever.

Maybe motorcyclists like to fly a little closer to the flame than the average civilian, and the soundtrack for that attitude toward life tends to exclude bland and risk-free music.

In any case, I see in the paper that Canned Heat is playing at our local Madison Blues Festival next month. Looks like I might finally get to see these guys play; I never did, being in Vietnam during their Woodstock period, when they were touring a lot.

And maybe our band can spring Paul out of the hospital and take him along to the festival for a little musical rehab.

As The Bear used to say at the end of every concert, shaking his finger at the audience like someone giving stern medical counsel, "And don't forget to boogie!"

Sound advice.

December 2003

SUSPENDED LOGIC

Had to drop off my Ducati ST2 for its 600-mile post-break-in checkup last Wednesday—just slightly overdue, as usual, at 1,100 miles—so I called up my good friend Jim to see if he wanted to ride along in my van.

"Thought I might make the rounds of three or four different dealerships in southern Wisconsin, as long as we're out and about, and look at some new bikes," I said. "Want to go?"

Jim said, "Well, I don't know. I might have to take a sick day to do it."

"How are you feeling?"

"Kind of feverish, all of a sudden."

"Better take a day off."

Luckily, Jim discovered he still had a useable vacation day, so he didn't have to feign death to get off work. I picked him up at 7:30 in the morning, stopped at a convenience store for a large coffee and a fried apple fritter about the size of a catcher's mitt, and we were on our way to a day of freedom and bike gazing.

I dropped off the Duck for service, and then swung home in a huge triangle that took us to a series of dealerships that handled, variously, BMW, Ducati, KTM, Triumph, Suzuki, Harley, Aprilia, and Kawasaki. Pretty much the full gamut, except for Honda and Yamaha, and I'd looked at those a few days earlier.

It was a wonderful day. We sat on bikes, wasted sales-staff time, drank tiny cups of gourmet coffee, looked at many bikes from many angles, collected brochures, and discussed the advantages and disadvantages of new designs and engineering ideas. Jim, who is an engineer himself, shares my belief that motorcycle design is somehow symptomatic of the relative health of Western Civilization.

On the way home, late that afternoon, Jim said, "Well, did you see any bike you can't live without?"

"Sure," I responded without hesitating, "lots of 'em. But I sometimes wonder if we aren't entering the Mannerist phase of motorcycle design."

"What does that mean?"

"Well, back when I was a D+ student in Art History 101, our professor taught us that artists spent centuries learning to depict perspective properly, so the feet of saints didn't point straight down and buildings didn't look all crooked and piled up on one another. Then, once they perfected realistic proportion, some painters felt they had run out of new things to do, so in the sixteenth century they started painting people with exceptionally long necks, exaggerated proportions, and their eyes too far apart. This was called the Mannerist school of art."

"I see where this is going," Jim said.

I shrugged. "There are still a lot of perfectly sensible, normal bikes out there, but in a day of looking at new bikes you can see quite a few cases of logic being stretched in the name of art, or clever design."

"For instance?"

"For instance, why would you build a BMW sport-tourer with an upswept muffler that cuts the volume of one of its two saddlebags in half? On a long, two-up trip, who's supposed to get that tiny saddlebag? You or your wife? It doesn't make any sense."

This, of course, touched off a discussion that lasted all the way home, based on various bikes we'd looked at. So Jim and I decided to help out the design staffs of motorcycle companies, in our own inimitable way, by setting down some Engineering Ideas that Never Go Out of Fashion. I thought it might help the modern sculptors who fashion our bikes leave us at least a semblance of logic and comfort. Here's a list of timeless good ideas that will almost always warm the hearts of potential motorcycle buyers (especially your slightly older ones, like me and Jim):

- Light weight. All but pure dirt and sport bikes seem to be getting larger and heavier each year, yet lighter is always better. I know of no exceptions; a heavy bike is a pig forever.
- An accessible battery. My Ducati and the BMW R1100S test bike I had a few summers ago both have the batteries buried deeply within the bodywork. Bad idea.
- A comfortable seat. The new Multistrada we looked at has the hardest seat I've ever sat on, and the KTM 950 Adventure isn't much better. Even the dealers are astounded by them. We are told

optional factory "comfort" seats may become available. Why not make the "discomfort" seat an option, just to see how many people would order one?

• A flat seat. Men, especially, don't like to be slid into the tank under braking, and I've never met a passenger who prefers a high perch.

• Centerstands. Those who fear ground contact while racing may easily take them off. The rest of us love them.

• Adjustable—or swappable tubular—handlebars. Fixed bars always make someone unhappy.

• Big gas tanks. I don't know a single living human—outside of drag racing—who likes small gas tanks. On a tourer or sport-tourer, 200 miles of range is a nice minimum goal.

• Windshields that don't make you deaf. Much wind-tunnel work needed here on most of the bikes I've owned and ridden.

• Clocks. Never mind Peter Fonda throwing his watch away in *Easy Rider*, most of us have places to go, and we hate unzipping jackets and gloves to get at a wristwatch while riding.

• Petcocks on gas tanks. Gas gauges are nice, too, but a petcock with reserve has a less vivid imagination.

• Good styling. If you think the bike you've just designed might be really ugly, ask around before you stick the poor dealer with it.

• Heated grips. You can probably skip these on a pure sport bike, but they are a wonderful thing on any bike intended for travel.

That about does it. Oh, yeah, I forgot reasonable seat height. If seats get any taller on adventure-tourers, I'll have to hire a Mannerist painter to draw me a longer set of legs.

And maybe take some of the gray out of my beard and lose the bifocals . . .

January 2004

ANOTHER GREEN TRIUMPH

I have often said—and probably at least once in these pages—that the next motorcycle we buy is very often a form of revenge for our last long trip. For instance, if the seat was too hard or the windflow over the windshield was too deafening on that last big ride, a person might be tempted to go out and buy a more luxurious and quiet motorcycle for the next cross-country adventure.

Last week, however, I bought a new motorcycle not because it's different from the last bike I took on a long trip, but because it's essentially identical: a reward rather than a revenge.

The trip in question was a travel story that editor Beau Pacheco asked me to do for *CW*'s sister annual, *Adventures.* "I'd like you to pick up a new Triumph Bonneville in Nashville," Beau told me, "and ride it down to Memphis, then take a long, rambling trip through the Mississippi Delta, and do a story on searching for the roots of the blues."

Persuasiveness is Beau's long suit, so I left about 15 minutes later on the trip. As a hard-core blues fan with a weakness for Triumphs and British bikes in general, I was an easy mark. Also, I'd been curious about the new Bonneville, wondering if it could flourish as an all-purpose, do-everything motorcycle, or if it were essentially a retro-toy for cruising around on warm summer evenings and trying to relive some elusive magic from one's youth.

Long story short, I was surprised how much I liked the new red-and-silver Bonneville on my trip to Mississippi. The weather was cool and wet, but even this failed to dampen the amount of fun I had on the ride. The road probably helped. Instead of shooting from Nashville down to Memphis on the interstate, I headed out on Highway 100. This is a winding, picturesque road that sweeps and dips through small towns in the tapering foothills of the Appalachians until it finally bottoms out in the flat, fertile cotton land of the

Mississippi Delta. Vine-covered bridges cross rivers whose names suggest the ghosts of Indian tribes and Stephen Foster songs.

You spend a long time on this road flicking through successive bends, lofting blind hills, and descending into curving tunnels of dark green trees hung with kudzu vines. It's a good place for a smooth, torquey twin you can move around on, a motorcycle with medium-wide bars, and a slightly upright riding position for maximum scenery absorption. It was perfect for the Triumph, and I would rate this as one of the four or five best rides I've ever taken—one of those rare times when your mood, the road, and the bike all coalesce into a kind of drip feed of inexpressible pleasure that lasts all day long, and into the next.

I spent long hours in the saddle of this bike and never found it tiring or boring. And each morning it was newly inviting, like the road itself. So I stuck that information about the Triumph in the back of my mind and let it ferment there, like a slow-bubbling vat of sour mash.

Then late this summer, I walked into Sharer Cycle Center, where my old friend and former ace Triumph flat-tracker Lyall Sharer holds court over a rurally located kingdom of Triumphs, Guzzis, and Kawasakis. And, lo, sitting there in the middle of the floor was a green Triumph Bonneville T-100 (deluxe version with proper knee pads and tach) with gold trim on the tank. "Goodwood Green and Aztec Gold," the brochure said. Robin Hood meets Montezuma.

Now, I have a strong constitution, but there are a couple of things that can make me instantaneously weak in the knees, as if I've been hit by one of Marlin Perkins' rhino darts. And those are first, any black-and-gold Norton Commando or bevel-drive Ducati 900SS, and second, any green Triumph. I stood around for an hour and kept saying, "Damn, that's a good-looking bike!" until Lyall was about ready to throw me out.

Of course, I went back and sat on the bike the mandatory seventeen times before making a decision, but last weekend, with winter closing in like an avalanche, Lyall informed me there was an enticing end-of-season discount on the bike and I simply said, "Okay!"

I added the slightly freer-flowing pipes and richer jets, and had the shop install a centerstand. I picked up the bike last Friday, then took an all-Saturday ride in clear, cool weather.

So, does the rose-tinted southern memory jive favorably with the chill Yankee riding experience?

So far, so good.

The new Bonneville is not at the edgy, outer limit of any single performance parameter, but I was ready and primed for what you might call a "conventional" motorcycle. There is a place in every small collection of motorcycles for a pure sport bike, a big tourer, or an off-roader, but there is something very satisfying about a motorcycle that has simply been built to ride around on, without pretending that it might win a MotoGP or go jumping over sand dunes on the way to Dakar. I don't ride in those places. I ride mostly on good pavement among the red barns and green hills of Wisconsin, on the winding ridge-and-valley roads that string them together. Strange to say, they are roads very much like those found in England. The Bonneville seems built for these roads.

The new Bonnie does not represent what my old 1960s Bonneville did—that bike was a little more "pure" and refined in some of its aesthetic details (but not others), and it was also a symbol of world-beating excitement and dangerous speed. To own one was to surround yourself with an aura of risk and wild-man angst and daring. The new one goes just about as fast—and runs, stops, and handles immeasurably better—but it is now a middle-of-the-road bike. Fast enough to be good fun, but not legendary. In any case, today's speed bar is now so high it's almost unreachable—and often unuseable.

But the Bonneville has brought back, just by its very conventionality, an element of fun and versatility I'd almost forgotten was missing from my garage.

And it's Goodwood Green, and it's made in England. Thirty-five years after the other green Triumph in my garage.

February 2004

LOST SUMMERS

It isn't every day you get a letter on cast-off official stationery from the palace of Saddam Hussein, but it happened to me last month.

I have been corresponding, you see, with one SP/4 Darrell Pacheco, who is an MP patrolling the streets of Baghdad. Some of you may recognize the Pacheco name, as Darrell is the brother of Beau Pacheco, editor of our sister publication, *Adventures*.

Like Beau, Darrell is an avid lifelong motorcyclist, but hasn't been riding much lately because of his job in Iraq. His story is an interesting one: He's a forty-nine-year-old veteran of the first Gulf War who stayed in the army reserves afterward and then retired two years before the September 11 attack. On September 12, he did what many of us felt like doing but did not have the means or the strength of will to accomplish—he rejoined the army and went back to the Middle East.

He's been there for about nine months now, and he isn't sure when he's coming home. "Just get me home in time for Daytona," he writes. "That'll be one year."

Despite dealing with the constant threats of ambush and land mines and the intense heat ("Woke up from a nap this afternoon and it was 132 degrees . . ."), he writes letters that are remarkably free from the sort of grousing and complaining in which I, personally, would be tempted to indulge. Still, you can tell, reading between the lines in Darrell's letters, that he misses his motorcycles back home.

He has a 1978 BMW R80 with R90S fairing and cycle parts on it and a Kawasaki ZRX1100 with the Eddie Lawson–replica paint scheme, both of which he rides on the Blue Ridge Parkway near his North Carolina home. He's also owned a Sportster and a VFR750 ("Wrecked it at Deal's Gap"), and is an avid roadracing fan. He's hoping to buy a Springer Softail when he gets out, to do some traveling.

Though we aren't that far apart in age (I'm just six years older), it's funny how the content of Darrell's writing reminds me of my own letters from Vietnam in 1969 and 1970. When we can't ride motorcycles, the dream of doing so fills our plans and sustains us.

My little army stint in Southeast Asia was the one period of my adult life when I didn't ride any bikes at all. Although the country was crawling with millions of Honda 50s and Super-90s, we troops had no opportunity to own motorcycles, and I was never seriously tempted to borrow one from our Vietnamese interpreters because these guys had most of their life savings tied up in their Hondas. They were not toys to the Vietnamese, but their only means of transportation. You didn't mess around with these bikes.

So in lieu of actually riding, I simply dreamt of riding. I sent away for Triumph and Norton brochures and had them taped on the inside of my foot locker, and I'd spend hours off-duty staring at those pictures and trying to decide which bike to buy when I got out, and where I would go with it. I also sent for brochures from a company in London called Elite Motors Limited, checking into the possibility of foreign delivery of a new Bonneville when I got out. A trip through England on a new Triumph sounded like an ideal way to quickly dispose of 14 months of overseas combat pay. Still does!

Then I hatched a new plan: I would get out of the army on October 8, 1970, at the Oakland, California, replacement center, buy a new Bonneville or Norton Commando from a San Francisco dealership, and ride home to Wisconsin. I wrote my parents and informed them of this scheme.

My dad, who seldom wrote letters, responded almost immediately:

"You will not (underlined three times) *buy a motorcycle in San Francisco and ride home in October. Your mother is worried sick and has hardly slept since you left for Vietnam, and she doesn't need one more thing to worry about. Have a little mercy. You will get on an airplane and fly home as soon as possible."*

I was twenty-two years old and free to do what I wanted, but when my dad used this tone, you didn't cross him unless you wanted to be swatted to death with your own hat. So I gave up on the San Francisco idea and flew home. A few weeks later, it snowed in Wisconsin and I bought a rusty old Volkswagen instead of a bike. Triumphs and Nortons would come later, in better weather.

Still, those bikes in the brochures had done their job, which was boosting morale about the future. I think with my friend Darrell in Iraq, they are serving the same function.

As they are for me, even now.

Last spring, I was diagnosed with Hepatitis C, an unpleasant little virus whose eradication requires six months of injections and pills that make you too queasy and tired to do much but lie on the sofa and stare at the ceiling. (I should really do something about that cobweb and those plaster cracks.) As of this writing, I have five weeks of this delightful treatment left and, though the prognosis is good, the past summer was an almost total write-off for motorcycling. I was simply too tired and dizzy to ride most of the time. I took a few short rides into town, but didn't have the stamina to go very far.

If you look carefully at the sofa where I spent the summer, however, you will note that it is surrounded by stacks of motorcycle magazines, sales brochures, U.S. road atlases, and maps of Europe, England, and Mexico. Somewhere in the pile is a book about the Isle of Man . . .

I may not have ridden much this summer—a few hundred miles total, on the handful of days when I felt okay—but I have lived what is possibly the richest imaginary motorcycle life since my days in Vietnam. Never have I had so many plans.

It'll be winter when I'm done with this medication, but I'm already plotting a "Payback for the Lost Summer" tour in the Deep South with my new Triumph Bonneville.

I'll probably hit Daytona this year, too. Maybe finally get to meet SP/4 Darrell Pacheco, who I know only from his letters. With any luck, we'll both be home by then, back on our bikes.

March 2004

DIFFERENT DRUMMERS

"What do you know about the 1975 Suzuki RE-5 Rotary?" asked a caller on the phone the other night.

I immediately recognized the voice of my old friend Jim Buck, from Boise, Idaho. Who else, after all, would ask such a question?

Jim is sort of the Will Rogers of motorcycling—he never met an old bike he didn't like—and he has even less resistance to hopeless, cast-off relics than I do. He owns sheds filled with all kinds of odd and interesting bikes, some of which actually run.

He'll call me and say, "I just picked up an old CBX at a garage sale yesterday."

"Does it run?" I'll ask.

After thoughtful hesitation, "Well . . . I imagine it would," Jim will say, "if it had a cylinder head and a back wheel. Also, it could use a little detailing. The pigeon crap from the barn has pretty much eaten up the chrome and paint . . ."

You get the picture. Jim does own some nice clean classic bikes, but others Need Work. All are equally welcome.

I met Jim way back in the early 1980s, when he called *CW* from Missoula, Montana, where he lived at the time, and asked why we'd never tested the new Guzzi V-50.

"Can't get a test bike from the U.S. distributor," we replied.

"Well, I just bought one," Jim said. "Why don't you come up to Missoula and test mine?"

So managing editor Steve Kimball and I drove a Chevy Citation (remember those?) borrowed from our sister publication, *Road & Track*, all the way to Missoula with a trunk load of test equipment. Jim turned out to be a great guy and a complete bike nut, and we've been friends ever since, calling each other regularly with important news of another completely shot motorcycle discovery.

And now this question out of left field about the Suzuki RE-5 Rotary.

"I wish I could tell you something about that bike," I said, "but I've never ridden one. I never knew anybody who owned one, and the Rotary was out of production when I arrived at *Cycle World*. All I know is they had a Wankel engine, weird-looking instruments, and didn't sell very well. Why do you ask?"

"Oh, there's a local guy who's got one that might be for sale."

"Does it run?"

"He says it did before he put it away."

"Amazing," I said. "But then every old bike I've ever owned used to run at one time, according to the owner . . . "

I told Jim I'd consult my vast file of old motorcycle magazines, read some road tests, and get back to him.

So today I dug up a couple of old road tests in *CW* and *Cycle*. Both magazines featured the Suzuki RE-5 in 1975 comparison tests of large touring bikes, and *Cycle World* senior editor D. Randy Riggs even did a 3,000-mile touring story with the RE-5, looping down through Baja and taking the La Paz ferry across to mainland Mexico.

Unfortunately, no one had many good things to say about the bike. Testers liked its precise handling and engine smoothness at highway speed, but that was about it. The RE-5 was heavy for its class, complex, rough and raspy at idle, not particularly fast, and it got poor fuel mileage—twenty-eight to thirty-four miles per gallon—and had a rather short touring range. It also ran hot, despite its huge radiator, baking the rider in warm weather (Riggs had to deflect the heat with spare face shields taped to the tank). Fork seals blew out on the first test bike, coating the engine with oil, and the chain lubricator threw oil all over the back of the bike, but missed the chain. Styling was a bit odd, and no one liked the Thermos bottle–shaped instrument and taillight pods. It seemed to have been a classic case of a set of answers to a group of questions no one had asked.

But it was a bold move nonetheless. Suzuki, at that time, was known for well-engineered two-strokes that were more durable than some of the other nickel-rocket ring-dings of the era. Owners reported long, trouble-free miles out of bikes such as the Titan 500 Twin. Suzuki was also an innovative company, willing to try new, almost eccentric, designs to separate itself from the others. Such as the GT750 "Water Buffalo," a liquid-cooled two-stroke triple, an engine that soon became the darling of small race car builders.

By the mid-1970s, however, two-stroke road bikes were on their way out, thanks to new smog laws and an emphasis on fuel mileage because of the recent gas crisis. Suzuki, rather than imitate Honda and Kawasaki inline fours, decided to try something completely different.

You might call the RE-5 Rotary an interim step that really didn't lead anywhere, preceding the introduction of Suzuki's own well-respected GS750 and 1000 inline four-stroke fours. The GS1000 was Suzuki's flagship when I came to work at *CW* in 1980.

So I missed the RE-5 era. In those mid-1970s years when Suzuki was struggling to sell the Rotary, I bought a new Norton 850 Interstate instead. Which I see, incidentally, came in sixth in *Cycle*'s 1975 eight-bike touring comparison test. Right behind the fifth-place RE-5, but ahead of the Moto Guzzi 850-T Interceptor and the last-place Harley FLH1200. The BMW R90/6 and the Honda Gold Wing tied for first.

So of course I went right out and bought the Norton. I never was very good at taking advice.

And I don't think Jim is, either.

Even if I pass along all the reported shortcomings of the RE-5, he'll probably buy the old Rotary anyway. And who could blame him?

What could be more fun than to try an odd and unusual type of motorcycle you've never ridden before? Especially one that represents a lost, transitional phase in history. For some of us, it's almost what collecting old bikes is all about.

Maybe I'll have to run out to Boise and take a ride next summer, if Jim can get the bike running.

And he probably can. After all, it used to run, before it was put away.

April 2004

THE AGE OF TOUGH ENGINES

I cruised over to one of our two local Honda shops last weekend to take a look at a used red 2001 Honda VFR800 they have for sale. It's very clean, with about 8,500 miles on the clock.

I must admit to a weakness for this generation VFR, even though I've steered away from four-cylinder bikes in recent years, generally preferring the torque and personality of twins. But there is something in the sizzle and snap of that Honda V-four I find quite soulful.

Nevertheless, I'm still at the mulling and pondering phase, looking around at other bikes as well. It's a long winter, and what else have we got to do here in Wisconsin? If you think of anything else, besides drinking Guinness and watching the *V-Four Victory* Isle of Man video, send me a card.

Anyway, as I drove home from the dealership, it dawned on me that I had checked the VFR's digital odometer, duly noted the mileage, and dismissed that 8,500 miles as a piffling trifle (sounds like an English pastry the Scarlet Pimpernel might eat), hardly worth mention.

Eighty-five hundred miles a trifle? That's almost three full transcontinental crossings of the United States.

Yet the VFR is only about halfway to its first valve adjust. The O-ringed chain is still fine, and the bike looks clean enough to put back on the showroom floor as a new leftover. It's had one set of new tires, four oil changes, and that's its total service history.

As a guy who cut his teeth (and often his hands) on the bikes of the early 1960s, I find this sort of durability to be one of the biggest changes I've seen in motorcycling during my interminable, yet fleeting lifetime. Motorcycle engines have gotten so good now, we almost think of them as sealed units. We still change oil and adjust valves once in a while, but very few people feel compelled to buy a complete shop manual with a new streetbike any more. Imminent replacement of crank bearings or valve guides is not really in the picture.

It's a sobering thing to admit, but if you are my age or older (God forbid), the pistons and rings on your new bike will probably live longer than you will.

This is also true of the last bottle of aftershave you bought, but why be morbid? The plain fact is, unless you race—or spend your Golden Years entering Iron Butt rallies—you will probably never see the inside of your engine.

This is a nice change.

When I got into this sport, most non-Japanese bikes were still in the IVC (Infernal Vibratin' Contraption) phase. BMWs were smoother and longer-lived than most, but they seemed to have achieved this excellence through a devil's pact in which they'd traded zesty performance for dogged reliability.

Other brands had shorter lifespans.

I've done restorations on two Triumph twins and one Ducati single from the 1960s, all of them (curiously) with almost exactly 12,000 miles showing, and they all needed serious engine work. Both Triumphs had worn-out valve guides, valves, pistons, rings, rod bearings, primary chains, sprockets, and clutch baskets at that mileage. The Ducati had not been as hard on its own internals as the Triumphs, but it still needed cylinder-head work, and it had more electrical glitches than the Baghdad telephone exchange.

The point here is, all of them were disassembled and laid out on my workbench before they'd reached 13,000 miles. Or 3,000 miles before that modern VFR needs its first valve check.

Japanese bikes, particularly Hondas, were the force of change that raised everybody's expectations. They were oil-tight, civilized, easy to live with, and fast for their displacement. Critics (including me) pointed out that they were disposable consumer goods, generally not worth rebuilding once you wore them out, but you still got about three Triumph, Ducati, or Harley engine-rebuild lifetimes out of them before they had to be tossed. In the meantime, you had a lot of fun riding around and stayed out of the garage.

Depending upon your point of view, motorcycle engine rebuilding was either a Zen-like ritual of great spiritual importance or a huge drain on national productivity, like workdays lost to the flu. Most riders, once they realized there was no excuse for bad engines, came to see it as a version of the flu.

Now, of course, almost no one will put up with engine trouble from a bike, and manufacturers know it.

Triumph, once the poster bike for English Troubles (though certainly not the worst or only one), has resurrected itself on a bedrock of reliability. My riding buddy and fellow Slimey Crud, Toby Kirk, now has 90,000 miles on his 1995 Triumph Sprint without a single engine repair, and last year he blasted flat-out to the Southwest and back, just for some good Mexican food.

Imagine doing this on a 90,000-mile 1965 Bonneville. Assuming there ever was one.

I've had three modern-generation Ducatis and have yet to experience engine troubles with any of them (okay, a bad clutch cover gasket on the 900SS), despite long road trips and the relentless pounding of track days on my 996. At 12,000 miles they feel just broken in.

Harleys? Well, every time I say Harley engines are bulletproof, I get about four letters from owners who've had some kind of cam trouble, but I never have. My Evo and Twin-Cam engines have been flawless on long, hot cross-country trips. Until personal experience proves otherwise, I consider them sealed units, as do most modern Harley owners.

This sort of progress is okay with me.

I still like to restore old bikes from the 1960s, but I don't have a single gene in my body that longs to tear down a two-year-old engine, just off warranty. Or to leave my greasy fingerprints on the "exploded view" of the engine cases in a shop manual—got plenty of those already; my Norton manual looks like the phone book at Al's Lube Rack.

In fact, if I get that VFR, I might just pass on the shop manual entirely. At least until my aftershave runs out.

June 2004

WHAT TO DO IN WINTER

People who don't know me very well often say, "Egan, you're a gearhead; you must survive those long winters in Wisconsin by getting out on your snowmobile."

I usually tell them that while I have many motorcycle-riding buddies who are also complete snowmobile nuts, the appeal of these machines has never really caught on with me. I've spent a lot of time on "sleds," riding trails with my dad and father-in-law, and I actually went snowmobiling with the entire Unser family in Eagle River one winter while doing a story for a magazine—but I've never become fanatical about them.

Why not?

I've analyzed this in my mind (a process not unlike alchemy, in which nothing turns to gold) and decided that I've avoided the snowmobile addiction simply because I don't get quite enough tactile satisfaction out of the way they handle.

I realize there are wizards who can do amazing things with snowmobiles, but at my low level of riding competence they don't seem to require as much finesse as a good dirt bike. As my riding buddy Pat Donnelly says, "You don't so much steer a snowmobile as estimate where it's going to go."

But then I feel the same way about quads. My fearless (not to say insane) friend Paul Roberts can actually fly down a forest trail faster on his four-wheeler than I can ride a dirt bike, to my eternal shame, but I'd still rather be on the bike. I just like the dynamics better.

Which is all a long-winded way of saying, no, I'm not an avid snowmobiler.

But to be perfectly honest, my biggest problem with snowmobiles, and with certain other invigorating winter sports such as ice racing, is simply that I hate to be cold.

When I was in the army, I nearly froze to death in winter basic training, my teeth chattering like castanets. Since then, I've lost all desire to shiver continuously for periods of more than 12 hours. After a winter in the freezing rains of Kentucky, I actually enjoyed the steamy heat of Vietnam and never, ever complained about it—while grousing about virtually everything else.

No, I'd rather spend my winters in a warm garage, working on a bike, and dreaming about summer, than running around in the snow. The only winter sport I really like is skiing, and I sometimes suspect the main attractions of even *that* are the bar near the fireplace and the hot tub back at the lodge. Ice fishing, of course, is out of the question. There are limits.

My personal philosophy is that if the good Lord had wanted us to go outside in the winter, he would have made it a lot more pleasant.

So how do narrow-minded, closely focused motorcyclists like me manage to get through the long, dark, and dismal nonriding season here in the upper Midwest?

Well, with spring in the air at the present moment and the snow slowly melting on our lawn, I have looked back at this particular winter and come up with a few helpful suggestions, based on recent experience:

- Throw a Tropical Party. My friends at Corse Superbikes in Saukville, Wisconsin, did this at their Ducati/Aprilia/KTM bike dealership during February in the absolute depths of winter. They hired a musician/DJ to sing and play a mixture of Jimmy Buffett, Reggae, and Hawaiian music, catered in a luau-type smorgasbord (there's a cross-cultural combination: Don Ho meets Ingmar Bergman), and required everyone to wear Hawaiian shirts. While we feasted on pork ribs and pineapple, dressed in our Parrot Head best, gazing fondly upon exotic red and orange motorcycles, winter raged outside, all but unnoticed.
- Go to a motorcycle show. All of us in the Slimey Crud Motorcycle Gang (SCMG) migrate southward to the Chicago bike show every year, and so do thousands of others. This gives you a chance to sit upon and ponder the merits of virtually every new motorcycle in the universe while wandering around with your friends in the huge

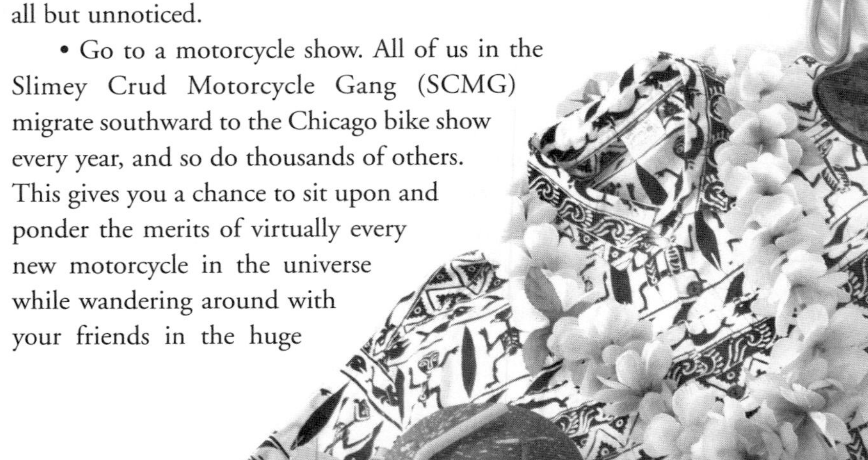

heated Rosemont Center. If you stay in one of the connected hotels, there are heated swimming pools, and our hotel bar even had a happy hour, though your actual happiness may last considerably longer than that. For those on the Atkins diet, Morton's and Gibson's famous steak houses are right across the street. A weekend of self-contained paradise, with minimal outdoor exposure.

• Throw a Slip & Slide Party. My friend Rob Himmelmann did this last weekend. He got out five or six of his huge dirt bike collection—including a couple of amazing Rokon two-wheel-drive Trail Breakers—and led a series of mercifully short rides on nearby trails through the snowy woods. Naturally, most of the time was spent in Rob's garage, looking at all the great old bikes he's accumulated over the years. A bunch of us hung out for the day, with all our critical motorcycle synapses firing like faulty Lucas ignition points, despite the cold outside. A little risk of too much fresh air here, but nothing lethal.

• Form or join a motorcycle club that holds casual weekly meetings at a friendly bar that has free popcorn and peanuts and at least twenty ales, stouts, and lagers on tap, including Guinness and Sprecher Black Bavarian. Discuss motorcycles, Nietzsche, or the important role of the Hawker Hurricane during the Battle of Britain. Let it snow.

• Go to Daytona, Southern California, or anyplace the water is not frozen. Take a bike with you, or rent one. Send home postcards with palm trees on them.

With any luck at all, these simple strategies will allow you to get through the winter without having to demean yourself by participating in any winter sports that require more than a few moments of exposure to the cold and snow, thereby preserving your precious reservoir of enthusiasm for the important work of riding motorcycles on warm, sunny days in summer, as nature intended.

July 2004

QUIET CLASSICS OF THE SHOWROOM

"What are those things like?" I asked my friend Lee Fleming, nodding toward a brand-new black Kawasaki Concours. "I know they've been around forever, but I've never had a chance to ride one."

We were standing just outside the showroom of Champion Motorcycles, Lee's dealership in Costa Mesa, California. Lee and I go way back, having raced motorcycles together in prehistoric times, and I always drop by for a visit when I'm in California.

I had just escaped from the character-building rigors of the dark Wisconsin winter, flying into the Golden State for a writing assignment. Barb had driven me to the airport in her Jeep on a day when schools were closed because of high winds and drifted snow across the highways. Meanwhile, here in Costa Mesa, it was seventy-two degrees and the sun beamed down upon my shoulders like God's own electric vest. A blonde woman drove by in a red Alfa convertible, the boulevard flanked by palm trees. Strains of a Randy Newman song wafted through my brain.

Where was I? Ah, yes . . . motorcycles.

Lee folded his arms and looked at the Concours thoughtfully. "Well," he said, "it's comfortable, reasonably fast, and has good wind protection. It's basically a bike that gives you about ninety-five percent of the performance of a current-generation sport-tourer, but it costs about $5,000 less. It's a steady seller for us, with a dedicated following."

"I remember when these things came out, in 1986," I said.

Lee nodded. "It's one of those bikes I enjoy selling, because the owner is always happy. Same for the KLR650. It's not the latest thing, but it does exactly what people want it to, and it doesn't cost too much. And you know, at any given moment, there are half a dozen people going around the world on KLRs and having a great time."

Lee went off to help a customer, and I wandered around the shop looking at bikes. It seemed to me that in his description of the Concours and the KLR650 he had touched on a whole segment of the motorcycle market—the often-overlooked modern workhorse that keeps selling, year after year, because it fulfills a real need and there is no exact replacement.

These are both bikes that get very little (or no) advertising and promotion from their mother company, and not much ink in magazines. We announced and tested them years ago, included them in various comparison tests with their contemporaries, and then moved on to newer products. But the bikes are still in production, still being bought by a loyal coterie of fans who appreciate their virtues.

I have three friends—in Wisconsin, Colorado, and Alabama—who all ride KLRs. One went to Alaska and back on his, and the others ride fire roads on the weekends. The KLR isn't much of a dirt bike for hard-core off-roading, but it works fine on unpaved roads, and it comes right off the showroom floor with a big gas tank, a cushy seat, and a luggage rack. It's comfortable on the highway, has a relatively low seat height and, when dropped, can be picked up by a single human being. These are all details that don't go unnoticed by people who adventure-tour, so the bike stays in production year after year.

Looking around Lee's showroom, I spotted another often-overlooked gem, the Honda XR400. Lee said sales of these bikes have been pretty slow, because many riders prefer to buy newer, lighter, and more powerful liquid-cooled enduro bikes. It's hard to argue with more horsepower and less weight, but the old XR still has a few things going for it.

When I was trail riding in Baja with my buddy Pat Donnelly last year, we kept running into off-road tour groups who were mounted almost exclusively on XR400s. I asked a couple of the tour guides about this, and they said, essentially, "We use XRs because you can't kill them. They have kick starters and they're air-cooled. No hoses, radiators, or water pumps to break in the middle of nowhere, and maintenance is minimal."

Dirt bike technology marches on, but as long as there are places like Baja, I suspect there will always be a market for a bike like the XR, whose very lack of complexity and exotic plumbing is the reason people buy it. Too much technology is not always a good thing when you're thirty miles from a reliable source of drinking water. Or coolant.

That rugged, air-cooled appeal also holds true for another bike I think is an unsung budget classic, the Suzuki DR650—which, like the XR400, has been with us since 1996. It's on about the same adventure-tourer/fire road wavelength as the KLR650, but is a little more dirt-oriented and not quite as posh on the highway. It also has a smaller gas tank and doesn't come with a luggage rack, but it has a higher level of fit and finish than the KLR and is a bit more agile. Also, the motor is wonderful, torquey yet willing to rev, and has a nice snap to it.

Others?

Well, on the road-bike side, there's the Yamaha YZF600R (introduced in 1996 also), which I'm glad to see is still in production. The YZF isn't nearly as intense or track-worthy as its R6 stablemate, but it makes a better all-around streetbike. It has a low price (under seven grand), laser-sharp steering, great torque for a high-revving four, and it's as comfortable to tour on as a Honda VFR800, while feeling somewhat lighter and sportier. And I worry that when it's gone, there won't be anything quite like it.

But that's true of all the bikes I've mentioned, and a few others as well (the V-Max comes to mind). The funny thing these motorcycles have in common is that they are all amazingly cheap, by any modern standard, yet the people I know who own them are experienced riders who could probably afford any bike on Earth. You'd think, based on price, that these perennial survivors might be aimed at novices, yet they are just as often bought by people who aren't easily dazzled and know exactly what they want.

People who, as Lee put it so nicely, always leave the dealership happy.

September 2004

ADVENTURES IN FUEL MILEAGE

Scene One: It is a beautiful warm morning in 1967 and the lawns around my college dormitory at the University of Wisconsin have finally turned a brilliant, almost artificial Easter-basket green. Fat robins are hopping around the campus. I'm flying high, having just taken my last semester exam (Geology 101) at 7:45 in the morning. My freshman year is finished. Summer is almost here.

I head back to my empty dorm room in Sullivan Hall. My roommate is already gone, and there's nothing left in the room but a geology textbook, a World War II surplus A-2 brown leather flying jacket, a Bell 500 TX motorcycle helmet, an official Boy Scout knapsack, and some dust mice under the bed. My parents had stopped by two days earlier and hauled away my guitar, typewriter, and other earthly belongings in their Falcon wagon. Now my room looks like a barracks at the end of a war.

In the parking lot across the street, my chariot awaits. It's a silver-and-black 1965 Honda Super 90 motorcycle, purchased just a few weeks earlier with money earned by washing pots and pans every night for the residence halls food service. I got the bike from a high school kid named Ronnie Coke (don't ask me why I still remember his name) for $180.

I put on the helmet, zip up my jacket, swing the pack onto my back, turn on the fuel, pull the choke lever up, and prod the kick start lever. The lovely little single-overhead-cam engine fires immediately and I'm on my way. I cruise by another dorm nearby and join forces with my old high school friend, Dave Schroeder. I ran into him on campus the day before and discovered he *also* just bought a Honda S-90 and planned to ride home the next morning, so we decided to ride together.

We head into the green Wisconsin hills, running flat-out at about fifty-five miles per hour on Highway 12, stop for breakfast in Sauk City, then motor toward my home town of Elroy, Wisconsin (pop. 1,502). Dave lives to the north, in Kendall, six miles farther up the road.

When we get to Elroy, Dave waves goodbye and keeps rolling toward home. I pull into Garvin's Mobil station, which still has a flying red horse in front. Bob Garvin comes out, cranks the pump back to zero, lifts the nozzle, and trips the switch.

There are no self-service gas stations at this point; the only people who pump their own fuel are employees or owners of service stations. I'm nineteen years old and have never operated a gas pump. Bob would be offended if I tried, and it would be taken as a rude demonstration of impatience, like going behind the counter to bag your own popcorn at a movie theater. It just isn't done.

I remove the gas cap and Bob carefully tips the nozzle into the Honda tank. "All done with college for the year?" he asks, and in the time it takes to say that, the tank is full. Bob peers into the tank and back at the pump and looks baffled. The bike has taken a tick over .7 of a gallon, and the pump says I owe twenty-three cents.

"When did you fill this up last?" he asks.

"Yesterday afternoon, in Madison."

"You really went ninety miles on twenty-three cents worth of gas?"

"I guess I did," I reply, feeling somewhat guilty for making Bob come out of the station to pump so little fuel.

"That's well over a hundred miles per gallon," he says. "More like one twenty-something . . ."

"Yeah, I guess that's right," I say, nodding in solemn commiseration. I take two dimes and three pennies out of my blue jeans pocket and hand them to Bob. It doesn't feel like a fair exchange for two hours of carefree motoring on a beautiful spring morning.

Bob hefts these tiny, almost weightless coins in the palm of his hand and then looks at the Honda. "Well," he says, "I hope they don't make too many more of those things."

Scene Two: Yesterday afternoon, almost exactly thirty-seven years later.

I'm leaving this coming weekend for Colorado to do some fire-roading in the Rockies with my friend Mike Mosiman, so I've been prepping my dual-sport Suzuki DR650 for the trip—DOT knobbies, skid plate, heavy-duty handguards, etc. The last step is to install a plastic 4.1-gallon Clarke gas tank to replace the stock steel 3.4-gallon tank.

I throw a splash of gas into the new tank and ride to the nearest station, where the sign out front says unleaded regular is now $2.09 per gallon, up five cents from yesterday. You are allowed (required) to pump your own gas now, so I slide my credit card in and out of the pump at exactly the right speed, then fill the tank with a further 3.9 gallons of regular, for a cost of $8.18.

I look at the pump and then stare at my receipt numbly, trying to comprehend that I've put more than eight dollars worth of fuel into a moderately sized motorcycle tank.

But my bad fuel day is not yet over. I return to the station later to top off the thirty-five-gallon tank in my Ford Econoline van for the trip. It takes thirty gallons, or $62.97 worth of fuel. Then I fill up all the plastic five-gallon gas cans we keep at our rural home for running lawnmowers, chain saws, weedwackers, etc. The total on those is $71.29. Now I've spent $142.44 for gasoline in one day—without going anywhere!

So it turns out Bob Garvin needn't have worried about Honda making too many more of those fuel-sipping Super 90s and putting him out of business.

He couldn't possibly have foreseen that an entire generation of riders who bought those bikes would later escalate to much larger motorcycles that get about one-third the mileage of the S-90.

Or that some of us would feel compelled to haul our bikes 1,000 miles to Colorado and back in a sixteen-miles-per-gallon van for a few days of trail riding.

Or choose to spend perfectly good motorcycle funds on lawn mowers, chain saws, and weedwackers, using up our rare, remaining riding days to groom real estate bought with our own money.

Who could have guessed?

Certainly not that free-and-easy college kid with the little Honda.

December 2004

A MINOR ODYSSEY

Since September 11, things have been different. There was a strange shift in American psychology following that murderous event, and it seemed for many months that no one, including Barb and me, wanted to venture very far from home.

Lavish trips and endless hours in airports suddenly seemed pointless. Why lose long days in transit when our families and friends were right here? Why go halfway around the world when virtually all of us in North America live in places that are never more than a few hours' drive or ride from some small (or spectacular) natural paradise we've never fully explored?

Since those dark days, American travel patterns have gone, more or less, back to normal, but the tendency to look into our own backyard for diversion has not entirely gone away.

Barb and I are much more likely, these days, to get out a map of Wisconsin (where we live) or the Great Lakes region when planning a vacation. We've been taking more short, fun motorcycle trips and fewer road-pounding forays into the Great Plains or beyond. We've also found it's nice to be within a single day's ride of home when the housesitter calls and says, "Your dog ate three pounds of cat treats, and I think he's hallucinating."

So it was an easy sell when our friend Randy Wade called a few weeks ago and said, "Marilyn and I are thinking of taking a four-day motorcycle trip to Michigan on our Honda VFR800. It might be fun to take the high-speed Lake Express ferry from Milwaukee to Muskegon and then ride up the Lake Michigan coast and explore the Leelanau Peninsula. I found a cabin we could rent on a bay near Manistee. You guys interested?"

"That clattering you hear is our touring gear falling out of the closet," I said. Or something less clever, possibly.

Randy did the legwork (i.e., Internet work) of getting ferry tickets—$240 round trip, per couple and motorcycle—and securing the cabin. All Barb and I had to do was pack.

Ah, but what motorcycle to take?

I walked out to the garage, where my two choices were the new KTM 950 Adventure and my 2003 Triumph Bonneville. Not too difficult a choice; the KTM's free hard bags—part of a sales promotion when I bought the bike in May—still had not arrived after two and a half months of waiting. (You'd think an Austrian company might grasp the concept of a short riding season, but no . . .) Soft luggage was out, because the high pipes tucked under the seat would set the bags on fire. Also, Barb found the stock KTM seat too hard for a long trip, and I hadn't yet ordered a costly aftermarket one.

So, I strapped our set of soft bags on the conventional, comfortable Bonneville, and off we went on a bright and sunny Saturday morning, riding two-lane back roads all the way to Milwaukee with Randy and Marilyn. We ate lunch at an outdoor cafe downtown, then rode down to the ferry terminal. About ten bikes were waiting—all of them Harleys—beside the line of cars. We were loaded first, parked in a special bike area with D-rings built into the steel floor. The crew gave us ratcheting tie-downs to secure the bikes, and we went above to the nicely furnished passenger lounge.

A long and honorable tradition, carrying bikes on a ferryboat. Barb and I had taken the Liverpool ferry to the Isle of Man in 1982 for the TT, and just two summers ago Pat Donnelly and I had ferried our Ducatis across Lake Michigan to Ludington for a track day at Grattan. But this new Lake Express ferry was something special. It was fast. We blasted across the lake in two and a half hours at forty miles per hour. I went outside on the deck and nearly lost my hat and sunglasses in the wind. Women in dresses fled back into the cabin, or at least the modest ones did. Disembarking, we rode through the city of Muskegon—a strange mixture of lovely lakeside homes and lost industrial magnificence in an eerily quiet downtown—and then headed north along the coast on the sinuous and charming two-laner that is BR-31.

Checking into our deluxe cottage on Portage Lake (actually a bay, with a narrow outlet), we went off to dinner at a grand old lakeside lodge called Portage Point Inn, then returned to watch a moonrise on our bay. Moonrises on bays are seldom bad.

Sunday's loop around the Leelanau Peninsula was one of the nicest rides I've ever had. The twisting and dipping coastal road took us past huge sand dunes, high cliff vistas, fishing villages, and deep woods that reminded me, alternately, of California's central coast and parts of New England, but with their own wild, northwoods flavor. We returned to our cottage right at sunset and rode to dinner at a superb-yet-reasonable restaurant called The Blue Slipper Bistro in nearby Onekama.

A leisurely ride down the coast on Monday brought us back to the ferry, where we killed some time until our 10:30 p.m. departure by dining very slowly at a good bayside restaurant called Dockers. We were supposed to leave on a 4:30 ferry, but got bumped off because the Kerry/Edwards campaign entourage had taken it over. This is a sacrifice I didn't mind making because *(a)* I'm a patriotic American voter; and *(b)* the ferry company kindly refunded our full fare and gave us a free trip.

When we got to Milwaukee at midnight, Randy and Marilyn rode home to Madison on the interstate, but Barb and I got a motel room so we could rest up and take a meandering back road trip home the next morning.

As we pulled into our driveway at noon on Tuesday, I looked at the odometer and realized we'd gone only 700 miles on the bike. Not very far, really, yet we'd had a wonderful trip, with spectacular scenery, a high-speed lake voyage, great meals, good friends, endless curves, and not one mile of boring road.

It hadn't been a relentless blast toward the far horizon, but it didn't have to be. One thing I've discovered over the past three years on these short weekend trips is that the lakes don't get exponentially bluer as you get farther from home.

INDEX